Chilcotin Chronicles

T0287507

Copyright © 2017 Sage Birchwater

02 03 04 05 06 22 21 20 19 18

All rights reserved. No part of this publication may be reproduced, stored in a retrieval system or transmitted, in any form or by any means, without prior permission of the publisher or, in the case of photocopying or other reprographic copying, a licence from Access Copyright, the Canadian Copyright Licensing Agency, www.accesscopyright.ca, 1-800-893-5777, info@accesscopyright.ca.

Caitlin Press Inc.
8100 Alderwood Road,
Halfmoon Bay, BC V0N 1Y1
www.caitlin-press.com

Edited by Catherine Edwards
Text and cover design by Vici Johnstone
Map by Demian Pettman

Front cover bottom: Image 62182 courtesy Canadian Museum of History. Top right: Old George Turner (circa 1930). Photo courtesy Al Elsey. Top left: Louisa One-eye Turner. Photo Bill Mouat. Back cover: Domas Squinas portrait by Harlan I. Smith, Image 62147, courtesy Canadian Museum of History.

Printed in Canada

Caitlin Press Inc. acknowledges financial support from the Government of Canada and the Canada Council for the Arts, and the Province of British Columbia through the British Columbia Arts Council and the Book Publisher's Tax Credit.

Canada Council for the Arts / Conseil des Arts du Canada
British Columbia Arts Council
Funded by the Government of Canada
Canada

Library and Archives Canada Cataloguing in Publication

Birchwater, Sage, author
Chilcotin chronicles : stories of adventure and intrigue from British Columbia's central interior / Sage Birchwater.

ISBN 978-1-987915-33-4 (softcover)

1. Chilcotin Plateau (B.C.)—History. 2. Chilcotin Plateau (B.C.)—Biography. I. Title.

FC3845.C445B57 2017 971.1'75 C2016-907720-9

Chilcotin Chronicles

Stories of Adventure and Intrigue From British Columbia's Central Interior

Sage Birchwater

Caitlin Press

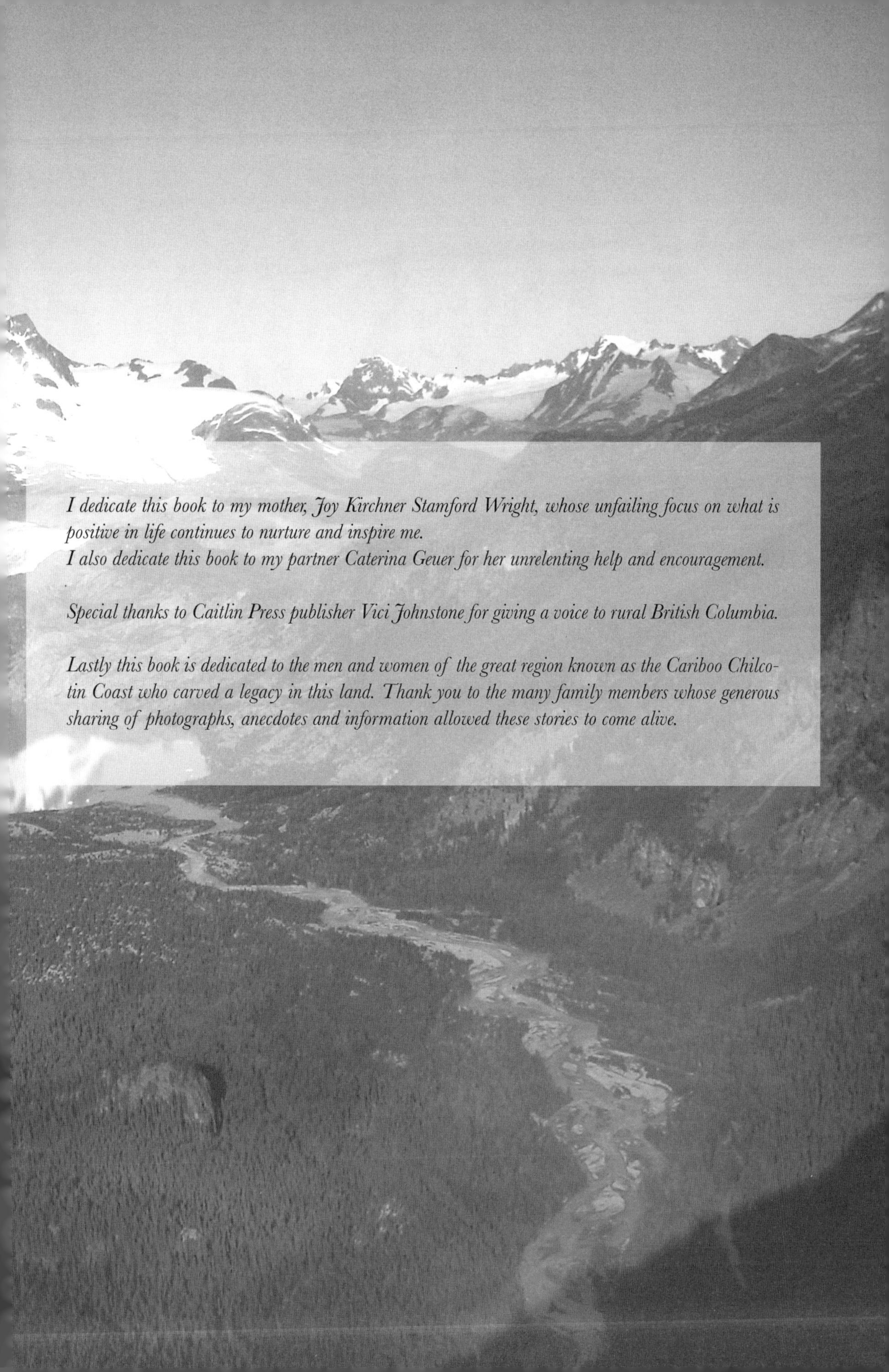

I dedicate this book to my mother, Joy Kirchner Stamford Wright, whose unfailing focus on what is positive in life continues to nurture and inspire me.
I also dedicate this book to my partner Caterina Geuer for her unrelenting help and encouragement.

Special thanks to Caitlin Press publisher Vici Johnstone for giving a voice to rural British Columbia.

Lastly this book is dedicated to the men and women of the great region known as the Cariboo Chilcotin Coast who carved a legacy in this land. Thank you to the many family members whose generous sharing of photographs, anecdotes and information allowed these stories to come alive.

Contents

Opposite: Lester Dorsey was one of the great backwoodsmen of the Chilcotin who arrived from the United States after the First World War. Image courtesy of Hank Winning.

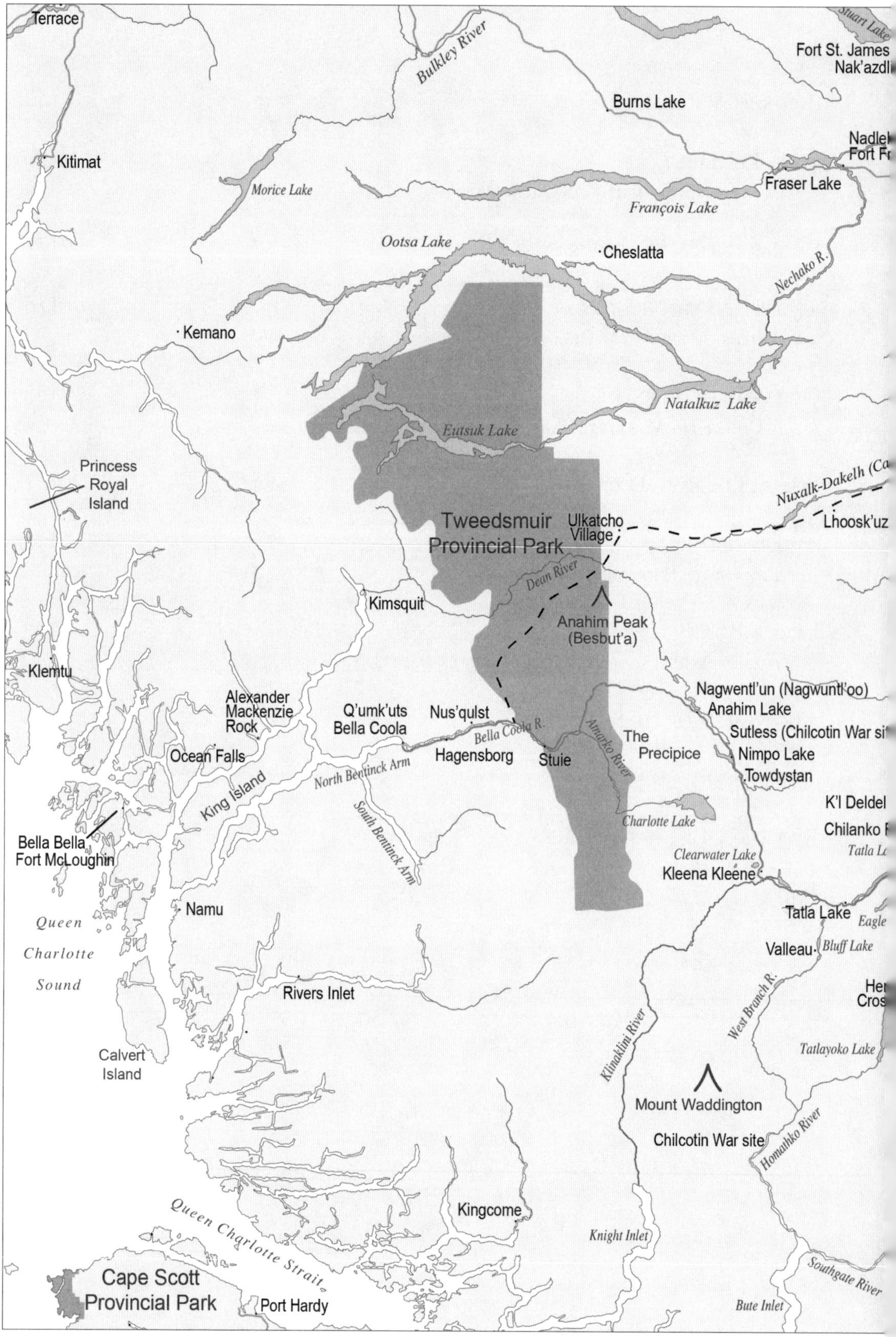

Terrace
Bulkley River
Stuart Lake
Fort St. James
Nak'azdli
Burns Lake
Kitimat
Morice Lake
Fraser Lake
François Lake
Ootsa Lake
Cheslatta
Nechako R.
Kemano
Natalkuz Lake
Eutsuk Lake
Princess Royal Island
Nuxalk-Dakelh
Tweedsmuir Provincial Park
Ulkatcho Village
Lhoosk'uz
Dean River
Kimsquit
Anahim Peak (Besbut'a)
Klemtu
Alexander Mackenzie Rock
Q'umk'uts Bella Coola
Nus'qulst
Bella Coola R.
Nagwentl'un (Nagwuntl'oo)
Anahim Lake
Sutless (Chilcotin War si
Ocean Falls
Hagensborg
Stuie
Atnarko River
The Precipice
Nimpo Lake
Towdystan
King Island
North Bentinck Arm
South Bentinck Arm
Charlotte Lake
K'l Deldel
Chilanko
Bella Bella
Fort McLoughlin
Clearwater Lake
Kleena Kleene
Namu
Tatla Lake
Eagle
Queen Charlotte Sound
Valleau
Bluff Lake
Rivers Inlet
West Branch R.
Calvert Island
Klinaklini River
Tatlayoko Lake
Mount Waddington
Chilcotin War site
Homathko River
Kingcome
Queen Charlotte Strait
Knight Inlet
Southgate River
Cape Scott Provincial Park
Port Hardy
Bute Inlet

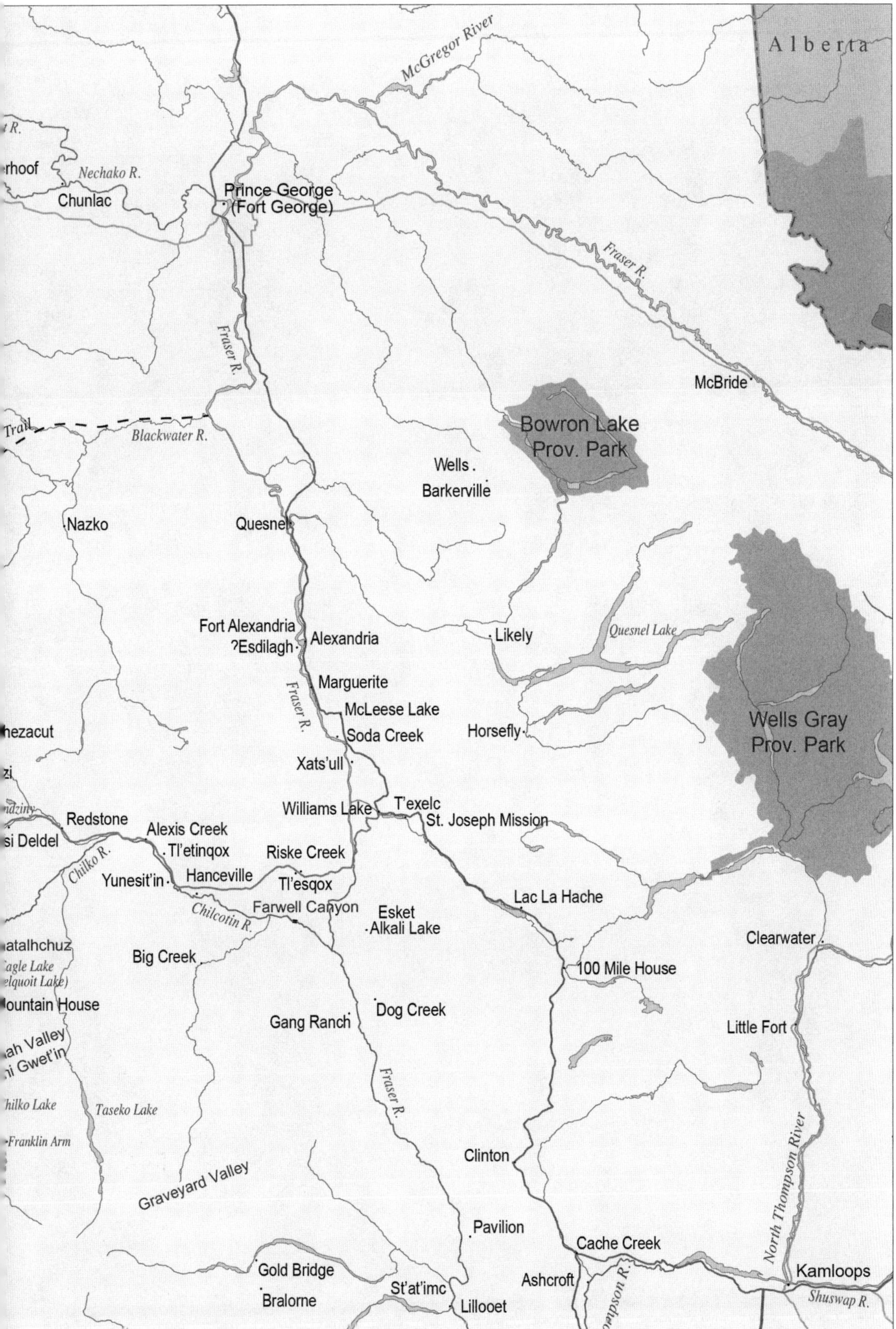

Alberta
McGregor River
Nechako R.
Prince George
(Fort George)
Chunlac
Fraser R.
Fraser R.
Fraser R.
Fraser R.
McBride
Bowron Lake
Prov. Park
Trail
Blackwater R.
Wells
Barkerville
Nazko
Quesnel
Fort Alexandria
?Esdilagh
Alexandria
Likely
Quesnel Lake
Marguerite
McLeese Lake
Soda Creek
Horsefly
Wells Gray
Prov. Park
Xats'ull
Williams Lake
T'exelc
St. Joseph Mission
Redstone
Alexis Creek
Tl'etinqox
Riske Creek
Chilko R.
Yunesit'in
Hanceville
Tl'esqox
Chilcotin R.
Farwell Canyon
Esket
Alkali Lake
Lac La Hache
Clearwater
Big Creek
100 Mile House
Gang Ranch
Dog Creek
Little Fort
Taseko Lake
Franklin Arm
Clinton
North Thompson River
Graveyard Valley
Pavilion
Cache Creek
Gold Bridge
Ashcroft
Kamloops
Bralorne
St'at'imc
Lillooet
Shuswap R.
Thompson R.

Introduction

I grew up in Victoria, BC, on the southern tip of Vancouver Island. In the mid-twentieth century, it was an idyllic place to spend my early years. It's still an amazing place actually. It strikes me as a refugium of civilization.

In my youth, I had a passion for studying maps and was particularly intrigued by the immense and varied landscape of British Columbia. Its mountain ranges, rivers, valleys, fjords, lakes, plateaus, deserts and trackless wilderness that seemed to stretch forever instilled a sense of wonder.

When I was 19, I got a job for a year in Port Alberni and regularly travelled over the spine of Vancouver Island past the magnificence of Mt. Arrowsmith. To the west was the Pacific Ocean and to the east across the Strait of Georgia and the Salish Sea was the mainland of British Columbia, with the great massifs of the Coast Mountains serrating the skyline. I knew from my study of maps that Mt. Waddington lay out there in the midst of these snowy crags, almost due north of Campbell River. Maps always mentioned this as the "highest peak completely within British Columbia."

I was curious about what lay beyond Mount Waddington and the great array of mountain ranges that stretched 750 kilometres from Vancouver to Prince Rupert. They formed a natural barrier and cultural divide between the interior of British Columbia and the coast.

Fate brought me to Williams Lake in 1973, and determination and good luck allowed me to spend more than four decades in this region that locals refer to as the Cariboo Chilcotin Coast.

I found myself in a place where few stories had been written down; rather, it was a country richly steeped in oral storytelling traditions. History was conveyed and passed on by word of mouth. Accounts told around kitchen tables or while staring into the embers of campfires were so vivid and alive that we took them for granted. They would always be there, we figured.

But time changes everything.

When I moved to my wilderness trapline sixty kilometres into the mountains south of Tatla Lake in 1977, rural electrification had just laid the first power lines down Tatlayoko Valley from a generator station in Tatla Lake. The only telephones in the country were the crank variety strung along Highway 20, where you'd ring three longs and a short or some other configuration to get your party. Of course, the phone system was one great party line from Anahim Lake to Alexis Creek and dozens of neighbours could be listening to your phone conversations. Some people had radio telephones, but most of us didn't have phones at all for another dozen years or so. We stayed in touch

Opposite: Patrick Charleyboy points out remnants of ancient fish trap on Big Eagle (Choelquoit) Lake to radio interviewer Keith Watt. Photo Sage Birchwater.

Mount Waddington and the buttress of the Coast Mountains inspired a fascination and wonder to the author growing up on Vancouver Island. Photo Sage Birchwater.

via a radio CB (Citizens Band) system, which was very neighbourly and friendly. Since everybody could hear your conversations, the CB radio kept us informed.

When I moved from my trapline in the West Branch to Tatlayoko Valley in 1987, Harry and Fran Haynes ran the Tatlayoko Post Office in their home about eight kilometres down the road from my cabin. Besides the local CB radio system, Fran and Harry had the only telephone in the valley. It was actually a public radio pay phone located in front of their house next to the main road. An extension of the pay phone went into Harry and Fran's house, and of course they would answer it when it rang and would take messages for people.

Needless to say, Harry and Fran's place was the social centre of the valley. Their CB handle was "Coffee House" and people gravitated there to make phone calls, pick up their mail and post letters. They also went there to visit with Harry and Fran. The coffee pot was always on and Fran made an endless supply of cookies.

It was probably around Harry and Fran's kitchen table that I first realized the immensity of the country's cache of stories. Harry would spiel them off one after the other. He would bring long-forgotten characters of the region to life with his colourful descriptions. Harry also had a wonderful photograph collection of the old-timers he told stories about.

Harry's mother, Del Naomi Haynes, was the postmistress when she came to Tatlayoko Valley from Victoria in 1929, a single mother with five young sons. So Harry got a taste of the busy social scene associated with the post office when the Hodgson Freight truck delivered the mail every two weeks. People would come from all around the country, riding over on mail day from Henry's Crossing, Eagle Lake, Tsuniah Lake, Mountain House and Chilko Lake.

Harry had stories about them all.

Like the time when Eileen Lulua showed up at his mother's house all drenched in sleet and rain after spending three hours in the saddle riding over from Neghatalhchuẑ along the Chilko River to pick up the mail. Eileen was also a single mom with offspring fathered by several different men, and Del Haynes had recently arrived with her five boys, having separated from her husband. Eileen took off her drenched top coat and hung it by the heater to dry. After observing Del's kids playing on the living room floor, she suddenly spoke up: "What's the matter, you white woman? All your kids got same papa!"

This simple statement spoke a thousand words—describing the two cultural solitudes living side by side in that country.

I spent twenty-four years living in the Chilcotin, tracking down stories, interviewing old-timers, covering events and documenting history. My travels took me to the far reaches of the Cariboo Chilcotin Coast, a vast region intrinsically tied together with as much biodiversity as the rest of Canada combined.

Five distinct Indigenous nations have occupied this landscape over the past 10,000 years, working out their differences, finding things in common, and developing their languages and cultural traditions in harmony with the land on which they lived. The Dakelh occupy the northern part of this region; the Secwepemc, the eastern part between the Cariboo Mountains and the Chilcotin Plateau; the Nuxalk evolved on the Central Coast; the St'at'imc live in the canyons and mountains along the southern fringe of the Chilcotin Plateau; and the Tŝilhqot'in live in the midst of

Harry Haynes at his 80th birthday potluck in Tatlayoko Valley in 1993. Photo Sage Birchwater.

the other four nations on the high Chilcotin Plateau between the Fraser River and the Coast Mountains.*

There are stories of fierce conflicts between these peoples stretching back before the first Europeans arrived. Peace was maintained by mutual respect, protocols and the recognition of their respective traditional territories.

This is the setting for these stories, which chronicle a relatively recent past. These are tales portraying the convergence of cultures and very different ways of seeing the world. They are about the aftermath of colonization and settlement over the past two hundred years and about the strength and resilience of individuals who learned to contend with changing times.

On a recent stop at Hat Creek Ranch near Cache Creek, my partner Caterina overheard a German tourist remark how very recent the story of British Columbia actually is. In her country, people still occupy buildings 500 years old, while here, only 200 years ago, Indigenous societies dominated the landscape.

* The Tŝilhqot'in have also been known historically as the Chilcotin, the Secwepemc as the Shuswap, and the Dakelh as the Carrier.

Oral History: An Important Source of Knowledge and Information

Perhaps the most important source of pre-contact knowledge—one largely overlooked by conventional historians till recently—is information contained in the oral histories of Indigenous peoples. Stories passed down from generation to generation, repeated over and over, become part of the collective memory and understanding of Indigenous communities. These stories penetrate deeply into the past.

The extent and significance of this knowledge was realized during the Tŝilhqot'in land title case initiated in 1989 by the Xeni Gwet'in First Nation and Chief Roger William. The 339-day trial that ended on April 11, 2007, relied extensively on oral history provided by Tŝilhqot'in Elders. On June 26, 2014, the Supreme Court of Canada awarded the Xeni Gwet'in and Tŝilhqot'in Nation title to 1,900 square kilometres of land. While this area represents only 2 per cent of traditional Tŝilhqot'in territory, it was the first time in Canadian history that Indigenous title to the land had been recognized outside of a reserve.

Oral history also played an important role in arguing the Xeni Gwet'in and Tŝilhqot'in historical claim to their territory during the Prosperity Mine and New Prosperity Mine environmental review hearings held in 2009 and 2013. Once again, the judicial process was swayed by the evidence brought forward by these oral records of the past.

Much of the information in this book relies on the oral tradition of the Indigenous peoples of the Cariboo Chilcotin Coast.

First Contact

The Royal Proclamation of 1763

The Garden of Eden is always teetering on the brink. Once you reach the summit of a mountain, the only way forward is down.

The Indigenous people of North America, living in harmony with the land and the forces of nature of which they were a part, played a quintessential role in the survival of the first Europeans to come into their midst. It's a story that's been told over and over across the continent, but it didn't take too many generations for this generosity to be forgotten. Like an avalanche thundering down a mountainside wiping out everything in its path, the arrival of European civilization ultimately spelled an end to the Indigenous subsistent societies it encountered.

From the European perspective, the vast tracts of virgin forest, wide-open prairie, rivers, lakes, valleys and natural resources were theirs for the taking, to be exploited by the "manifest destiny" mindset of the newcomers. The Indigenous people and their way of life were seen as expendable or subservient.

The colonization of North America didn't happen overnight. Indigenous people in what is now British Columbia continued to inhabit this varied landscape with its rich biodiversity as they always had for another two centuries without interruption after the first white settlers established themselves on the eastern shores of the continent. Slowly but surely, however, the encroachment on the Indigenous domain pushed ever-westward.

In 1756, England and France were immersed in a global conflict known as the Seven Years War. It was fought in Europe, the Americas, West Africa, the Philippines and India. In North America, it was also known as the French and Indian War, fought between France and Great Britain along the frontier of the Thirteen Colonies of British America and the colonies of New France that occupied Canada from Acadia to the Great Lakes and as far south as New Orleans at the mouth of the Mississippi River. Both sides were supported by various Indigenous allies. The British colonies, which had a population of two million, had a distinct advantage over the French colonies, which numbered only 60,000 inhabitants.

The war ended with the Treaty of Paris, signed on February 10, 1763, between England, France, Spain and Portugal. It formalized Great Britain's victory in the war, and, in North America, marked the end of France's rule in Canada.

In divvying up the spoils, France had the choice of retaining Canada or acquiring a couple of islands in the Caribbean. It chose the tropical islands of Guadeloupe and Martinique, as well as the islands of Saint Pierre and Miquelon in the Gulf of St. Lawrence, along with fishing rights in this area. The French declared that the sugar

Coronation of King George III in 1760. Three years later he issued the Royal Proclamation of 1763 that continues to impact Indigenous rights in Canada today.

plantations of the Caribbean were easier to defend, and their economic value outweighed the worth of the fur trade. French philosopher Voltaire summed up Canada: little more than a few acres of snow.

Eight months later, England's young monarch, King George III, then only 25 years old and three years into his reign, issued a royal proclamation that continues to reverberate in Canada today.

The Royal Proclamation of 1763, signed on October 7, set out the guidelines for European settlement of Indigenous lands in North America. The proclamation affirmed under British law that Indigenous title existed in North America, and that all land would be considered the property of Indigenous nations until it was ceded to the British crown by treaty. Only the Crown, and not colonists, could make deals for Indigenous land.

For the Thirteen Colonies, the proclamation was seen as an affront to their ambition of self-determination. Land speculators like George Washington were already pushing into "Indian" territory towards the Mississippi River, west of the Appalachian divide, when King George made the proclamation. Thirteen years later, in 1776, the United States declared independence from Great Britain, and were no longer prevented from making their own deals for land with Native Americans.

The American War of Independence ended in 1783, but the Royal Proclamation of 1763 was still the law in British-controlled Canada as the Hudson's Bay Company and the North West Company competed to extend their fur trading empires ever westward. While the fur trade had significant impacts on Indigenous societies, it didn't dispossess them of their homeland or way of life. For the most part, the relationship between the fur traders and the Indigenous inhabitants was mutually beneficial.

In the Cariboo Chilcotin Coast, the first physical contact between Indigenous people and Europeans occurred in 1793 when Alexander Mackenzie made his historic crossing of North America from Montreal to Bella Coola. A dozen years later, in 1806, Simon Fraser established the first fur trading posts west of the Rocky Mountains at Fort McLeod, Fort St. James, Fort Fraser and Fort George. Fraser named this region west of the Rocky Mountains New Caledonia after his ancestral homeland of Scotland, which had been called Caledonia by the Romans in the second century CE. In 1808, Fraser made his historic journey down the river later named after him to its mouth in the Salish Sea.

Fort St. James in 1913. Image NA-08367 courtesy of the Royal BC Museum and Archives.

In 1814, a trading post, later named Fort Alexandria in honour of Alexander Mackenzie, was established along the Fraser River at ʔEsdilagh close to the junction of the territories occupied by the Secwepemc, Dakelh and Tŝilhqot'in peoples. This is approximately where Mackenzie abandoned his descent of the Fraser River and headed overland to Bella Coola.

Chris Wycotte Sr., a T'exelc (Williams Lake Indian Band) councillor and treaty negotiator, says the Secwepemc people were interested in trading with the Hudson's Bay Company when the fur traders first arrived. "They had items such as metal pots and pans for cooking, knives, guns and steel traps. In exchange, we gave them fur and salmon."

He says the fur traders relied heavily on salmon and other food sources provided by the Secwepemc. "You look at Hudson's Bay journals, and there are records that show that 10,000 salmon had been taken out of Farwell Canyon and traded during one season."

It was the gold rush of 1858 that changed everything for the Indigenous peoples of the Cariboo Chilcotin and Central Coast. Up until then, the Hudson's Bay Company had managed to discourage settlement of New Caledonia to protect its lucrative fur trade. But when news of the first gold strikes along the Fraser River reached San Francisco, the floodgates opened. Within a month, 30,000 gold seekers had descended upon Victoria, then a village of 500. Soon after, the new arrivals started swarming up the gravel bars of the Fraser Canyon and British Columbia was changed forever.

First Contact

Alexander Mackenzie's Great Journey West

Alexander Mackenzie followed a path to the Pacific coast forged by friendship. It was no accident that he took the route he did, following the Nuxalk-Dakelh Grease Trail from the Fraser River near present-day Quesnel to Bella Coola in 1793. He was seeking a route across North America to the Pacific Ocean when he portaged from a tributary of the Peace River into the upper reaches of the Fraser River watershed.

Coming down the Fraser past present-day Quesnel, his Indigenous guides advised him to abandon his descent of the great river because of rapids and unfriendly peoples and instead take the well-travelled overland route west, following the trail system up the Blackwater River through the Coast Mountains to Bella Coola. It was such a well-defined route that Mackenzie named the Blackwater River the West-Road River.

The Columbia River was still unknown to Mackenzie or European interests when he first plied the waters of the Upper Fraser River in 1793. Only a year earlier, in May 1792, American merchant sea captain Robert Gray had confirmed the existence of the Columbia and that it entered the Pacific Ocean at latitude 46° North. By the time Mackenzie reached home and published his memoir in 1801, Captain Gray's great river was fully on the European radar. Mackenzie concluded—incorrectly—that it was the Columbia headwaters in which he had paddled on his journey.

The open avenue to Bella Coola that Mackenzie travelled is evidence that the Cariboo Chilcotin Coast had a regional identity even then. The friendship and political alliances between the Athapaskan-speaking Dakelh from the high interior plateau and the coastal Nuxalk was key to the existence of this major thoroughfare.

The lifestyle and culture of the Nuxalk and Dakelh couldn't have contrasted more. The Nuxalk way of life was moulded by the temperate rainforest of giant cedar trees and an abundance of fish in the swift-flowing rivers. The Dakelh had to contend with a more severe climate and the necessity to move over a broad expanse of territory throughout the year to gather everything they needed to survive.

It wasn't uncommon for a Dakelh family to travel from the Fraser River to the Central Coast, and from the Nechako River to the Potato Mountains in the Chilcotin in a single year. In their semi-nomadic seasonal round, each family occupied several permanent homes and camping sites as they moved across the landscape following various hunting, fishing and gathering opportunities.

The Nuxalk were more sedentary, living in great longhouse villages along the Bella Coola, Kimsquit, Teleomy, Noeick, Kwatna and Dean rivers, all of them teeming with fish. They let the resources come to them. Their mastery of the dugout spoon river canoe allowed them to navigate these waterways as their highways. These narrow, tippy craft gave them a means to escape the Haida, whose great ocean-going canoes couldn't follow them up the swift-flowing streams.

Perhaps it was the great differences between them in their lifestyles and cultures that allowed the Nuxalk and the Athapaskan-speakers from the high plateau to be such good friends and allies. The Dakelh and Tŝilhqot'in were invited as honoured guests to the great Nuxalk winter potlatches. Their role was to serve as witnesses to the bestowal of names, the dancing of new masks, and the mysteries of the Nuxalk ceremony.

They would arrive in the Bella Coola Valley on horseback with their colourful clothing and buckskin, bringing a nomadic freshness to the more stay-at-home valley dwellers. Like a fresh breeze from the mountains, they would arrive with tanned buckskin, obsidian, dried meat and soapberries to trade for the products of the sea. They also brought love. Intermarriage was a natural consequence of this intermingling and this helped cement tribal solidarity even further.

By far the most coveted trade item from the coast was oolichan grease. It was such a vital commodity that the trading trails between the coast and the interior were called grease trails. This delicacy and food staple was prized by Indigenous people across the region. The Nuxalk ate it with everything, and it was a vital part of the

Ulkatcho elders Mac Squinas and P. L. West work with youth Vincent Toney to uncover an ancient line of warrior rocks at Detna Lake north of Ulkatcho Village and the Nuxalk-Dakelh Grease Trail. Photo Sage Birchwater.

Children in front of Clelliman House, Q'umk'uts Village at the mouth of the Bella Coola River. Photo Simon Bangen. Image 46919 courtesy of Canadian Museum of History.

Dakelh and Tŝilhqot'in diets because it fortified their bodies against the bitterly cold winters. It was also valued by the people on the high plateau for tanning buckskin from deer, moose and caribou hides.

Oolichan grease is a polyunsaturated oil very good for human health. Every spring Nuxalk families took pride in rendering their own distinguishable brand of grease at the mouth of the Bella Coola River. A discerning connoisseur could tell which family the grease came from.

The smelt-like oolichans were caught by the ton in long, conical nets made from stinging nettle fibre. They were placed in pits lined with cedar boughs, known as stink boxes, and allowed to ferment for up to ten days. Once they had ripened sufficiently, the rotted fish were shovelled into bentwood cedar boxes that were used to cook the brew. Hot rocks brought the water to a boil, allowing the oil to separate from the fish.

As Alexander Mackenzie observed in 1793, the Nuxalk-Dakelh Grease Trail passed through Ulkatcho Village, located on Gatcho Lake at the western edge of Dakelh territory. Ulkatcho Village was a potlatching and trading centre located 160 kilometres inland from the coast. It was unoccupied most of the year as large extended Ulkatcho families wintered in their own hunting and trapping areas in the surrounding countryside where they could obtain enough sustenance to survive. In later years, they used these isolated meadows to cut hay for livestock.

The Culla Culla House in Ulkatcho Village. Photo by George Dawson 1876. Image 3609 courtesy of Canadian Museum of History.

Spoon canoe in the Bella Coola River in front of Q'umk'uts Village. Photo courtesy Peter Solhjell from Simon Bangen original prints.

Mackenzie described the Nuxalk-style artwork and designs on the Culla Culla potlatch house at Gatcho Lake in his journal. This represented the cultural blending that occurred between the interior and coastal peoples. This longhouse was the only permanent structure occupying the site. When Ulkatcho people gathered at the Culla Culla House for important occasions, they would stay in tents or temporary brush houses covered by skins or tarpaulins. Eighty-three years later, in 1876, the Culla Culla House was still standing when surveyor George Dawson took the only known photograph of it. The image coincides with Mackenzie's description of it.

Ulkatcho Elders say there were other potlatch houses throughout their territory. Mac Squinas said his grandfather, Captain Harry, told him of a big potlatch house at Qualcho Lake, between the Dean River and Tetachuck Lake.

Theresa Holte said her grandmother told her about a potlatch house at Nagwuntl'oo on the shores of Anahim Lake. "Way before my grandpa Chief Domas Squinas, they used to have feather dances at Nagwuntl'oo Potlatch House," Theresa said. "They would play the drum and sing and feathers used to fly up. This was way before the war between the Tŝilhqot'ins and the Waddington survey men."

Despite having had no formal education, Ulkatcho old-timers like Domas Squinas, Antone Capoose, Baptiste Stillas, Captain Harry, Old Cahoose and Old

By 1927 a Catholic church had replaced the Culla Culla House as the dominant structure at Ulkatcho Village. Photo Frank Swannell. Image G-00872 courtesy of the Royal BC Museum and Archives.

Sundyman were multilingual and could converse in the languages of their neighbours. Their mother tongue was Dakelh, but they also knew Nuxalk, Tŝilhqot'in, Chinook, English and the universal sign language used in trading with other nations.

With the colonization of British Columbia, change was in the wind. European influences quickly impacted the Indigenous lifestyle. In Bella Coola, frame houses built with sawn lumber replaced the great communal longhouses. On the plateau, log cabins finished with whip-sawn lumber replaced the underground pit houses and brush houses.

By the early 1900s, a Catholic church replaced the Culla Culla House as a prominent place in Ulkatcho Village. Surrounding the church, each family built their own log house finished with whip-sawn lumber and cedar shakes hauled in from Burns Lake. Even with permanent structures like the church and log houses, Ulkatcho Village was still only occupied periodically during special occasions—like Priest Time in June, Christmas or funerals. The rest of the time, the village remained as it always was, mostly deserted except for a few Elders too frail to travel with their families.

First Contact

New Caledonia

British Columbia has always been defined by its rugged topography. The movement of tectonic plates over millions of years pushed the landmass into an accordion-like formation, and a rich biodiversity was the result.

Indigenous cultures evolved from the land they were part of. It is only natural, then, that British Columbia, with its many ecosystems and pockets of habitat truncated by mountain ranges, raging rivers and impenetrable rock canyons, would be home to the most diverse number of distinct Indigenous societies in Canada.

In other parts of the country, where the landscape didn't impede movement, fewer Indigenous peoples occupied larger tracts of land. When Europeans first intruded into western Canada in the 1600s, the Great Plains, for example, were teeming with buffalo and the Indigenous peoples there, aided by their recently adopted horse culture, moved freely over the wide open spaces.

Navigable rivers feeding the Great Lakes and Hudson Bay offered accessible routes for European voyageurs and fur brigades to push ever westward. But access into British Columbia was a different matter. The Rocky Mountains drew a line in the sand that stymied easy entry. It's no wonder, then, that British Columbia was one of the last places on earth to become enveloped by European colonization.

Similar to the way the morning sunshine hits the tops of the mountains before it reaches the valley bottoms, the Indigenous peoples of British Columbia knew about the existence of the white-skinned Caucasians long before the first European newcomers showed up to "discover" them. Trade networks brought trade items, and lightning-fast word-of-mouth communication and storytelling made sure of that.

In northern British Columbia, the Sekani people had never seen white-skinned humans before meeting up with Alexander Mackenzie and his voyageurs in 1793. But the Scottish explorer observed that they already possessed a number of European tools and trade items. They had obtained metal axes and knives from the Dakelh, who in turn had received them from coastal traders and brought them inland along their grease trails.

Anthropologist Wilson Duff noted that Indigenous people in the BC Interior felt the effects of the white men's presence long before they had any direct contact with them. "Horses, guns and other trade items passed quickly from tribe to tribe from the south and east in advance of the first explorers," he wrote. "So did diseases such as smallpox and some European religious ideas."

Most of the written knowledge of pre-contact Indigenous life in British Columbia comes from the journals of explorers like Alexander Mackenzie and Simon

Father Adrien-Gabriel Morice spent nearly twenty years at Stuart Lake Mission. He learned to speak various Dakelh dialects and developed a syllabic alphabet so Dakelh speakers could enjoy a written language. Photo courtesy OMI Lacombe Canada Inc.

Chief Louis Billy Prince at his grandfather Chief K'wah's grave, refutes many of the beliefs postulated by Father Morice. Particularly the tradition that Dakelh widows carried the charred bones of their dead husbands around with them. Photo courtesy Lizette Hall.

Fraser and the writings of missionaries like Father Adrian-Gabriel Morice. Through their eyes, we get a glimpse of what life was like before this convergence of cultures. At the same time, these accounts are told with unavoidable cultural bias.

Take Father Morice, for example.

He was born in Mayenne, France, in 1859 and joined the Oblates of Mary Immaculate missionary order in Nancy, France, in 1877. As a seminarian, he was inspired by Father Émile Petitot, a French Oblate who spent many years in the Canadian north before returning briefly to France. Morice likewise set himself the goal of becoming a missionary and explorer in northwestern Canada.

He left France for British Columbia in 1880, where he was ordained as a priest in 1882. His first posting was to St. Joseph's Mission near Williams Lake, where he spent three years working among the Tŝilhqot'in, Secwepemc and Dakelh peoples, learning their languages and ministering to their spiritual needs. At St. Joseph's Mission, he befriended a student named Jimmy Alexander, the son of a Dakelh woman and a fur trader father, who helped him begin his study of the Dakelh language.

In 1885, Morice was sent to Fort St. James and placed in charge of the Stuart Lake mission. There he spent the next nineteen years learning the Dakelh language in depth, and becoming acquainted with the dialects spoken in the various Dakelh villages. During that time, he became familiar with the origins and customs of his "flock."

Like Father Petitot before him, Father Morice was a scholar and a linguist. He was convinced that the message of the gospel could best be conveyed to his "children of the woods" (as he called them) in their mother tongue. To this end, he developed a syllabic alphabet the Dakelh people could readily learn.

Given the choice, Father Morice would have remained in Fort St. James for his ecclesiastical life, but complaints from the Hudson's Bay Company factor convinced the bishop to withdraw him from New Caledonia in 1904. Morice was sent

Lizette Hall, author of the 1992 book, *The Carrier, My People* said the Dakelh people got the name "Carrier" because they had to pack their stuff on their backs over the rugged mountain trails. Harlan I. Smith photographed a demonstration of this technique in Bella Coola in 1922. Image 55694 courtesy Canadian Museum of History.

Taya, son of Chief K'wah, and father of Chief Louis Billy Prince. Photo courtesy Lizette Hall.

to Kamloops, but he was unhappy there and unable to get along with the other priests. After several years of conflict, the church set him up in a house in Winnipeg where he spent the remainder of his life as a scholar, writing extensively on Dakelh language and culture.

In 1906, Father Morice published his definitive work, *The History of the Northern Interior of British Columbia (1660 to 1880)*. While extremely informative and entertaining, Morice's writing must be read with discrimination. He speaks with the bias of someone who believed his own western European culture was superior to the cultures of the Indigenous people with whom he was working.

Lizette Hall, a Dakelh citizen and author of the 1992 book, *The Carrier, My People,* debunks many of Father Morice's beliefs. Hall was a direct descendent of

Lizette Hall and her father Chief Louis Billy Prince in 1959 when he was 95 years old. Photo courtesy Lizette Hall.

the legendary Dakelh chief, K'wah, of Nak'azdli Village, located near the outflow of Stuart Lake. Her father, Chief Louis Billy Prince, born in 1864, was Chief K'wah's grandson.

Hall said that there were a lot of things Father Morice got wrong in his book about the Dakelh people. "Like my tribe, the Carrier [Dakelh]. He [Father Morice] says we got that name [Carrier] because widows carried the bones of their dead husbands on their backs for a year. I asked my father about that and he said it wasn't true. He said they used to bury the charred bones of their dead in trees."

She said her father told her that the people who gave Father Morice that information were so tired of and annoyed by all his persistent questions that they made up that story just to get rid of him. Hall says the name "Carrier" comes from the Sekani name for her people, "Aghelh Ne," which means "ones who pack." She goes on to say that in the early days the Dakelh had no other means to transport their goods overland except on their backs or in canoes along waterways. "So they called us 'Carriers.' We used the hide from the shin bone of a deer or moose as a head-strap for packing."

The Sekani, an Athapaskan-speaking people who lived east of the Rockies, had adopted the horse culture of the plains and used horses with travois for packing their goods. Hall says, "So we called them Tsek'ane, which means 'Dwellers on the rocks' in our language. They lashed a pole on either side of their horse, then lashed two cross pieces of wood to the ends of the poles and covered it with a piece of hide for a platform. Their burdens were then lashed onto this platform with babiche."

FIRST CONTACT

SIMON FRASER ARRIVES IN NEW CALEDONIA

Fifteen years after Alexander Mackenzie's historic 1793 crossing of North America, Simon Fraser followed the river later named after him to its mouth in 1808. The journals kept by both explorers provide poignant insights into the lives, culture and interrelationships among the Indigenous peoples they met as they travelled through the rugged landscape that would become British Columbia.

When Simon Fraser was born on May 20, 1776, in the village of Mapleton near the boundary between New York State and Vermont, the American Revolution was poised to erupt. He was the last of eight children born to Captain Simon Fraser and Isabella Grant.

Captain Fraser was a member of the 84th Highland Regiment who had crossed the Atlantic on the *Pearl* and arrived in the Thirteen Colonies in 1773. The Frasers had family in New York and established a farm near Mapleton.

Simon Fraser was just a boy when he and his family settled in the small town of Cadillac, Quebec, in 1783. Simon Fraser University Archives F-208-4-0-0-0-2. Charcoal drawing donated to Simon Fraser University in 1965 by his great-great grandson Donald C. Fraser of Fargo, North Dakota.

Young Simon was less than 2 months old when the Thirteen Colonies declared independence from Great Britain in July 1776, and the new nation of the United States of America was born. Unfortunately for the Fraser family, they were on the wrong side. Simon and Isabella were committed loyalists to the British cause, and on August 16, 1777, Captain Fraser was captured in the Battle of Bennington and thrown into prison. A year and a half later, he died in captivity before his youngest son, Simon, had turned 3 years old.

British Columbia was largely unknown to Europeans during this settling of accounts in eastern North America. Simon Fraser Jr. was only 2 years old when Captain James Cook anchored in Nootka Sound on the west coast of Vancouver Island in 1778, gaining a first glimpse of British Columbia for Great Britain.

Cook traded with the Nuu-chah-nulth and made repairs to his ship, remaining for a month at Nootka Island. Then, in late April, he set out, mapping the northwest coast of North America all the way to the Bering Strait. In a single visit, he became the first mariner to chart the majority of this coastline on world maps.

After the Revolutionary War ended in 1783, widowed Isabella Grant Fraser, assisted by her brother-in-law, Judge John Fraser of Montreal, moved with her dependent children to Quebec. Simon was 8 years old when they arrived in the small northern Quebec town of Cadillac, and when he was 14, he attended school in Montreal in the care of his uncle. At 16, he entered the service of the North West Company, apprenticing as a clerk.

Little is known of Simon Fraser's first decade with the Montreal-based fur trading company, during which he worked his way up the ranks. He had only been in the company's employ for a year when Alexander Mackenzie made his historic 1793 journey across the continent to the Pacific coast.

Fraser's own dance in the historic limelight occurred over a brief three-year span, from fall 1805 to August 1808. His commission by the North West Company was to follow the Peace River to its headwaters, cross the Rockies, and establish trading posts in what is now the interior of British Columbia. His main objective, however, was to follow Mackenzie's so-called "Columbia River" to its mouth.

It was assumed, of course, that the great river that Mackenzie had paddled in 1793 on his journey to Bella Coola was the upper reaches of the Columbia. Fraser eventually proved otherwise.

He continued to perpetuate Mackenzie's misunderstanding as he led a party of twenty men up the Peace River in fall 1805 to establish a post at Rocky Mountain Portage at the foot of the turbulent Peace River Canyon. The community of Hudson's Hope occupies that site today and the W.A.C. Bennett Dam was constructed nearby in the 1960s. Fraser recognized this as an excellent location for a trading post and supply base to launch exploratory forays into the unknown region beyond the Rocky Mountains.

Leaving most of his men to build Rocky Mountain Portage House that fall, Fraser set off with a smaller party to explore the upper reaches of the Peace River. Following the Parsnip tributary, the party reached Trout Lake, now known as McLeod Lake, where they met a band of friendly Sekani people. Fraser decided to build Trout Lake Post, later renamed Fort McLeod, and this became the first permanent European settlement in British Columbia west of the Rocky Mountains.

That winter, one of Fraser's men, James McDougall, set off from McLeod Lake on a reconnaissance trip west into the lands of the Dakelh. After a three-and-a-half-day trek he got as far as Stuart Lake, and met a Dakelh man by the name of Toeyen, who described how Stuart Lake drained into the large river system Mackenzie had paddled in 1793. McDougall told Toeyen that a party of white men would be coming to found a trading post on the shores of Stuart Lake the following summer and gave him a piece of red cloth so he could identify himself when they arrived.

When McDougall brought the news of his discovery to Rocky Mountain Portage, Fraser was committed to taking the longer, more circuitous water route to Stuart Lake, to stay true to his quest to follow Mackenzie's great "Columbia" River. With a party of a dozen men in two large birchbark canoes, Fraser set out in early June 1806, as soon as the rivers were navigable. It took them more than a month to reach Stuart Lake.

Though Toeyen had warned his people about the impending arrival of the fur brigade, the Dakelh community was alarmed when Fraser's two large birchbark canoes hove into sight.

Father Morice wrote an account of this memorable event as it had been described to him:

> The 26th of July 1806 was a rather windy day on what the Dakelh called Lake Na'kal... The soapberries were ripening and most of Chief K'wah's people were camped at the mouth of Beaver Creek... when what appeared to them, two immense canoes were descried struggling against the wind around a point.
>
> ... Immediately great alarm arises as such large canoes have never plied on Dakelh waters... and lo, a song like of which has never been heard before strikes their ear...
>
> Toeyen... donning his red piece of cloth as an apron, seizes a tiny spruce bark canoe lying on the beach... and fearlessly paddles to meet the strangers...
>
> On landing, Fraser's men, to impress the natives with a proper idea of their wonderful resources, fired a volley with their guns, whereupon the whole crowd of Dakelh fell prostrate to the ground...

That was the dramatic first contact on Dakelh soil.

Despite being low on provisions, Fraser set his men to building a trading post on Stuart Lake near Chief K'wah's Nak'azdli Village, which he named Fort St. James. Chief K'wah was one of the key defining figures at the time of first contact in New Caledonia. He was chief at Stuart Lake when Simon Fraser arrived in 1806 to build Fort St. James and a second post along the Nechako River near the Dakelh village of Nadleh, which became known as Fort Fraser. Chief K'wah is credited with saving the lives of Fraser and his party from starving to death by supplying 30,000 dried salmon to feed them their first winter. Fraser's plan was to resume his major task of exploring Mackenzie's "Columbia" River to its mouth as soon as he amassed enough provisions for the journey.

It was the great distance across the continent that made it essential for the North West Company to find a practical route to the Pacific coast to reduce the costs of maintaining its far-flung fur empire. The remoteness of New Caledonia made it difficult to keep the posts adequately supplied. It took nearly a year to bring trade goods across the continent from Montreal.

It was this delay in bringing provisions west that forced Fraser to wait until the spring of 1808 before attempting the final leg of his perilous and fantastic journey south.

CHIEF K'WAH AND JAMES DOUGLAS

Twenty-two years later, K'wah was to save the life of another prominent European—James Douglas. In 1828, Douglas was working as a clerk for the Hudson's Bay Company at Fort St. James. K'wah entered the fort with a group of Dakelh men to confront Douglas over the brutal killing of a Dakelh man in K'wah's camp while K'wah was away. This man had been accused of murdering a Hudson's Bay Company employee two years earlier in Fort George, and Douglas and his men rousted him out of K'wah's tent and bludgeoned him to death.

During the encounter at the trading post, one of K'wah's men grabbed Douglas by the throat and held a knife over him, waiting for K'wah to give him the signal to strike. Douglas's wife, Amelia, who was half-Indigenous herself, pleaded with K'wah for her husband's release. After a few tense moments, K'wah granted Douglas mercy, but life for Douglas in New Caledonia after that was never the same. He had lost the trust and respect of the Dakelh people and was soon reposted to Fort Vancouver in the Columbia District.

In the push and shove of frontier life in early British Columbia, history could have been rewritten in the blink of an eye without K'wah's intervention.

At Fort Vancouver, Douglas worked his way up the chain of command to eventually become the Hudson's Bay Company's chief factor for the Columbia District. Then, when the Oregon Treaty of 1846 set the boundary between Canada and the United States at the 49th parallel, Douglas established a new post for the Hudson's Bay Company at Fort Victoria on Vancouver Island. He later became the first governor of the crown colony of Vancouver Island.

FRASER'S JOURNEY TO THE SALISH SEA

A new urgency had arisen for the North West Company when American President Thomas Jefferson commissioned Meriwether Lewis and William Clark to explore and map the newly acquired Louisiana territory purchased from France in 1803, and to find a practical route to the Pacific Ocean. Lewis and Clark set out from St. Louis in May 1804, bound for the Columbia River, with the intention of establishing an American presence on the west coast where Captain Robert Gray had claimed the land for the United States. The Lewis and Clark expedition took two years to complete and the American explorers returned to St. Louis a year after Fraser departed from Fort William for the land beyond the Rockies.

During summer 1807, Fraser made final preparations for his trip down the great river by building Fort George at the mouth of the Nechako River, where he would launch his expedition. He constructed canoes and amassed a cache of trade goods and supplies he would need.

Simon Fraser navigating the rock face suspension bridge trail in the Fraser Canyon assisted by Indigenous inhabitants who, according to Fraser, scaled the lashed scaffolding like sailors climbing a sailing ship's rigging. John Innes painting, "Simon Fraser in the Fraser Canyon on His Journey to the Sea, 1808." Image MSC130-19236-01 courtesy of the Philip Francis British Columbia Postcards Collection, a digital initiative of Simon Fraser University Library.

On May 28, 1808, Fraser's party of twenty-four men set out from Fort George in four canoes. Joining Fraser were his two lieutenants, John Stuart and Jules Maurice Quesnelle, nineteen French-Canadian voyageurs and two Indigenous guides and interpreters. The strong current of the spring freshet took them quickly downstream through Fort George Canyon and Cottonwood Canyon to the grassland benches and open vistas downstream of present day Quesnel.

To Fraser's surprise, the land was fully occupied, with many Indigenous dwellings and villages on both sides of the river. He observed the first domesticated horses west of the Rockies and passed the place where Mackenzie had turned back to follow the Nuxalk-Dakelh Grease Trail to the Pacific coast.

When Fraser pulled ashore in front of a large house on the banks of the river, he was cautioned by the Dakelh inhabitants not to proceed any farther until he made his intentions known to the people who lived farther downstream. "Should you surprise them, they might take you for enemies and attack," he was warned.

Mounted couriers were sent to the people living farther down the river, and soon a party of Dakelh and Secwepemc arrived to meet the newcomers. They were curious about the white strangers intending to visit their country, yet were friendly because of the respect shown by giving advance notice. For the rest of his journey, Fraser followed this sage advice and had the chiefs from each preceding community introduce him to the communities he would be visiting.

As Fraser entered the domain of the Secwepemc near the present community of Xats'ull, he was introduced to the great Chief Logshom, who offered to guide the party for the next 300 kilometres through Secwepemc territory to Lillooet and act as their ambassador. Here the river got narrower and more dangerous, and Fraser's guides told him the river ahead was a series of waterfalls, fast water and rock canyons, with tremendous whirlpools capable of swallowing a canoe and all its people and contents.

Though Fraser brought a vast store of dried salmon and other provisions to sustain his men, for the most part, the party relied upon food they were able to obtain from their Indigenous hosts along the way. A favourite food of the voyageurs was dog meat, and when the opportunity arose, they feasted on this delicacy.

Just past the mouth of the Williams Lake River, they encountered a very long and dangerous rapid. Fraser asked Chief Logshom if his people were in the habit of running this rapid, and the chief said no. Fraser chose to run it anyway with one of his canoes and was sorry he did. The five-man crew managed to stop their craft before it got swallowed up by the turbulent waters and were forced to cut a path up the canyon wall with their knives. Using ropes, they managed to haul and lift the canoe up the perpendicular rock face.

Chief Logshom advised Fraser to abandon the river route entirely and travel by horseback to the east where they would find a great river and smooth water all the way to the sea. As it turns out this would have taken Fraser to the Columbia River he was seeking. Instead he stuck to the task at hand. "Going to the sea by an indirect way was not the object of the undertaking," Fraser wrote in his journal. "I therefore would not deviate, and continued on our route."

A few kilometres farther on, they reached the Iron Canyon between Riske Creek and the Chilcotin River. This time they portaged completely and didn't attempt to run the swirling rapids. At the mouth of the Chilcotin River, a group of Tŝilhqot'in people gathered to witness the passage of the white-skinned strangers they had heard about.

Finally, at Leon Creek just north of Lillooet, Fraser took Chief Logshom's advice to abandon his canoes. He overturned the two craft on scaffolding and covered them with branches to protect them from the scorching sun. As he had at other locations along the river, he buried a cache of dried salmon and supplies for their return journey.

The party then continued on foot to the land of the St'at'imc at Lillooet, where Chief Logshom took his leave, and Fraser bartered for the use of Indigenous dugout canoes. The St'at'imc chiefs from Lillooet passed Fraser's party into the care of the Nlaka'pamux (the Canyon Salish) at Lytton, where 1,200 people awaited to meet them where the clear water of the Thompson River joins the muddy Fraser. Then at Yale, they were handed over to the Coast Salish Stó:lō.

The Indigenous inhabitants along the route helped with the heavy lifting by carrying loads over portages, guiding them over the precipitous trails, paddling the canoes, and providing food. "We had to pass many difficult rocks, defiles and precipices," Fraser wrote. "There was a kind of beaten path used by the natives, and made passable by means of scaffolds, bridges and ladders."

He said navigating these structures required no small degree of dexterity and courage. "For instance we had to ascend precipices by means of ladders composed of two long poles placed upright and parallel with sticks tied crossways. These ladders were placed up to any height, and often were so slack that the smallest breeze put them in motion."

He said sometimes the ladders were so narrow it took great concentration to place your foot on each rung. "Most perilous was when another rock projected over the rock you were leaving. The Indians deserve our thanks for their able assistance through these alarming situations. We had to trust all our things to them. Even our guns were handed from one to another, yet they thought nothing of these difficulties, but went up and down these wild places with the same agility as sailors do aboard a ship."

"It took a man of great courage and determination to forge alliances, wheedle, barter, buy, and in some instances extort the help he needed to complete his mission," writes Stephen Hume in his 2008 book, *Simon Fraser*.

Needless to say, Fraser was disappointed when he read his sextant at the mouth of the river in the land of the Musqueam and determined he was at the 49th parallel north. This was not the Columbia River he was seeking, which entered the Pacific Ocean at 46°N, but another stream altogether.

To make matters worse, the route, because of its difficulty, was not suitable for the fur trade. In that sense, Fraser felt the expedition was a failure. But he completed the 800-kilometre journey down the river from Fort George to the Salish Sea in thirty-six days, and returned to Fort George and New Caledonia in thirty-five days.

His party travelled through the harshest conditions imaginable, passed through the territories of half a dozen Indigenous nations, and never lost a man.

Simon Fraser and his party were the first Europeans seen by the Indigenous nations of the Interior who lived along the great river. Though the various nations had a long history of warfare with each other, it was the co-operation, assistance and diplomacy of the Indigenous inhabitants that allowed Fraser to achieve his goal.

Fraser's journey knit a thread through the cultural and geographical diversity that would become British Columbia. It is perhaps fitting that this great stream, known by different names to each Indigenous people along the way, should ultimately bear Fraser's name.

The Twans of Fort Alexandria

One of the grand families of the Cariboo can trace its roots back to the fur trade. John Sanford Twan was born at Fort Alexandria in 1853 and grew up there. His children were also born there.

John's mother, Mary (Marie) Cletses, came from ʔEsdilagh, a Dakelh village next to the fort, and his father, Charles Touin (as his name was originally spelled), was a Métis voyageur from Montreal.

Charles was 17 when he joined the fur brigade in 1833 and made his way west to New Caledonia. Hudson's Bay Company records show him employed as a middleman in a canoe in New Caledonia and the Columbia District, a fur-trading region that extended from Fort St. James on Stuart Lake to Fort Vancouver at the mouth of the Columbia River.

Charles Touin (later anglicized to Twan) and his Dakelh wife Mary (Marie) Cletses. Photo courtesy Danny Twan.

Fort Alexandria was built in 1814 near McAllister on benchland above the flood level on the east side of the Fraser River to serve as a terminus for the Columbia River–New Caledonia brigade system. The river below this point was too treacherous for canoe travel and the large meadows nearby provided ample pasture for brigade horses.

Then in 1821, when the Hudson's Bay Company and the North West Company amalgamated under the Hudson's Bay Company banner, the fort was moved farther upstream because there was better agricultural ground there. (The fort grew all its own grain, with 2,300 acres under cultivation.) In 1836, the fort was moved again, to the west side of the Fraser, which was more accessible to the fur trade with the Tŝilhqot'in people from the Chilcotin Plateau. Land was cultivated there and a small flour mill had been established by the time Marie Cletses gave birth to John Sanford Twan in 1853.

When the gold rush of 1859 began, the quiet trading post was transformed overnight. Gold rush traffic converged on Alexandria, and the Hudson's Bay Company set up a store on the east side of the river to cater to the rush of hopeful miners. Three or four saloons sprang up there as well, but the hustle and bustle was short-lived.

In 1862, construction of the sternwheeler *Enterprise* got underway on the banks of the river next to the fort. It was anticipated that Alexandria would be the head of navigation for the Upper Fraser and become a thriving economic centre. But when *Enterprise* Captain Doone discovered he could safely navigate the river as far downstream as Soda Creek, aspirations for Alexandria evaporated.

Mary (Marie) Cletses Twan. Photo courtesy Danny Twan.

Fort Alexandria, the birthplace of John Sanford Twan in 1853. Image F-05775 courtesy of the Royal BC Museum and Archives.

John Sanford Twan and Rosalie Sam Hunt Twan. Photos courtesy Danny Twan.

Times were changing quickly. By 1867, Quesnel had replaced Alexandria as the Hudson's Bay Company supply centre for the region, and the trading post at Fort Alexandria closed. The company continued to farm the land around the old fort to supply Quesnel and the Cariboo with produce.

Over the years, the Hudson's Bay Company started selling off its trading post properties. Finally, in 1895, the company executed a "quit claim" to Fort Alexandria, relinquishing its last holdings at the fort and returning it to the Crown.

On April 1, 1895, John Sanford Twan, by now 42 years old, pre-empted the old fort and the 44 hectares (109.5 acres) that surrounded it. Two years later, he and 18-year-old Rosalie Sam Hunt were married. Rosalie, a woman of Dakelh lineage, had been born at ʔEsdilagh, next to Fort Alexandria.

Despite their 26-year age difference, Rosalie and John Sanford spent nearly fifty years together. They had a dozen children beginning with a daughter, Suzanne, born in 1899, followed by Eva (1901), Irvin (1903), Emma (1905), Dave (1907), Jeanette Rose (1909), Nora Martha (1911), Bill (1913), Clarence (1916), Allan (1917), Evelyn (1919) and Charlie (1922).

Like most men of his time, John Sanford Twan made his living in a number of ways. The 1890 voters list identifies him as a shoemaker. In 1894, he was listed as a harness-maker. Various land pre-emption applications refer to him as a farmer. He was also a rancher and a guide for police, government officials and land surveyors.

Over the years, he added other pre-emptions and hay and grazing leases to his holdings.

The Twan children grew up playing in the ramshackle loop-holed old Fort Alexandria and exploring its underground passages leading to the storehouse and powder magazine. By the 1920s, the fort had become pretty dilapidated and dangerous, so John Sanford tore it down. The old log walls and huge squared corner posts made excellent firewood—except for the accumulation of lead bullets and flints deeply imbedded in the wood, which played havoc with his crosscut saw.

Eventually John Sanford turned the old fort property over to his eldest son, Irvin, who also raised his family there. Irvin later sold to the property to Terry Exshaw, who turned most of the contents of the old warehouse over to the Quesnel Museum. The property was eventually sold to the ʔEsdilagh First Nation after a forest fire razed the buildings, and it sat vacant for a number of years.

St. Paul's Catholic church on the east side of the Fraser River overlooking the Twan family burial plot, is where John Sanford Twan and his wife Rosalie are buried one grave apart. Photo Kris Andrews.

John Sanford Twan lived to the great age of 93 and got to know two generations of his descendants. His grandson, Danny Twan, was 3 years old when the old man passed away in Quesnel in 1946. He had a vague memory of his grandfather being laid to rest in the Twan Family Cemetery in Alexandria on the east side of the Fraser River. John Sanford had traded land on the west side of the river for land on the east side for the family burial grounds, which is shared by the ʔEsdilagh community as well.

Granny Rosalie Twan also lived to a great age. She was 97 when she passed away in Quesnel in June 1976 and was interred in the Twan burial plot. She wasn't placed right next to her husband though. She always insisted she didn't want to sleep "next to that man" so the family honoured her request and laid her to rest one grave over from her husband.

The Twan family, prominent now throughout the Cariboo and other parts of British Columbia, proudly embraces its First Nations and settler roots that link Indigenous society with the newcomers of the early fur trade.

Fort Chilcotin

The Tŝilhqot'in developed a reputation for being independent, hard bargainers in their dealings with European newcomers. As early as 1825, the Hudson's Bay Company looked into opening a trading post in the Chilcotin, but didn't find the Tŝilhqot'in overly eager to do business with them.

Finally, in 1829, the company opened Fort Chilcotin as a satellite to Fort Alexandria. It was built west of Bull Canyon on the north side of the Chilcotin Valley between the mouth of Alexis Creek and the junction of the Chilcotin and Chilko rivers. The post operated on a sporadic and seasonal basis until it shut down in 1843. The fur company's attempts to do business there were continually fraught with difficulty.

There was an expectation that the Tŝilhqot'in would supply the fort with fish and fresh game, and that the fur company would pay for the privilege of fishing in Tŝilhqot'in territory.

Company officials figured the Tŝilhqot'in were demanding too high a price to supply provisions to the fort, and workers there complained that they were little more

A memorial ceremony at the site of Fort Chilcotin. Every year, on October 26 the Tŝilhqot'in nation gathers to commemorate the six war chiefs who were hung in 1864 and 1865. Photo courtesy Tŝilhqot'in National Government.

than slaves to the Tŝilhqot'in, who they found "difficult to keep in check." In 1839, the Tŝilhqot'in people completely barred the river downstream of the fort, preventing Fort Chilcotin workers from catching fish.

The Tŝilhqot'in people were astute in business and had a broad view of their territory ranging from the Fraser River to the Central Coast. Rather than automatically trade their fur at Fort Chilcotin because it was closer and more convenient, they'd shop around for opportunities where they could get a better deal. They were aware that trade goods at Fort Alexandria and Fort Chilcotin were double the price of goods at Fort Kamloops or Fort McLoughlin near Bella Bella. A memo from James Douglas notes that 40 per cent of the furs traded at Fort McLoughlin came from the Interior.

In 1840, Fort Chilcotin clerks complained the Tŝilhqot'in continued their practice of trading with other First Nations rather than dealing with the company. Historian Tom Swanky, in his 2012 book *The True Story of Canada's War of Extermination on the Pacific*, says the Tŝilhqot'in people wouldn't have taken their fur all that distance from the Chilcotin through middlemen to the Central Coast if it weren't for the enormous prices asked at Fort Chilcotin and Fort Alexandria for trade goods.

Swanky says most of the difficulties experienced at Fort Chilcotin came as a result of the bad characters of its first and third fort managers. He says the Tŝilhqot'in people ran the first one out because he refused to pay for furs he had accepted on credit with a promise to pay later. He also made threats about punishment by the Christian God.

Under the command of the second trader, William McBean, Swanky says that the fort was comparatively well accepted. "McBean ingratiated himself with the people and did not fight Tŝilhqot'in public policies. In other words, he made no attempt to keep them in check. He employed Alexis from Bendziny (Puntzi Lake) when he was a young man and hired several other Tŝilhqot'in youths as well. Alexis later became a chief. There is no evidence that the Tŝilhqot'in were against the fur trade or the Hudson's Bay Company in principle," Swanky says.

It was the fort's third trader, Donald McLean, notorious for his disrespect, that became Fort Chilcotin's Achilles heel. It was the fort's failure under McLean's tenure that caused it to be closed down permanently in 1843. The next year, the fur company moved its satellite post from Fort Chilcotin to Lhoosk'uz (Kluskus) in Dakelh territory.

The First Priests

Christianity made its first inroads into the Cariboo and New Caledonia in 1842 when Roman Catholic missionary Father Modeste Demers arrived at Fort Alexandria with the fur brigade from Fort Vancouver. He had first been sent to the Columbia District by Quebec's archbishop, Joseph Signay in 1838, to answer the call of Roman Catholics in Oregon for their own missionaries and priests. Signay indicated that his primary duty was to the Indigenous peoples and had instructed him to learn the Indigenous languages as swiftly as possible.

Demers learned to communicate quickly. After twelve months in the Columbia District, he had compiled a dictionary, a catechism, a prayer book and hymns in the Chinook jargon and had acquired an elementary knowledge of more than one of the local dialects.

Father Demers made his first foray into British Columbia three years after his arrival, when he visited Fort Langley in 1841. A year later he accompanied Hudson's Bay Company factor, Peter Skene Ogden, to the Cariboo, following the Columbia River up the Okanagan Valley to Fort Kamloops, then on to Fort Alexandria, where he spent the winter. He baptized converts throughout New Caledonia and oversaw the building of chapels at Williams Lake, Fort Alexandria and Fort St. James.

Born in St. Nicholas de Lévis, Quebec, in 1809, Demers was 33 years old when he set foot in the Cariboo and he got along well with the Indigenous people there. He wrote a letter to Archbishop Signay, dated December 22, 1842, telling him how the T'exelcemc people of Williams Lake were already living in houses built after the European tradition when he arrived and had been doing so for several years. "The old Chief William reserved his own house for me and moved in with his son, the young Chief William," he wrote.

At Williams Lake, the priest baptized several children and commissioned Chief William to build a chapel in the T'exelcemc village site beside Missioner Creek, where the city of Williams Lake is today. The next time Father Demers visited, a 41-by-19-foot chapel had been completed, along with a large fireplace and window openings covered with animal skins. There was no glass available so the translucent rawhide served to keep out the bugs and cold and let in sufficient light.

But when he returned in January to give his first communion, Demers was devastated to discover that the hides covering the windows had been eaten by dogs. "Oh vexatious disappointment," he wrote. "Some miserable starved dogs ate our windows. We had to set traps to catch several guilty ones to put a stop to this scandal."

Demers returned to the Columbia District later that year, and after the Oregon Treaty of 1846 set the boundary between the United States and Canada at the 49th parallel, he moved to Fort Victoria with James Douglas. In 1847, he was named the first bishop of Vancouver Island and British Columbia.

Most Reverend Modeste Demers, first bishop of Vancouver Island and British Columbia 1846–1871, was the first priest to visit the Cariboo and New Caledonia in 1842. Photo used with permission of the Roman Catholic Diocese of Victoria.

Father John Nobili, a Jesuit from Italy, was the next priest to visit the Cariboo in 1845. Like Father Demers, he arrived with the fur brigade from the Columbia District and stayed two years. He kept meticulous records, registering 629 baptisms among the Dakelh, Secwepemc and Tŝilhqot'in before returning to Oregon in 1847.

Gold discovered in California in 1849 whisked Father Nobili away to San Francisco, and for nearly twenty years after that, no Catholic missionaries visited the Cariboo or New Caledonia.

These three grave markers next to St. Andrews Roman Catholic Cathedral in Victoria, BC, designate the final resting place of three eminent church icons: Bishop Modeste Demers, the Colony of Vancouver Island's first bishop; Bishop Charles John Seghers, the second and fourth bishop of Victoria and second archbishop of Portland; and Vicar-General Father John J. Jonckau, pioneer parish priest of Victoria. Bishop Demers' colourful vexation condemning "miserable starved dogs" for eating the hide-covered windows of the first chapel in Williams Lake, is well-remembered in the Cariboo. Father Demers called the incident a scandal. But scandal seems to have followed the esteemed bishop to the grave. The memorial marker carved in stone gives the incorrect year of his death, 1861 instead of 1871. The Roman Numeral MDCCCLXI is missing an "X." However, linguistic expert Bill Poser suggests the wavy line over the single "X" may in fact indicate a multiple of "X's."

Dunlevy

The First Gold Strike in the Cariboo

If it wasn't for Margaret "Ma" Lally Murray, the intrepid newspaper publisher from Lillooet, the story of the first gold rush discovery in the Cariboo would have been lost forever.

Alex P. McInnes was the postmaster at Marguerite when Ma Murray and her MLA husband, George Matheson Murray, made his acquaintance in the mid-1930s. Alex lived in a rambling old log house, one of the original stopping places on the Cariboo Road.

Alex McInnes had been born in Barkerville on April 11, 1868. His father, Alexander Douglas McInnes, was the colony's first gold commissioner during the most spectacular days of the Cariboo gold rush, and one of his father's best friends was Peter Curran Dunlevy, the gentleman gold miner who was party to the first gold strike in the Cariboo.

Once Dunlevy retired from active mining, he used his fortune to establish a prosperous ranch, hotel, store and stopping house at Soda Creek. Alex attended school at St. Joseph's Mission with Dunlevy's children, and, as a boy, he heard many first-hand accounts of the gold rush from Dunlevy and the old-timers clustered around the spittoon in Dunlevy's Soda Creek store swapping tall tales.

He learned how Dunlevy and his party of five miners made the first big strike of placer gold in the Cariboo on the Horsefly River in June 1859. This predated the big strike in Barkerville by several months. Alex promised Dunlevy he would someday write his stories down.

"Alex was keenly planning to chronicle the life and times of the early gold seekers in six sections," Ma Murray recalled in a book she later published about Dunlevy. "Every time my husband and I made a trip north, a call at Marguerite was a must and a visit with McInnes likely the most exciting encounter along the way."

Alex was fretting that his stories weren't arranged and he had no way of getting them typed. Then George Murray handed him a ream of foolscap and encouraged him to write the stories out longhand. "We weren't back in Lillooet six weeks when the first installment of the promised six arrived in the mail," Ma Murray stated.

A short time later, a second installment titled "Indian Games" arrived at the post office. These were followed by several thumbnail drawings of the characters in Alex's narrative.

"We were very excited with the McInnes manuscript," Ma Murray said. "The copy was written in a fine, steady hand, and in 1938 we published the first volume of

Peter Dunlevy, an early miner in the Cariboo, and owner of the Exchange Hotel in Soda Creek. c1870. Image A-01383 courtesy of the Royal BC Museum and Archives.

Alex McInnes' writings." It was typeset in 7-point type on linotype and the Murrays printed 1,000 copies of the booklet in soft cover. "We called it *Chronicles of the Cariboo Number One*, subtitled *Dunlevey's Discovery of Gold on the Horsefly*."

Ma Murray used Alex's misspelling of "Dunlevey" in the booklet, and awaited further volumes of the manuscript, but they never came. "Mr. McInnes advised us that each manuscript was in fairly good order but that he was going to the hospital for a short rest," Ma Murray stated. "We never heard from him again."

Alex's short rest turned into an eternal one, and the whereabouts of the old box of manuscripts he brought with him to the hospital was never discovered. "Whoever disposed of that old box when Alex was discharged from his last stay in hospital removed a more accurate history than will ever be written about this colourful era in the Cariboo," Ma Murray lamented.

In 1971, Ma Murray published an expanded version of Alex's chronicles, compiled by Edith Beeson, enshrining two of his diaries, the "Dunlevey" story and "Indian Games." The book, titled *Dunlevey From the Diaries of Alex P. McInnes*, is an insightful read.

Peter Curan Dunlevy, born in Pittsburgh in 1835, was 24 years old when he and four partners were sifting gravel on a sandbar at the mouth of the Chilcotin River in the spring of 1859. They were so engrossed in their work, examining the gravel for signs of gold in the washings of their rocker that they didn't notice a tall Secwepemc man, Tomaah, walk into their midst.

"Klahowya Whitemans," Tomaah greeted them in Chinook. Then pointing to the rocker, he asked what they were doing with it.

The five miners were startled by the appearance of the intruder and immediately grabbed their Kentucky long rifles, which were propped within an arm's reach of each man.

Alex P. McInnes's mother, Lizzie, at the McInnes roadhouse in Marguerite. Image E-05513 courtesy of the Royal BC Museum and Archives.

Tomaah, a runner for the Hudson's Bay Company, carried his own rifle lightly in the crook of his arm. When he noticed the alarm of the miners, he dropped his gun butt to the ground to indicate he had come in peace.

"Who the hell are you?" Dunlevy asked tersely. Then, greatly relieved when the intruder didn't pose a threat, he dropped his own gun butt to the sand.

Tomaah stated his name and said he was the son of Secwepemc Chief Lolo of Kamloops. He explained his business as a runner for the fur company bringing papers from Fort Yale to Fort Alexandria.

The young Secwepemc man was knowledgeable about the dealings of the white man in the business of the fur trade, but was puzzled by the feverish activity of the men working the gravel of the river. He expressed his surprise that they neither saw nor heard him coming and warned them about the Tŝilhqot'in people who lived on the high plateau to the west, up the Chilcotin River, who were not friendly towards newcomers and could easily have attacked them.

Then he examined the rocker more closely to see what these strangers found more important than protecting their lives. He asked what they were doing with the rockers.

"We are miners and we're looking for gold," Dunlevy explained. "You understand, gold?"

Tomaah shook his head. Dunlevy knelt in the wet sand and dug out a flake of gold from the bottom of the rocker. "That is gold. Gold is money. Good money."

Tomaah squatted on his haunches next to Dunlevy and carefully examined the tiny flake between his fingers and thumbnail. Then, taking out his knife from its rawhide sheath, he chipped at it with his knifepoint. Finally he looked up and said he knew what they meant by gold.

The other members of Dunlevy's party, Jim Sellars, Ira Crow, Tom Manifee and Tom Moffitt, all Americans who had migrated north from the goldfields of California, finally relaxed. Dunlevy, with his usual hospitality, invited Tomaah to stay and take food with them. As the shadows deepened around the campfire, Tomaah said at last that he knew where to find bigger pieces of gold.

If Tomaah had touched off a keg of dynamite, he couldn't have got the attention of the miners any quicker. The attitude of the men changed instantly. "Big ones! How big?" they queried.

Poking a bean on the side of his plate, he said they were as big as the bean.

The miners were in a frenzy.

Tomaah offered to show them where to find it in payment for the hospitality he had been shown and arranged to meet them in two weeks at a big gathering on the shore of Lac La Hache. There the Secwepemc, Tŝilhqot'in and Dakelh would come together to trade, play traditional games, discuss politics and socialize.

The next morning, in record time, the miners loaded their canoe and paddled back to Lillooet. "Be careful not to say anything of our plans to anyone," Dunlevy cautioned. "Appear in no haste when we reach Lillooet or we'll trigger a rush before we've had a chance at it ourselves." They then sold their boat and most of their equipment and obtained a couple of horses to pack their supplies overland.

True to his word, Tomaah was at Lac La Hache to meet Dunlevy and his party when they arrived. The five Americans were spellbound by the Indigenous games, particularly the intensity of the fight-to-the-near-death wrestling matches and the mysterious bone game of lahal. They also witnessed an intense debate that could have decided their own fate right there. Nits'il?in ?Anahim, chief of the western-most Tŝilhqot'in community of Nagwentl'un (Anahim Lake), raised concern about what to do about the flood of gold seekers invading the country. He attempted to rally the Secwepemc and Dakelh chiefs to join with the Tŝilhqot'in to oppose them. Edith Beeson paraphrases his words:

> For some time our scouts have been bringing us news of white men who are coming up our rivers. We have tolerated these men, thinking them to be weak-minded and therefore entitled to the reverent regard which all aboriginal people have for weak ones as dictated by the Great Spirit.
>
> However we have found out that these men are really not crazy and are washing out little pieces of yellow stone which they call gold

> and which they use for what we call seniya (money), to use as we use skins to trade for other goods.
>
> The St'at'imc from Lillooet have already been corrupted. It is said they have learned the white man's skill and are finding little pieces of yellow stone also.
>
> This seniya really belongs to us and the white men are taking it without asking us for it. The priests tell us this is stealing. If we steal they tell us that their God will punish us. But these white men are stealing from us. Will their God punish them for this bad act or have they made a convenient arrangement with this God? Has he one law for the natives and another law for the white man?
>
> We must keep these white men out. We must act together. If we do not act immediately we will only have to drive them out later. This will result in much bloodshed, for them and for our own people. We must act now or we are lost!

Dunlevy and his four companions were justified in fearing for their safety. Somehow they were reassured when ʔAnahim addressed them directly. As Beeson imagined it, he said to them: "This is not my country or my camp. If it were, I would say go back to the country you come from and induce your white brothers to do likewise. You are not wanted here. If you still choose to come and disregard my warning, then with sorrow I say your blood and our blood will be upon your hands and not ours."

Secwepemc Chief William and Dakelh Chief Lolo shook their heads, indicating their reluctance to enter into a battle they knew they couldn't win.

Chief Lolo spoke of his childhood growing up in the Dakelh community of ʔEsdilagh where Fort Alexandria was constructed forty-three years earlier at the boundary of the three nations. In Beeson's words, "I have studied the white man and his ways, and I do not know him yet but I know my people must learn to live in contact with him. To attempt to stop him is impossible. We Dakelh are not crazy enough to start a war that we cannot finish."

Chief William sided with the Dakelh leader. He said the smartest strategy was to work in co-operation with the white man. He declined to join the Tŝilhqot'in in a bloody, hopeless war and he stated that he wished to be friends with the newcomers so that his people could make a fair bargain with them.

The three leaders agreed to disagree, but history was about to tell a bitter tale.

The Miners' Strike in Horsefly

Once the council was over, Tomaah and his Dakelh friend, Baptiste, a fellow runner for the Hudson's Bay Company, led Dunlevy and his party east to the Horsefly River. The river was in flood in mid-June, and there Ira Crow, the most seasoned miner in the group, dug away the turf on a bench above the river to check the gravel beneath the overburden.

"This is it," he shouted. "This is the kind of stuff she's found in."

In short order, the men produced the first samples of shot gold in their pans, not the flat flakey stuff found along the Fraser River. Below the shot gold, they knew the bigger nuggets of coarser gold could be found.

The men staked their claims and struck it rich—but none too soon. Twelve hours later another party of gold seekers who had been following their tracks, arrived and staked claims of their own.

The Cariboo gold rush was on.

Chief William's Demise

The following year, in 1860, a frenzy of gold seekers continued to flood into the Cariboo following the strikes in Horsefly and Barkerville.

One day Chief William was approached by a settler, Thomas W. Davidson, who asked permission to build a cabin next to the chief's house and garden at Missioner Creek. The chapel the chief had built for Father Demers eighteen years earlier stood nearby.

True to his agreeable nature, Chief William welcomed the man. But when he arrived home from fishing for salmon on the Fraser River, he was shocked to find that Davidson had staked the whole area, and Chief William was pushed from his land.

Chris Wycotte Sr. says Davidson turned around and pre-empted all the land around there, including Chief William's house and garden. "There was a church and a village there as well. Davidson tried to pay Chief William twenty dollars for his land, but Chief William refused the money and said he wanted to keep his father's land."

Despite the colony's pre-emption laws, fashioned after the Royal Proclamation of 1763, that forbade the alienation of First Nations village sites, the pre-emption went through anyway, Wycotte says. "That's how our people lost that land. They had a policy or law that specifically said Indian graveyards and villages shouldn't be alienated, but they turned around and didn't abide by their own laws and allowed those pre-emptions to happen. The whole town of Williams Lake was our village site that got pre-empted. It's a very nice site. You can see why we were there."

Things went from bad to worse for Chief William. Two years later he died in the 1862 smallpox epidemic that swept across the region from Bella Coola to the Cariboo, wiping out two-thirds of the Indigenous population. He was succeeded by his son, Young Chief William, who continued to struggle against the tide of newcomers and an alien political system taking over his home and land, which had once been the exclusive domain of the Secwepemc people.

SMALLPOX

AND THE CHILCOTIN WAR

It's hard to characterize the Cariboo gold rush of 1858, the smallpox epidemic of 1862, and the Chilcotin War of 1864 as being anything but a single pivotal moment in history. These three events, which occurred in a span of just six years, worked in tandem to transform the heart and soul and nature of British Columbia.

Although Tŝilhqot'in Chief Nits'il?n ?Anahim failed to convince his Dakelh and Secwepemc counterparts at the Lac La Hache gathering in 1859 to take up arms against the flood of gold seekers swarming up the rivers into the Cariboo, the resolve of the Tŝilhqot'in leaders to maintain the sovereignty of their territory remained strong. But whatever misgivings Chief ?Anahim might have expressed in 1859 about newcomers invading the region, by 1861 the Tŝilhqot'in communities had given consent for both the Bentinck Arm Road from Bella Coola to the Cariboo and the proposed Bute Inlet Road up the Homathko River, consent that proved very costly.

In September 1860, according to Tom Swanky, land speculators led by George Cary had staked land at Bella Coola harbour. In October, the post manager from Fort Alexandria crossed Tŝilhqot'in territory buying fur and scouting out a road to Bella Coola. The following spring, Chief ?Anahim provided a party of nine men to guide road surveyors to Bella Coola where Chief Pootlass hosted a great feast at Q'umk'uts to welcome the land speculators and road-builders. The road from Bella Coola to Fort Alexandria in the Cariboo was given approval by the Nuxalk, the Southern Dakehl and the Tŝilhqot'in. "There was both consultation and consent," Swanky says, noting that all three Indigenous nations received passing miners in peace. In August 1861, Governor James Douglas issued Ranald McDonald a licence to create a toll road from the Bentinck Arm to the Fraser River, and in November, George Cary purchased this licence, which became the foundation for the Bentinck Arm Road.

Swanky says Chief ?Anahim and the Tŝilhqot'in leadership gambled that they would benefit from the gold rush while maintaining control of their territory, and hundreds of miners and many thousands of dollars in trade goods did pass successfully and peacefully along the Bentinck Arm Road in both directions during 1862 and 1863. But the introduction of smallpox in spring 1862 changed everything.

"It betrayed the trust the Tŝilhqot'in had extended to the newcomers," says Swanky, who is convinced that the introduction of smallpox along the Bentinck Arm Road from Bella Coola to Fort Alexandria by Francis Poole was no accident. Swanky says Poole led a party sponsored by the Bentinck Arm Company, and he is certain smallpox was spread intentionally at the behest of land speculators to wrest control

of the country from its Indigenous inhabitants. Until that point, the Indigenous population had far outnumbered the newcomers. With the Nuxalk, Tŝilhqot'in and Secwepemc numbers greatly diminished and their communities in disarray, it left the country open for pre-emption, settlement and colonial domination.

Historians trace the start of the 1862 smallpox epidemic to two passengers from San Francisco who stepped off the steamer *Brother Jonathan* in Victoria on March 13, 1862. Swanky says this sailing took place through arrangements made by George Cary, and members of a committee promoting the Bentinck Arm route were also on board. The disease spread to a group of Tsimshian camped nearby, and at the beginning of May, colonial authorities ordered them to leave at gunpoint. They returned to their home communities, taking the smallpox with them.

Poole's party left Victoria on May 21 and arrived in Bella Coola on June 5 with several smallpox-infected men in the company. They left Bella Coola on June 15, arrived in Fort Alexandria on July 4, and made it back to Victoria by July 20.

In their wake, the party left three smallpox-stricken men at Nanaimo, two at Fort Rupert on northern Vancouver Island, two at Nautlieff (Alexander Mackenzie's Friendly Village in the Bella Coola Valley), and two at a large Tŝilhqot'in village at Chilcotin Lake in Chezacut. In his memoir, Poole would also take responsibility for introducing the disease at South Bentinck Arm and Bella Coola. His passage through the country introduced the seeds of infection that spread throughout the region.

By the end of the year, smallpox had decimated two-thirds of the Nuxalk, Tŝilhqot'in and Secwepemc populations. Tŝilhqot'in communities at Bendziny (Puntzi Lake) and Chilcotin Lake and the villages of the Canyon Secwepemc along the Chilcotin and Fraser rivers were virtually obliterated.

The Bute Inlet Road

Meanwhile, at Bute Inlet Alfred Waddington received permission from British Columbia's Commissioner of Lands and Works, Colonel Moody, to build a toll road up the Homathko River through Tŝilhqot'in territory to the Cariboo goldfields. In spring 1862, he hired an exploratory expedition to map a route from Bute Inlet to Fort Alexandria, and Tŝilhqot'in Chief Telad, who lived in a village along the Homathko River at the edge of Tŝilhqot'in territory, agreed to serve as a guide for the survey crew.

Later that year, Chief Telad established a rancherie at the mouth of the river to take advantage of employment on the road. Construction began in September and continued until November, while the smallpox infestation continued to rage across the Chilcotin Plateau.

In 1863, Waddington had a workforce of eighty-five road-builders from April to the end of the year. Chief Lha Tŝ'aŝʔin (Lhatsassin), who had a fishing ground on the lower Southgate River, arrived at the Homathko in September with several

Opposite: Clellamin House (behind) and Pootlass House in Q'umk'uts Village where Chief Pootlass welcomed early land speculators in Bella Coola. Image 46917 courtesy Canadian Museum of History.

Tŝilhqot'in people, who would work with the road-builders. This group included the chief's brother, Qaqezʔ (Ka-kus).

The main party of workers returned to Victoria with Waddington in November, leaving a group of twenty-two men behind to continue blasting on the rock face. At Christmas, Waddington sent a boat to pick up the remaining men and it didn't return to Victoria until after the New Year.

Swanky speculates the boat was well supplied with liquor and that it was during this time that the work gang raped Chief Lha Tŝ'aŝʔin's daughter. This incident was described in oral testimony by Tŝilhqot'in Elders at the Prosperity Mine hearings in 2009 and 2013, and naturally raised the ire of Lha Tŝ'aŝʔin.

Trouble continued for Waddington as he made preparations to resume work on the Bute Inlet Road in spring 1864. Besides the grievance Lha Tŝ'aŝʔin had over the abuse of his daughter and other Tŝilhqot'in women and children by men on the road crew, things came to a head when the road-builders arrived at Bute Inlet on March 22 to discover that a cache of food left behind over the winter had been broken into and some flour had been taken.

Many Tŝilhqot'in were starving in the wake of the smallpox epidemic that had left their support network in disarray. Their traditional food sources had also been depleted by pressure from newcomers hunting and fishing in their territory and destroying spawning grounds, so hungry people helped themselves to the food in the locked storehouse. Swanky also notes that those who took the flour justified their actions by seeing it as a tax: "You are in our territory, you owe us bread." So they took some flour in payment.

This didn't sit well with the colonial authorities, who threatened that if the stolen food wasn't returned, more smallpox would be inflicted on the Tŝilhqot'in people. Swanky traces this sinister threat to Captain Edward Howard, skipper of the boat that delivered the work crew on March 22. He says this became the flashpoint for the Chilcotin War, which erupted six weeks later in the Homathko Canyon.

Road-builders continued construction, advancing the road several kilometres into Tŝilhqot'in territory, unaware that the powder keg was about to blow. On April 28, the ferryman manning the crossing on the Homathko River was killed. Then, in the early dawn of April 30, War Chief Lha Tŝ'aŝʔin's war party killed thirteen members of the road crew.

Lha Tŝ'aŝʔin then took the war campaign from the Homathko road camp to the Chilcotin Plateau, where William Manning lived at Bendziny with his Tŝilhqot'in wife, Nancy Tsholiralna. Manning, a business associate of the road-builders, had constructed a stopping house at Puntzi Lake, where many Tŝilhqot'in trails converged.

The Tŝilhqot'in village at Bendziny had been devastated in 1862 by the smallpox epidemic, and Manning and several partners, including Alex McDonald and Peter McDougall, had staked the land previously occupied by Nancy's family at the mouth of Bendziny Creek. Swanky says it was only because of Nancy's presence that Manning and his partners were given permission to be there by Chief Alexis, Nancy's brother.

In 1927 members of Frank Swannell's survey crew enact the Chilcotin War standoff at Sutless. Photo Frank Swannell. Image I-59567 courtesy of the Royal BC Museum and Archives.

A witness at the trial of the Chilcotin chiefs said that Tahpitt, accompanied by Chief ʔAnahim, was the marksman who "executed" Manning. Swanky says Tahpitt and his family were the long-time occupants of the spot where Manning and McDonald had built their roadhouse at the mouth of Bendziny Creek. Neither Tahpitt nor ʔAnahim had been part of the war party in Homathko Canyon.

Swanky says that during the 1862 epidemic Manning and McDonald had threatened Tahpitt with smallpox if he and his family didn't vacate the area they wanted to stake. Then they introduced the disease to the Tŝilhqot'in village at Bendziny anyway, where all but two young girls died. In late September 1862, Alfred Waddington said he saw 500 graves at Bendziny.

Swanky says when Lha Tŝ'aŝʔin decided to purge the Chilcotin of the men responsible for spreading smallpox, he gave Manning a chance to save himself by seeking exile with Chief Alexis.

Lha Tŝ'aŝʔin sent a message to Manning the morning before he was shot, saying he was to leave the area or face certain death. Nancy also tried to convince her husband to leave, but he didn't take the threats seriously.

A few days later Lha Tŝ'aŝʔin confronted McDonald's pack train near the Tŝilhqot'in village of Sutless (Nimpo Lake). The packers subsequently built a dugout refuge on the top of a small hill overlooking the Dean River to ponder their next move.

Jimmy Guichon, the boy on the left, and Young Guichon at Towdystan in 1927. As a boy Young Guichon witnessed the MacDonald pack train massacre at Sutless in 1864. Photo Frank Swannell. Image H-06536 courtesy of the Royal BC Museum and Archives.

The War Chief specifically targeted McDonald and McDougall for their role in introducing smallpox at Bendziny.

Swanky says Lha Tŝ'aŝʔin sent a message to McDonald offering him exile if he left his possessions and departed. McDougall's Tŝilhqot'in wife, Klymtedza, urged the packers to wait for Chief ʔAnahim to return from Bella Coola to seek sanctuary with him, but the packers bolted. "It was only when McDonald tried to flee with his pack train that Lha Tŝ'aŝʔin attacked it," Swanky says.

Killed in the attack were McDonald, McDougall and a man named Higgins, who had been present during the 1862 smallpox epidemic along the Bentinck Arm Road. Klymtedza also died in the action. Five other members of the party were allowed to escape with only light wounds and they returned to Bella Coola.

When Chief ʔAnahim arrived back at Nagwentl'un from Bella Coola, he collected the pack train horses and returned most of them to the colonial authorities, along with money collected from the bodies of the men who were killed.

THE COLONIAL MILITIA

Upon learning of the killings, the colony's new governor, Fredrick Seymour, launched a military campaign to capture the Tŝilhqot'in chiefs who were behind the attacks. In early June 1864, he formed two militia groups, one headed by Colonial Police Chief Chartres Brew and the other by William George Cox, gold commissioner and police magistrate in the Cariboo. For a month and a half, the militia scoured the countryside looking in vain for Lha Tŝ'aŝʔin.

Swanky says the Tŝilhqot'in let the militia defeat itself, by leading their pursuers on several fruitless forays, which benefited only the mosquitoes. "The hunted knew the ground from a long intimacy," he writes. "To the Colonial mercenaries, every unfamiliar curve seemed more like tomorrow's anonymous harlot."

He says the closest encounter occurred when a militiaman revisited a camp to find an overlooked item and discovered the Tŝilhqot'in strategy. "He found the wanted men enjoying the still hot coals of the militia's very own fire. In other words, the hunted Tŝilhqot'in hid in the militia's footsteps and shadows. The hunters became and remained, the hunted."

Swanky goes on to say that both Chief ʔAnahim and Chief Alexis made sure they had alibis when the warriors made the attacks, but he believes both Tŝilhqot'in leaders were fully complicit with Lha Tŝ'aŝʔin's actions. "Precisely when the wanted men were killing settlers in a war of self-defense at Bute Inlet, Alexis ensured that the Fort Alexandria Post Manager journalized his presence there."

Similarly, he says ʔAnahim made sure his presence was known in Bella Coola at the time McDonald's pack train was attacked at Sutless. "This allowed both chiefs to act as ambassadors for their people with the colonial authorities."

The man hired as second-in-command of Cox's militia was retired Hudson's Bay Company trader Donald McLean, who by then owned a stopping house at Hat Creek. As a fur trader, McLean had a reputation for brutality. He adhered to the

Engraving of Lha Ts̑'as̑ʔin. Courtesy of the Ts̑ilhqot'in National Government.

informal company policy of "club law," and it was widely known how he ruthlessly killed a Dakelh family near Quesnel while tracking down another man, because they wouldn't reveal where he had gone. He was in charge of the failed Fort Chilcotin trading post when it finally shut down in 1843, and it was there that he earned the enmity of the Ts̑ilhqot'in people.

McLean was only too eager to join Cox's crew as an "Indian hunter" when Governor Seymour sent word for him to hire as many men as he could at Hat Creek and rendezvous with Cox at Soda Creek. McLean arrived on May 29 with twenty-four recruits carrying fifty rifles and as many revolvers. He was accompanied by Rod Finlayson, regional head of the Hudson's Bay Company from Victoria, who arranged for the company to underwrite the Chilcotin expedition through Fort Alexandria.

McLean was known to the Ts̑ilhqot'in as Samandlin and was a marked man as he pursued Lha Ts̑'as̑ʔin through the Chilcotin. It was his brazen manner that led to his downfall. On July 17, he disobeyed Cox's orders to stay in camp and got lured into a trap by his Ts̑ilhqot'in adversaries on the Potato Mountain side of Big Eagle (Choelquoit) Lake. The day was hot and he left his bullet-proof vest open at the front. When he bent down to examine a broken branch left purposely on the trail by the men he was pursuing, his vest opened just enough for a Ts̑ilhqot'in marksman to shoot him through the heart.

McLean was the final colonial casualty of the Chilcotin War, and Swanky speculates that his demise was the final purging required by the Ts̑ilhqot'in. Three days later, on July 20, Chief Alexis met with Governor Seymour at the militia's camp at Bendziny to discuss a resolution to the uprising. This was the first-ever meeting between a colonial head of state and the Ts̑ilhqot'in leadership in Ts̑ilhqot'in territory. Alexis knew the exact whereabouts of the wanted men but, as a pretext to establishing good faith with the governor, he supplied Seymour with maps and places the fugitives might be found, knowing full well they were not there.

When Seymour left for a tour of the goldfields, he promised to return in three weeks. It was this unkept promise that foiled Lha Ts̑'as̑ʔin's attempt to establish amnesty for himself and his followers.

Enthused with the new intelligence supplied by Alexis, the militia split into two forces. One was led by Brew and the other by Cox. Brew took his contingent deep into the mountains employing a "scorched earth policy" by burning any Tŝilhqot'in camps and food caches they found. His intent was to make it difficult for people to supply the warriors with food.

Driven from their fishing grounds, innocent Tŝilhqot'in families trying to accumulate vital food supplies for winter became the victims of this brutality. As Judge Begbie later acknowledged, the militia employed the hand of famine as its executioner. Swanky says Brew's party eventually outran its supply line chasing its elusive prey and was forced to dine on its own horses for survival.

Anticipating Governor Seymour's return to the Chilcotin, Chief Alexis made arrangements with Cox for a meeting between the governor and the War Chief Lha Tŝ'aŝʔin to discuss a resolution to the conflict. Cox gave Alexis some tobacco as a gift for Lha Tŝ'aŝʔin as a sacred gesture of good faith so they could commence peace talks.

On August 15, as arranged, Lha Tŝ'aŝʔin and seven members of his party arrived at Cox's camp unarmed. They were accompanied by Chief Alexis and a number of his people, but Governor Seymour wasn't there. On entering Cox's camp, the War Chief followed the customary protocol of smoking the tobacco with Cox that had been sent to him a few days earlier. "I feel safe now," are Lha Tŝ'aŝʔin's fabled words. Nothing could have been further from the truth.

When Lha Tŝ'aŝʔin addressed the gathering, neither the Tŝilhqot'in-to-French translator nor the French-to-English translator was present. According to Cox, Lha Tŝ'aŝʔin stated, "I have brought seven murderers with me and I am one myself."

Swanky says the War Chief would never have put it that way because he saw himself engaged in a war of self-defence, not criminal activity. "He would more likely have said, these are the Tŝilhqot'in concerned in the matters we have agreed to discuss in good faith, and I am one of them."

The Tŝilhqot'in warriors came to the fort under a flag of truce, expecting a conference with the colonial head of state, but were instead overpowered by the militia, arrested and put in chains like common criminals. Swanky says the ambush by Cox violated the sacred conventions of the pipe ceremony and dishonourably violated the mores of both cultures. "There was no sense of surrendering or submitting," Swanky writes. "And no turning themselves in, to accept offers of personal immunity. They expected to have Tŝilhqot'in sovereignty recognized."

The eight Tŝilhqot'in prisoners were transported to Quesnel for what Swanky says was a "show trial." They appeared before Judge Matthew Baillie Begbie on September 28 and 29, and the judge released two of the prisoners, Tnananski and his son Cheloot because there was no evidence against them. He sent another, Cheddeki, to New Westminster for trial, but he escaped en route and was never recaptured.

The other five, Head War Chief Lha Tŝ'aŝʔin, Chief Biyil, Chief Tahpitt, Chief Telad and Chief Chayses were sentenced to hang on October 26, 1864. Anglican missionary Lundin Brown was sent to minister to the five condemned men. "They said they meant war, not murder," Reverend Brown later wrote. "Lha Tŝ'aŝʔin said he would have never killed the whites if they had not killed his people first by sending smallpox, and threatened to kill more of his people by sending it again. Lha Ts̑'as̑ʔin could not see they had done wrong."

A year later, in New Westminster, two more Ts̑ilhqot'in chiefs, Chief Ahan and Chief Lutas, stood trial for the attack against the pack train at Sutless. Chief Lutas was pardoned by Governor Seymour, but Chief Ahan met his fate on the gallows.

Tom Swanky says the illegal capture and "show trial" of the Ts̑ilhqot'in chiefs were designed to intimidate Indigenous people across British Columbia by the might of the colony. "The Governor made no bones in his reports to London that this was all about political control of territory and had nothing to do with law enforcement except as a pretext."

With their numbers reduced by smallpox, Indigenous people no longer occupied every facet of the land as they once had. This left the country open to pre-emption and settlement by white newcomers.

On October 23, 2014, nearly 150 years to the day after the hangings in Quesnel, British Columbia Premier Christie Clark acknowledged on the floor of the legislature that the six chiefs sent to the gallows in 1864 and 1865 were wrongfully arrested, wrongfully subjected to trial, and wrongly put to death.

> Madame Speaker, today we acknowledge that these chiefs were not criminals and they were not outlaws. They were warriors, they were leaders, and they were engaged in a territorial dispute to defend their lands and people… We confirm without reservation that these six chiefs are fully exonerated of any crime or wrongdoing. The Tsîlhqot'in people rightly regard these chiefs as heroes of their people.

Xeni Gwet'in Chief Roger William today says the martyrdom of the Ts̑ilhqot'in chiefs continues to strengthen his people. "Their sacrifice is still supporting us. The warriors keep us together. Our culture is preserved."

Yunesit'in Chief Russell Myers Ross confirms that, without the warriors' sacrifice, the Ts̑ilhqot'in people might not be here today. "We wouldn't be here without them. Their sacrifice helped stop the road and protected our culture."

Tribal Chair and Tl'etinqox Chief Joe Alphonse says the Chilcotin War defines who the Ts̑ilhqot'in people are today. "The communities of Tl'etinqox, ʔEsdilagh, Yunesit'in, Tsi Deldel, Tl'esqox and Xeni Gwet'in work as a nation to continue the fight of our six War Chiefs of 1864. The War Chiefs stood against the Canadian government in an effort to gain Aboriginal Rights and Title to our Ts̑ilhqot'in lands."

A Dakelh Medicine Woman

Narrowly Escaping Smallpox

One reason the Dakelh people weren't as badly impacted by the smallpox epidemic as some of their neighbours is that they lived off the beaten track of the Bentinck Arm Road between Bella Coola and the Cariboo goldfields. They were also dispersed across the landscape in isolated extended family groups.

A story told by late Ulkatcho Chief Jimmy Stillas points out how people with unusual spiritual powers of discernment were able to protect their families. He said a medicine woman in his family saved his kin from the smallpox epidemic in Bella Coola. These are his words:

> Indian doctors at one time were really powerful. I wouldn't be standing here today if one of the women in our family wasn't an Indian doctor.
>
> A group of our family was travelling on foot to Bella Coola during the time of the 1862 smallpox epidemic. There were four or five of them, maybe seven in all.
>
> They were following the Nuxalk-Dakelh Grease Trail, and had gone past Tanya Lakes and were just approaching the big drop-off down the steep switchback trail into the Bella Coola Valley, when our medicine woman said, "Everybody stand back. Something bad is happening down in Bella Coola. A lot of people are dying. Look at that smoke."
>
> Everybody looked for the smoke but only the old woman could see it. Then she said, "We've got to find a cave and get in there until that cloud goes away."
>
> The young people in the group figured the old woman was crazy and didn't know what she was talking about. "There's no cloud. There's no smoke," they said.
>
> But one man, the hunter of the family, believed the old woman. He knew she was an Indian doctor, and he told the rest of the family to do what she said. They found a cave and stayed in there for seven days. Every morning the old woman would go outside and look.
>
> "No, that smoke, that cloud is still there. We can't go yet."
>
> Finally, on the morning of the seventh day, the medicine woman went out to check the situation and came back into the cave and said it was safe to come outside.
>
> "We can go out and find food now. That smoke is still there. It's still a little bit bad, but it's starting to go away."

The next day she said it was safe to continue travelling. When they got to Bella Coola a few days later, many people had died from smallpox. But our family was saved.

Ulkatcho Chief Jimmy Stillas hosted a traditional gathering at Tanya Lakes in August of 1987. Here he lashes a spear hook to a pole used to snag salmon from the river. Photo Sage Birchwater.

Nancy Swanson

Chilcotin War Matriarch

Occupying a place of honour on the living room wall of Bev and Lee Butler's home, located in the West Branch Valley of the Homathko River south of Tatla Lake, is a photograph of Lee's maternal grandmother, Annie Mackill, and his great-grandmother, Nancy Tsholiralna Swanson. Nancy was the spouse of William Manning, who was killed in the Chilcotin War uprising of 1864 at Bendziny (Puntzi Lake).

The photograph was taken around 1928 at One Eye Lake, three years before Lee was born. Nancy was close to 100 years old then and Lee takes great pride in the fact that his great-grandmother survived that turbulent time when the Tŝilhqot'in people stood up for their sovereignty on the Chilcotin Plateau.

Nancy Swanson, close to 100 years old, poses with her two daughters, Jessie Swanson on the left and Annie Mackill on the right in 1928. Photo courtesy the Butler/Mackill family.

He feels it's a story that needs to be told.

Nancy Tsholiralna Swanson was a central figure in that conflict of 1864 in which nineteen people died over a three-month period, including her husband, William Manning.

After Tŝilhqot'in War Chief Lha Tŝ'aŝʔin (Lhatsassin) led an attack on Alfred Waddington's road-building crew in the Lower Homathko canyon, killing fourteen workers in late April 1864, his party headed up to the Chilcotin Plateau and killed William Manning at Bendziny a few days later.

Nancy was at Bendziny with Manning when members of her family warned her that Lha Tŝ'aŝʔin had vowed to kill all the white people in the Chilcotin associated with building the road from Bute Inlet and spreading smallpox across the Chilcotin Plateau two years earlier.

Manning was identified as being involved in intentionally spreading smallpox at Bendziny that wiped out the Tŝilhqot'in village there in 1862.

Lee Butler said Nancy's relatives told her that she had better escape before the war party got there, because they might kill her too. He said his great-grandmother tried to convince Manning to flee with her, but he refused to leave. She was pregnant with Manning's child when she headed down through the country to Riske Creek.

When Lha Tŝ'aŝʔin was taken prisoner at Fort Chilcotin after being tricked into putting down his weapons on the pretext of attending peace talks with colonial officials, he and his seven followers were taken to Quesnel to stand trial for their acts in defending their homeland.

Lee said colonial authorities then rounded up Nancy at Riske Creek and took her to testify at the trial. "Nancy and one or two of her relatives were chained to the horses and mules they rode to Quesnellemouth to be forced-witnesses," Lee said. "Whenever they had to pee or something like that, there was an armed soldier right there with a rifle. It doesn't sound like she was too willing to testify. I can't see her testifying against other natives."

At the trial, Lha Tŝ'aŝʔin professed that the killings were an act of war to defend his homeland from invaders who had threatened his people with smallpox and to avenge the abuse Tŝilhqot'in women, including his young daughter, had suffered at the hands of the road-builders. But Judge Matthew Baillie Begbie ruled it was murder, and on October 26, Lha Tŝ'aŝʔin and four of his fellow chiefs died as martyrs on the gallows on the banks of the Fraser River. A sixth Tŝilhqot'in chief, Ahan, was hanged a year later in New Westminster.

Lee said that before the trial, Nancy gave birth to Manning's son, Moleese, in Riske Creek country, but the family lost track of where the baby went to. "She had to leave him behind and he was raised by others at Riske Creek."

After the Chilcotin War, Lee said things were pretty wild among the Indigenous people in the Chilcotin. Archival records show that Nancy and two other Indigenous people who had been called as witnesses at the trial were sent to Victoria to protect them from certain harm if they came back to the Chilcotin. There is no record of when Nancy returned.

Sometime later she met William "Billy" Swanson, a Scot in his mid-30s who had come to Canada to seek his fortune, possibly with the fur trade. "I don't know how they met," Lee said. "Perhaps at Toosey. For an Indian woman of that time, she spoke good English."

They eventually took up land on the west side of the Fraser River, opposite the mouth of Chimney Creek, and raised horses and grew potatoes there. Swanson operated a ferry crossing, rowing a barge-like boat across the Fraser. They eventually pre-empted their 160-acre homestead in 1891, which is still known today as Swanson Flats. William and Nancy had two daughters—Jessie, born in 1871, and Lee's grandmother, Annie, born in 1877.

When Billy Swanson died from pneumonia in January 1896, he was only 65 years old. His death registration was signed by Joe Isnardy, who worked for Swanson as a labourer and ferryman, and lived with Annie Swanson. Annie and Joe Isnardy had three children in quick succession: William Isnardy in 1895, Sarah in 1897 and Francis in 1898.

On June 28, 1899, Nancy was baptized by Father François Marie Thomas OMI (Oblates of Mary Immaculate). He recorded her age to be about 70 years old and wrote the phonetic spelling of her name as "Tsholiralna."

When Annie and Joe Isnardy parted company, Annie moved with her mother to Riske Creek. The 1901 census lists Nancy as the head of a household with her daughter, Annie, and Annie's three children, William, Sarah and Francis.

At Riske Creek, Annie formed a liaison with stopping house owner Fred Becher and bore him three children. First-born Henry died in infancy in 1901. Cecilia was born in 1903, followed by Amelia in 1908. When Annie and Fred Becher went their separate ways, Becher sent their two daughters to England.

The Isnardy children, William, Sarah and Francis, stayed with Joe Isnardy's family when Annie moved to Soda Creek to be with Jim Mackill. She bore Jim three children. Lee's mother, Hilda, was the eldest, born in 1909. Next was Clarence Mackill, born in 1911, followed by Jack Mackill in 1913.

Jim and Annie brought their family west to Kleena Kleene in 1923 after Jim corresponded with Cyrus Bryant in Tatla Lake looking for work out there. They left Soda Creek with all their family possessions, including a twenty-foot boat tied onto their horse-drawn wagon, and settled at One Eye Lake. They spent their first year in a tent while they built their first cabin. Jim hired Baptiste Dester and Frank Render to build the fabled Kleena Kleene Lodge, later named the Chilanko Lodge.

Three Mackill siblings: Clarence, Hilda and Jack. Photo courtesy the Butler/Mackill family.

Nancy remained at Riske Creek, living out the rest of her days in a small cabin by the road. Her daughter Jessie lived nearby with her many offspring, including her daughter Lillian Collier, the wife of trapper and famed author, Eric Collier, who wrote *Three Against the Wilderness* in 1959.

Collier referred to Nancy as Lala in his popular book, stating that she had been taken away from her family by a white man when she was 15 years old, and never lived with other Tŝilhqot'in people after that. Nancy was known to everyone around Riske Creek and liked to sit outside by a small fire and smoke her pipe. She died peacefully, some say at 102 years old.

"She died as some ancient oak might die that has stood too long in the forest," wrote Collier. "A moment or so ago she was resting comfortably on her straw-filled tick, puffing serenely away at her pipe. When the tobacco ceased to smoulder, and the bowl of the pipe grew cool, she placed it carefully on the stool by her bed and sighed, 'Me tired now, blimey me sleep.' And that's how Lala died." She was buried on the spine crest of a nearby ridge above the little cabin where she spent her last years.

With her passing one of the last living links to the Chilcotin War was gone forever.

But for her descendants, Nancy lives on in memory as an inspiration—a matriarch who survived tumultuous times, lived a colourful life, and brought forth a long line of proud descendants. Through his great-grandmother, Lee felt that the Tŝilhqot'in warriors didn't die in vain. He sees them as martyrs whose deaths have inspired generations of Tŝilhqot'in people in their struggle for justice in Canadian society.

Lee Butler, great-grandson of Nancy Swanson, with his wife, Bev, granddaughter Lea and daughter Kathy. Photo Sage Birchwater.

St. Joseph's Mission

The Plight of Chief William and the T'exelcemc

When the first gold strikes on the sandbars of the Fraser Canyon in 1858 brought a flood of 30,000 miners overnight into the colonies of British Columbia and Vancouver Island, the Oblates of Mary Immaculate (OMI) established its colonial headquarters at Esquimalt near Victoria on Vancouver Island. In 1865 the Order relocated its headquarters to New Westminster.

The mandate of the Oblates was to work among the Indigenous people. In August 1866, Oblate Superior Louis-Joseph d'Herbomez assigned 31-year-old Irish priest Father James Maria McGuckin to the Cariboo–Williams Lake mission district. The Catholic Church had been absent from the Cariboo and New Caledonia for nearly twenty years, since Father Nobili left in 1847.

Father McGuckin's task was to establish St. Joseph's Mission as a place to educate local Indigenous students and to teach Christianity, and he pre-empted land for this purpose in the San Jose Valley a few miles from the head of Williams Lake. He reasoned that this location would be convenient for the Secwepemc and other local Indigenous people to gather, far enough from the white settlements of Williams Lake and 150 Mile House.

Father James Maria McGuckin. Photo courtesy OMI Lacombe Canada Inc.

He later purchased a further 129 hectares (320 acres) from the Pomroys to be used as a school and farming village. The Oblate Brothers of St. Joseph farmed the land as a means of support and income, and hired local men to work on the ranch for fifty cents a day.

As the church was getting established at Williams Lake, the situation of the T'exelcemc (the Williams Lake Secwepemc) was becoming ever more

Interior Salish chiefs with Chief William back right. PDP- 01895 image courtesy of the Royal BC Museum and Archives.

dire. They had lost their village site at Missioner Creek in 1860, when Thomas W. Davidson pre-empted it out from under them. Then the smallpox epidemic of 1862 killed two-thirds of the T'exelcemc population, including their leader Chief William. He was the man who had built the chapel at Missioner Creek for Father Demers in 1842. His son, Chief William Junior, took over leadership of the T'exelcemc, but his people had no place to live.

As the flood of gold miners and settlers continued to pour into the Cariboo, the T'exelcemc had less and less land and resources to sustain themselves. Compounding the problem was the law that prevented Indigenous people from pre-empting land unless they became enfranchised or gave up their Indian status. In short, they were dealing with a foreign system they had little understanding of or access to.

On July 5, 1867, just four days after the birth of Canada, St. Joseph's Mission opened its doors to serve the Indigenous people and neighbouring miners. Church services were held and the first cemetery was created. The mission was given the responsibility for recording births and deaths in the region, and the first burials were made that year in the cemetery.

The Oblates allowed the homeless T'exelcemc to live on mission property, but this temporary fix was far from adequate. In 1870, the T'exelcemc were moved to Oblate land west of the San Jose River, but they were still without a home.

Finally, by 1879, the situation reached the boiling point. In desperation, Young

Chief William, who was by that time an old man, drafted a letter to the Victoria *Colonist* newspaper, describing how the land his people had lived on for centuries had been taken over by the white newcomers.

> The land on which my people lived for five hundred years was taken by a white man. He has crops of wheat and herds of cattle. We have nothing—not even an acre.
>
> Another white man has enclosed our graves in which the bones of our fathers rest and we may live to see their bodies turned over by his plough.
>
> Any white man can take three hundred acres of our land and the Indians cannot touch an acre.
>
> Her Majesty sent me a coat, two ploughs, and some turnip seed. The coat will not keep away the hunger, the ploughs are idle, and the seed is useless because we have no land.
>
> The whites have taken all the salmon and all the land, and my people will not starve in peace. A war with the white man will end in our destruction, but death in war is not so bad as death by starvation.
>
> Land… land… a little of our own land. That is all we ask from her Majesty.

Oblate Father Charles Grandidier supported Chief William's plea, and wrote to the superintendent of Indian Affairs. "The T'exelcemc have been shamefully despoiled of their lands in direct opposition to Her Majesty's Proclamation of 1858 when she took formal possession of British Columbia." He went on to say that the proclamation's guidelines forbid settlers from pre-empting land occupied by Indigenous inhabitants—specifically where they had houses, cemeteries, gardens and fisheries.

Judge Matthew Baillie Begbie, now Chief Justice of the Supreme Court of British Columbia, got behind the effort to find land for the T'exelcemc. The government purchased several ranches at the head of Williams Lake and, in the spring of 1880, the T'exelcemc moved onto 4,100 acres abutting the eastern shore of the lake. In 1884, the Sugar Cane Indian Reserve was formally designated by the Canadian government.

Today the T'exelcemc community and the Northern Secwepemc te Qelmucw (Northern Shuswap Tribal Council) are involved in the BC treaty process.

St. Joseph's Mission

Residential School

Father McGuckin established the first school at St. Joseph's Mission for white and half-Indigenous boys in 1872. Eleven boys were enrolled that first year, and four years later, in 1876, the Sisters of St. Anne opened a school for girls. By 1878, the mission schools had an enrollment of forty-two boys and thirty-three girls.

It wasn't until 1886 that St. Joseph's Mission became a residential school exclusively for Indigenous children. After that, the white children were forced to attend schools in Williams Lake or 150 Mile House.

Canada's residential school program for Indigenous children is a legacy few people can be proud of.

As colonization of the land once exclusively the domain of Indigenous societies continued, Canada was faced with the problem of what to do with the Indigenous inhabitants who were being displaced. The subsistence way of life had occupied the whole of the land base and the European concept of private ownership of land and centralized control of resource development was in direct conflict with this. These

St. Joseph's Residential School. Irene Stangoe collection.

two conflicting ways of life were on a collision course the moment Christopher Columbus planted the first Spanish flag on the Bahamas archipelago in the so-called New World in 1492, and in British Columbia the shift from Indigenous control of the land base to colonial rule occurred in a brief period in the mid-nineteenth century.

The premise of the residential schools across Canada was to teach Indigenous children how to fit into the now-mainstream Euro-Canadian society. More to the point, they were institutions set up to deprogram children from their Indigenous heritage. A popular slogan in residential schools was to "kill the Indian in the child." The belief that Indigenous societies were inferior to European traditions was reinforced over and over in these schools until many of the children believed it to be true. The term "cultural genocide" hadn't been coined yet, nor identified as a human rights crime.

To expedite the reprogramming process, Indigenous children were removed from their families and forced to attend residential schools for ten months of the year. They were punished for speaking their own languages and taught to be ashamed of their cultural traditions. There are many accounts of this.

Chris Wycotte, a T'exelc band councillor and treaty negotiator, said he went to residential school at St. Joseph's Mission only a few miles from his family home at Sugar Cane. "They wouldn't allow you to speak your language or practise any part of your culture. Once you got out for summer holidays, you reverted back to what you were before you went to the mission. That's how we managed not to lose it," he said, crediting his grandparents for keeping his knowledge of the Secwepemc

Class of 1903–04. St. Joseph's Mission residential school. Irene Stangoe collection.

language and culture alive for him. "My grandparents made sure we didn't lose it. They only spoke to me in Shuswap, even though my mom and dad only spoke to me in English." He said his parents knew he and his siblings would be punished for speaking Secwepemc when they returned to the mission so they were resigned to making it easier for them. "But our grandparents made sure they only spoke to us in Shuswap until we understood it."

Wycotte said Secwepemc was his parents' first language when they attended residential school, and English was their second language. But the opposite was true for him. "For my generation it slowly turned around into English being our first language."

He said that when he returned to the mission in September, some of the kids would have dried meat or dried salmon, or home-tanned buckskin moccasins, gloves or other clothing they brought from home. "To us the dried meat and fish was a delicacy—our highly valued food. At the start of school, the supervisors would go through our stuff and anything like that they'd just throw in the garbage. It never happened to me but I felt really bad and offended about it. How could they do that kind of stuff? How can they take something that valuable and just throw it in the garbage?"

The residential school was only four miles from Wycotte's home, but he was prohibited from seeing his family most of the year. "I couldn't even come home to see my mom and dad. One time we were brought from the mission to Sugar Cane for Sunday Mass at Easter. We could go to Mass and visit with our mom and dad for half an hour or so. Then we were brought back to the mission."

Sisters of the Child Jesus and students, Williams Lake residential school. Photo courtesy National Archives of Canada, image C-56765.

St. Joseph's Mission residential school existed for ninety-five years until it was finally shut down in 1981—but by then the damage had been done. Generation after generation of Indigenous children raised in institutions away from their families had been deprived of learning parenting skills and the day-to-day cultural activities that would naturally have been passed to them by their Elders. Like Chris Wycotte, many lost the ability to fluently speak their native tongue.

There was an overriding expectation that Indigenous culture and their ties to the land would eventually die out as Indigenous children were assimilated. But this didn't happen.

In 2008, Prime Minister Stephen Harper publicly apologized for Canada's role in the "aggressive assimilation" of Indigenous children through the government-supported, church-run residential schools. In 2015, Prime Minister Justin Trudeau stated that Indigenous people in Canada really do matter. His statement has raised hopes for the dawn of a better future.

For treaty negotiator Chris Wycotte, the proof will be in what happens on the ground. He's waiting to see how different things will actually be.

Susan Hance

Residential School at Anahim Lake

Dakelh speaker Susan Hance grew up in Ulkatcho country north of Anahim Lake. Her large extended family lived along the Dean River at a place known as Salmon River, about fifty kilometres north of Anahim Lake. The country was remote and left mostly to itself until the early 1950s when Susan was born. The Ulkatcho people continued to live much as they always had, travelling the trails in that roadless country from Anahim Lake to Chezlatta and from the Fraser River to Bella Coola.

Then two big changes impacted their territory. The Kenny Dam was constructed on the Nechako River in the early 1950s, flooding their trails to Chezlatta and blocking travel routes to family members in Burns Lake. It also put thousands of square kilometres of Ulkatcho and Chezlatta trapping and hunting areas under water.

The second big impact was the construction of the Bella Coola Road in 1953. Previously the main access to Bella Coola from Ulkatcho territory had been along the Nuxalk-Dakelh Grease Trail that wound its way over the Rainbow Mountains. The road made access into the Bella Coola Valley much easier and many Ulkatcho families were attracted to Anahim Lake, where ranching jobs could be found.

A school for Indigenous children was established in Anahim Lake and a dormitory built to house them while their parents engaged in traditional activities like trapping, hunting and raising livestock in the isolated meadows. Susan Hance stayed in the residential dormitory while she attended primary school in Anahim Lake in the late 1950s and early 1960s. "A whole bunch of us stayed there and went to school right up to Grade 7. All the kids who finished Grade 7 were sent to Williams Lake for high school and they stayed at St. Joseph's Mission.

"The truck would come along in September to pick up the kids and take them to the mission. Dad called it the cattle truck. After I finished Grade 7 and I was ready to start Grade 8, they were loading all the kids into the truck and we were all getting ready to go to town. Then out of nowhere Mom showed up with the team and wagon. 'You're not going,' she told me. 'You'll probably learn more if you come home with us.'

"I was devastated and felt I was getting robbed of my education. I had no choice. I was 13 years old and had to go back home with my parents to Salmon River. Now I'm really glad I did that. I never had to go to the residential school at St. Joseph's Mission where all the rest of the kids from Anahim Lake stayed. When I went home, my parents and grandparents taught me how to trap and hunt and speak the Carrier language and tell the old stories."

Susan Hance and her sister-in-law Beverly Charleyboy lift a spring salmon out of Takia Creek. Photo Sage Birchwater.

It took Susan a while to appreciate the gift her parents had given her by making her stay home and learn the traditions of her culture.

She was still a teenager when she met her future husband, Ray Hance, while picking asparagus in the Okanagan. In the mid-1960s, an agriculture program was set up to hire Indigenous people from communities in the Cariboo Chilcotin to work in the orchards and farms of the Okanagan. Susan's whole family took part in it.

When she met Ray, Susan despaired, telling him that she had been robbed of her formal schooling by her parents. Ray didn't agree. "You're lucky," he told her. "You'd better thank your parents."

Susan now sees the wisdom of her parents' decision. "Now that I know what was going on I feel lucky my parents insisted I come home with them."

Susan was 18 when she and Ray got married. Two years later they started their family of three children—Carmen, Jason and Ryan. In accordance with her traditional upbringing, Susan insisted on remaining home while her kids were in school.

"As soon as my youngest kid graduated from high school I went after my schooling again at Thompson Rivers University and got my Grade 12," she said. After graduating, she got a job as a bank teller and was training to be a loans officer when she got pressured by her family to teach her native Dakelh language and culture in the Williams Lake school system. At first she refused the teaching opportunity because she liked working in the bank. Then the fates conspired and Susan took the job in the school.

Because of those important years living the traditional life with her family at Salmon River instead of attending the mission where the mandate was to "kill the Indian in the child," she was ideally suited to pass on the knowledge of her culture and language to the next generation.

Working in a classroom was challenging at first, and Susan doubted herself. "At first I thought, what have I got myself into, but it didn't take me long to get busy. I ended up teaching in the elementary schools and high school. Besides teaching the language, I shared the stories and history of our people. I just love it."

Father François Marie Thomas

Apostle of the Chilcotin

Father François Marie Thomas was the first missionary priest to bring Catholicism to the Chilcotin Plateau and Blackwater country west of the Fraser River. Other priests like Father Morice, Father Le Jacq and Father McGuckin had tried, but none had success in converting the Tŝilhqot'in or Dakelh people in this region.

Father Thomas was different. He succeeded where other missionaries had failed and spent nearly six decades in the region transforming the country and its people.

Father Thomas was ordained into the Oblate Order of Mary Immaculate (OMI) in 1888 in his homeland of Brittany, France. The young priest was given the choice to serve in Brittany rather than risk his life in a raw new country, but he chose to come to Canada. He arrived in the Cariboo Chilcotin in 1897, and was posted to St. Joseph's Mission near Williams Lake.

His first order of business was to establish contact with the Indigenous people and gain their respect and trust. His next task was to build churches in the isolated villages across the region.

Veera Bonner remembered Father Thomas fondly. "He had a hearty manner," she said. "He wasn't mild-mannered at all—just the opposite. He always had something to tell you." Veera, a third-generation Chilcotin settler from the Hance family, grew up in Big Creek. Her mother, Hattie Witte, was born in Hanceville, where Veera's grandfather, Orlando Thomas Hance, was the first white settler in the Chilcotin River Valley. Hanceville was named after him.

Father Thomas rarely came to Big Creek because most of his flock lived elsewhere, Veera said. "Most of the people at Big Creek were Anglican, but he did visit occasionally."

Veera's older sister, Irene Bliss, remembered Father Thomas visiting them in Big Creek. "We weren't Catholics, but he used to come and have lunch with us. He would make his rounds twice a year, once for the whites and once for the Indians."

Irene remembered his hearty laugh and bushy white beard. "He was a wonderful man. Everybody knew him. He was known from one end of the country to the other." She said he would head out in all kinds of weather to attend to the needs of his parishioners. "It didn't matter what the weather was like, he'd go."

Father Thomas is best remembered by the Tŝilhqot'in and Dakelh people for his annual springtime trek known to them as Priest Time. He would head out in the spring as soon as there was enough green grass to feed his horses. He would start out from Quesnel and go west from there in a long circuitous route to Nazko, Lhoosk'uz, Ulkatcho Village, Anahim Lake, Redstone Flats, Anaham Flats, Stone, Toosey, and finally back home to St. Joseph's Mission. The epic journey would last six weeks.

Father François Marie Thomas. Courtesy Archives Deschâtelets-NDC.

St. Francis Catholic Church at Redstone Flats. Sage Birchwater collection.

What made Father Thomas's Priest Time trek unique was how each community would send an envoy to bring him to the next village. When Priest Time was over in Nazko, the people from Lhoosk'uz would show up to bring him to their community. When Priest Time was done in Lhoosk'uz, a delegation from Ulkatcho would arrive to escort him farther west along the Blackwater Trail to their home.

Each Priest Time session lasted about a week. Since Father Thomas only visited once a year, a whole year's worth of church business had to be conducted in seven days. Graves were blessed, babies baptized, and couples married, and catechism and church doctrine was taught. Because everything was done at once, it was common for several couples to share the same wedding anniversary date.

Birth dates and the ages of children were approximated, and sometimes the guess by the priest was obviously wrong. Josephine Gregg said she was born in the Klinaklini Mountains while her parents were goat hunting. The next spring the priest entered her birthday as October 21. Josephine always argued they had her birthday wrong. She insisted she would have had to be born in September because there would have been too much snow to be in the mountains in October. But the official record prevailed and Josephine was officially an October baby.

Priest Time was a celebratory occasion. People came from isolated meadows and traplines near and far to socialize and join in the festivities. The Indigenous bone game of lahal was a favourite pastime.

Ulkatcho Elder Theresa Holte remembered the excitement of Priest Time in Ulkatcho Village. "In June we'd all leave our camps and go to Ulkatcho Village. Father Thomas would come all the way from Quesnel. He'd use a saddle horse all the way. When he got to Ulkatcho everybody started shouting, 'The priest is coming, the priest is coming!' People started running and got their shotguns to salute the priest coming in."

Theresa said the priest's horse would start dancing around, scared of all the guns

The graveyard and church at Ulkatcho Village. Photo George Robson.

going off. "But Father Thomas was a good rider. He usually managed to stay in the saddle."

There were no churches when Father Thomas started his mission. One by one, each village built their own church for Priest Time. At Anahim Lake there was no church, remembered Theresa Holte. She said Father Thomas had a big tent under the jack pines to perform his ceremonies. "Lots of people got married under the jack pines," she chuckled.

Ulkatcho Elder Mac Squinas said Father Thomas would always arrive at Ulkatcho Village every year during the first week of June. "Once a year, every June, the priest came to Ulkatcho Village. He stayed seven days. Father Thomas was the first Father to visit our country. Lots of people went to Ulkatcho. All of Lhoosk'uz, some from Ootsa Lake, and some from Anahim Lake. He would teach you church, just like going to school for one week."

Mac said from Ulkatcho Village Father Thomas would continue on to Anahim Lake and stay for one or two days until the people from Redstone would arrive to pick him up. "Tŝilhqot'in people would meet Father Thomas at Anahim Lake and bring him down to Redstone Flats in a wagon."

You didn't have to be Catholic to be drawn into the delights of Priest Time. Mary Ann Ross grew up in an agnostic household in the Klinaklini Valley with her brother George and their parents Louisa One-Eye and Old George Turner. Old Turner certainly wasn't religious, but they often came out from the Klinaklini Valley after trapping all winter and invariably ran into Father Thomas conducting Priest Time at Redstone Flats. "We used big-wheel freight wagons," Mary Ann said. "No cars in those days. We stop maybe one day at Priest Time on our way down to Gang Ranch to get a load of stuff all the way from Ashcroft. That's the way they come and get together at Priest Time. The Indians all come out like that in big-wheel wagons. They go across the river in a wagon like that too. Stuff piled up high."

Father Thomas's grave near the old St. Joseph's Mission at Williams Lake. Photo Sage Birchwater.

Father Thomas spent nearly four decades cultivating the mission fields of the Chilcotin Plateau and the Blackwater country on his own before he was joined by Father Hennessy in 1935. Although Father Hennessy was a big man, the Indigenous people always referred to him as "Little Father Thomas."

Oblate brothers, priests and Catholic sisters who died in western Canada were normally laid to rest in the cemetery of St. Mary's Mission in Mission, BC. But not Father Thomas.

When he passed away in an Edmonton hospital in 1957 at the age of 89, an exception was made. At his request, Father Thomas was brought back to the Cariboo he loved and was buried in the little cemetery at St. Joseph's Mission. There he shares space with many of the region's pioneers.

Irene Stangoe wrote how hundreds of Indigenous people attended Father Thomas's funeral from Sugar Cane, Canim Lake, Soda Creek, Dog Creek, Canoe Creek, Alkali Lake and from across the Chilcotin. "They followed the procession, praying aloud in their own language as they walked, saying the very prayers Father Thomas had taught them."

Bella Coola

D'Arcy Christensen's Roots

When D'Arcy Christensen sold his general store in Anahim Lake in 1999, the retail business had been in his family for over 100 years. His grandfather, Adolph Christensen, started the store in Bella Coola in 1898. In the late 1920s, D'Arcy's dad, Andy Christensen, took over the store from his father and eventually moved it up to the Chilcotin Plateau where he owned the Cless Pocket Ranch near Anahim Lake.

D'Arcy remembered spending the summers at the ranch and going to school in Bella Coola during the winter. "My dad used to pack all the supplies for the store on horseback from Bella Coola. It took three days and I went on several of those pack trains when I was a little kid."

He said you had to be careful. "Sometimes a pack would slip, and down the zigzag trails it would come. I remember one time a horse came right by me, tumbling

D'Arcy Christensen's old store in Anahim Lake before it burned down. Photo courtesy D'Arcy Christensen.

Adolph and Marit Christensen and their seven children in Bella Coola. Photo courtesy D'Arcy Christensen.

down the hill. I had enough sense to crowd my horse into the bank. It got by me all right. Sometimes they'd fall and roll right down the hill. It didn't seem to hurt them too much, but fortunately that didn't happen very often."

D'Arcy's grandparents, Adolph and Marit Christensen, were part of the Norwegian colony that came to Bella Coola from Crookston, Minnesota, in 1894. They initially settled fifteen kilometres up the valley from tidewater where Adolph started his retail business near Hagensborg. Then in 1904 Adolph relocated his store to the new townsite that was established at the mouth of the Bella Coola River on the north side next to Necleesconnay Creek.

The location of the townsite on the north side of the east–west valley was ideal from the standpoint of good winter sunshine, but unfortunately it was susceptible to frequent flooding when the Necleesconnay overflowed its banks.

When a major flood washed out the town in 1924, Premier Duff Pattullo inspected the disaster and recommended moving the village to the south side of the river. Buildings were dismantled and rebuilt where the Bella Coola townsite is today. Adolph Christensen paid his sons a nickel a board to tear down his store. Then he reconstructed it where the Bella Coola Co-op is today.

D'Arcy said he came by his entrepreneurial tendencies honestly. "Businessmen were part of my lineage on both sides of my family."

His mother's father, John Clayton, was an enterprising Englishman who made his way to the Central Coast from the Cariboo goldfields in 1873. He started working at the Hudson's Bay trading post in Bella Coola, then took over as postmaster when the factor died in 1876. When the Hudson's Bay Company decided to close the post in 1885, John Clayton bought the store and property and ran the store until his death in 1910.

John Clayton (above); Elizabeth Orden Clayton (below). Photos courtesy D'Arcy Christensen.

D'Arcy was born in 1929, nearly two decades after his grandfather's death, and said he found it strange that John Clayton's name was rarely mentioned in his household when he was growing up. "Not a word was said about him, even though he was my grandfather."

Years later, D'Arcy learned that John Clayton had been a pretty astute businessman. Besides the store, he owned his own steamship and freighting business between Bella Coola and Victoria and was a partner in the first fish cannery in Bella Coola. "John Clayton's trading business with the local natives was well established when the Norwegian settlers arrived in 1894, so his business would have thrived."

D'Arcy also learned that John Clayton had had another family before marrying his grandmother. He lived with a Nuxalk woman named Q'uit, when he first came to the country. He met her at Port Alice on one of his trips to Victoria, and brought her back to Bella Coola where she had originally come from. They had a son together, Willie Mack, born around 1877.

"In those days an Englishman who married out of his class was frowned upon," D'Arcy said. "Many Englishmen came to Canada, got established, then went back to

Haida Frank in front of John Clayton's trading post where he worked. Photo courtesy Peter Solhjell from Bangen original prints.

England to marry." John Clayton was no exception. In 1890 he returned to England and married Elizabeth Orden, a minister's daughter much younger than himself, and brought her back to Bella Coola.

D'Arcy claimed that when she arrived, Elizabeth Clayton was the only white woman in Bella Coola. "She was always invited to the potlatches, and would have her hair all trussed up in a bun. Those were the days of big skirts, and the little children at the potlatches would hide under her skirt when they got frightened by the dancers."

By 1894, John and Elizabeth had two sons, Vincent (Vinnie) and Davenport, and the white population in Bella Coola numbered about sixteen. Then, at the end of October of that year, the demographics of the valley shifted radically. Eighty-four Norwegian settlers arrived from Minnesota and the white population ballooned to 100 overnight. The following year two more groups of Norwegian immigrants joined the colony.

In quick succession, Elizabeth and John Clayton had two more children: Margery, who later married Bert Robson, and D'Arcy's mother, Dorothy, who would marry Andy Christensen.

When John Clayton died in 1910, he was the largest landowner in the valley. Elizabeth kept running the store but sold much of the property to speculators, anticipating that Bella Coola would soon be developed into a railway terminus and port. These dreams faded when the Grand Trunk Pacific Railway was completed to Prince Rupert in 1914.

Meanwhile, Willie Mack grew up in the Nuxalk community of Bella Coola. He married Mary Samson, the last person born in Noosgulch Village, thirty kilometres up the Bella Coola River at the foot of Mount Nusatsum. They had seven children together, and two of their youngest sons, Clayton and Orden, were named in memory of John Clayton and his British wife, Elizabeth Orden. Clayton Mack was born in 1910, the year John Clayton died. Clayton Mack remembered his dad, Willie Mack, socializing with his younger half-brothers, Vinnie and Davenport. "I see them together all the time. Work together. Them Clayton boys liked us kids. My dad used to take me over to the Clayton store when I was a little boy. I don't buy nothing at all, they just gave it to me. I looked at the shoes. 'You want the shoes?' they said to me. Yeah, I said. They put it on me. 'Okay, you can go home. You have new shoes now,' they told me."

The marriage of D'Arcy's parents, Andy Christensen and Dorothy Clayton, had its obstacles and almost didn't happen. For the longest time Elizabeth Clayton rejected the idea of her daughter, with her British ancestry, marrying a man of Norwegian descent. At one point the young lovers even considered eloping. Finally Elizabeth gave her blessing and the marriage went ahead. On one of the coldest days of the year, Andy and Dorothy said their vows in the little church on the Nuxalk reserve on a blustery day in early January 1924.

Willie Mack family. Courtesy Mack family collection.

From Bella Coola to Berlin in 1885

When a group of nine Nuxalk men went from Bella Coola to Germany in 1885 to perform their dances and songs and demonstrate their culture, their presence there influenced the historical development of anthropology in North America.

The nine men, known by their Nuxalk names of Ham-chick, Pooh Pooh, Kah-che-lis, Huck-mulshe, Ick-Iehoneh, Elk-qut, Isk-ka-lusta, Ya Coutlas and Que-noh were heading to work in the hop plantations of the Columbia Valley when they met a Norwegian artifact collector, Bernard Fillip Jacobsen. Jacobsen was working for a German entrepreneur, Carl Hagenbeck, collecting cultural materials from Indigenous communities along BC's west coast and shipping them back to museums in Europe.

Hagenbeck was also involved in a lucrative scheme to bring ethnic groups from around the world to Europe to showcase their "otherness" and demonstrate their cultures. These ethnic shows or human zoos were known as *Volkershau*, and in 1885, Hagenbeck sent Jacobsen to British Columbia to find some willing Indigenous participants.

Nine Nuxalk men in Germany demonstrate Nuxalk culture to European audiences. Carl Gunther photo, courtesy Canadian Museum of History, image 62099.

Five men in Nuxalk regalia. Carl Gunther photo, courtesy Canadian Museum of History, image 62101.

After failing to convince some Kwakwaka'wakw people from Fort Rupert near Alert Bay to join him, Jacobsen ran into the nine Nuxalk men and offered them jobs for a year if they would come to Germany. He offered them $20 per month plus room and board and promised to cover all expenses and travel. This was considerably more than the men would have made labouring in the hop fields.

On July 25, Jacobsen signed a legal agreement with the Indian superintendent in Victoria, Israel Powell, allowing the men to travel to Europe. There was one condition, however. They would have to be returned home in a year's time. Hagenbeck had to post a $1,000 bond to assure this condition would be met. On July 28, the nine men caught the train in Portland, Oregon, bound for New York City, and on August 5, they boarded a steamship to Bremen, Germany.

Their year-long tour took them to twenty-two cities where they demonstrated many aspects of their culture, including the construction of a Nuxalk plank house, mask carving, the use of bows and arrows, and Nuxalk games; in addition, they performed songs and dances. Their "job description" was to exhibit Nuxalk manners, habits and customs for the German public.

One of the most popular parts of the Nuxalk exhibition was the Cannibal Dance. The owner of the Berlin hotel where they performed would joke that the cannibals ate two kitchen boys a day.

Ethnic shows were gaining popularity in Europe at that time. There was a great curiosity about physical otherness, special beauty or great ugliness, and other countries, like France, England and the Netherlands, were bringing in ethnic groups from their colonies. The act that drew the most attention across Europe was Buffalo Bill's Wild West Show featuring "cowboys and Indians" riding horses and duelling out the Great Plains drama of the American West.

The Nuxalk, with their masks, carvings and more sedate dance routines, didn't offer the glamour and excitement of the eye-catching "Indian Wars" enacted by Buffalo Bill and his entourage. So the public wasn't particularly drawn to the Nuxalk, whose traditions didn't include the Native American stereotype of long braids and feathered headdresses.

While the Nuxalk performances didn't generate the economic return Hagenbeck was anticipating, the scientific community and academic élite in Germany were excited by the authenticity of the Nuxalk demonstrations. One young scientist in particular, Franz Boas, was particularly struck by what he saw at the *Volkershau* in Berlin, and it inspired a life-long interest in Northwest Coast Indigenous culture.

Billy Jones mending his net. In 1934 he was the last surviving member of the troupe that visited Germany in 1885. Cliff Kopas photo.

Shortly after the Nuxalk men set out to return to Canada, Boas also left Germany, bound for North America. Inspired by the Nuxalk and the culture of the Northwest Coast, he went on to become one of the world's foremost authorities on ethnography. His contribution was so great that he is still considered the father of American anthropology today.

In an effort to spark more public interest in the Nuxalk show, promoters of the *Volkershau* added feathers to the traditional Nuxalk regalia and even created a fictitious "Burning of the Shaman" act to make their performance more enticing. It was pure entertainment. One of the men was placed in a box and it was set on fire, a charred skull would be retrieved from the ashes, then miraculously the shaman would reappear unhurt. The audiences lapped up this falsified Nuxalk representation.

The English identities of only three of the nine adventurers who spent a year in Germany are known today: Tom Henry, Billy Jones and Alec Davis. When ethnographer Harlan Smith arrived in the Bella Coola Valley to photograph the Nuxalk in 1920, only Billy Jones and Alec Davis were still alive. In 1934, Cliff Kopas took a photograph of the last surviving member of the group, Billy Jones.

As the Second World War erupted into its fury, someone joked with Billy Jones, asking if Adolph Hitler could possibly be his son. Billy's only reply was, "Maybe." Some cursory mathematical calculation reveals the impossibility of this, however, since the German Führer was born in 1889 and Billy Jones and his Nuxalk colleagues returned to Canada in August 1886.

There are a few other curious historical twists to this story.

Despite the fact that the Canadian government had banned potlatches, mask dances and the practice of Indigenous customs in Canada in 1884, the year before the nine Nuxalk men set off for Germany, the government gave its consent for the nine men to demonstrate their culture in Europe.

And ironically, two years before they set out for Europe, Tom Henry, the leader of the group in Germany and their translator, had converted to Christianity. According to former Nuxalk Chief Ed Moody, Tom Henry had given up his cultural practices in 1883 and burned two wooden boxes of regalia in front of Methodist missionary Reverend William Henry Pierce.

Tom Henry's conversion caused quite a schism among the Nuxalk people. After he returned home from Germany, he led a lot of other Nuxalk people to Christianity, and founded a new Christian Nuxalk village on the north side of the Bella Coola River. There he spearheaded the building of the Emmanuel Methodist Church. Nuxalk traditionalists who still wanted to practise the old traditions of their culture remained on the south side of the river at the old Q̓umk'uts Village.

Bella Coola's Norwegian Colony

By the time Bernard Fillip Jacobsen returned the nine Nuxalk men home to Bella Coola, the community was changing. Postmaster John Clayton had purchased the old Hudson's Bay trading post and other white settlers like Tom Draney were moving in. In 1892, the BC government hired Arthur Cotton and Robert Palmer to survey a trail fifty kilometres up the Bella Coola Valley to Firvale.

Jacobsen, a born promoter, convinced the provincial government that the Bella Coola Valley was suitable for farming. Then he began publishing articles about Bella Coola in Norwegian-language newspapers across North America, comparing the fjord landscape of Bella Coola with that of Norway.

One of Jacobsen's articles caught the eye of Reverend Christian Tollefson Saugstad, the leader of a Norwegian colony in Crookston, Minnesota. Reverend Saugstad was in the midst of a political revolt in his religious community, and he looked favourably on Bella Coola as a place to make a new, utopian start. On October 30, 1894, he arrived in Bella Coola on the side-wheeler steamship SS *Princess Louise* with his first group of eighty-four Norwegian colonists. The new arrivals were mostly men who had left their wives and children behind in Minnesota while they went ahead to carve out a place for them in the raw Canadian wilderness.

When the ship dropped anchor at the end of North Bentinck Arm a kilometre from the mouth of the Bella Coola River, there was no wharf or sign of human habitation that any of the passengers could see. Then Captain John Irving let loose his ship's whistle, and a flotilla of dugout cedar canoes emerged from the mouth of the river to transport the new arrivals to shore.

The Nuxalk paddlers were members of a rich west coast Indigenous society that had developed a sophisticated culture in the region over millennia. Their mastery of the dugout spoon canoe was unrivalled as they used the tippy craft as their primary means of travel eighty kilometres inland up the Bella Coola River beyond Stuie, where the Talchako and Atnarko rivers met. They had little need for an extensive trail system through the rainforest near the mouth of the river, and this protected them from invasion.

The arrival of the Norwegian settlers was about to dramatically change the demographics and way of life in the Bella Coola Valley. Prior to the ship's arrival the white population was sixteen and the Nuxalk, numbering about 400, were still suffering from the fragmentation caused by the smallpox epidemic thirty years earlier. The numerous villages of their once-robust society had occupied the inner coast from Kimsquit to South Bentinck before their population of about 3,000 was diminished by the disease.

Three decades earlier, Norwegian immigrants had settled in farming communities in the American Midwest, in Minnesota, North Dakota, South Dakota, Iowa and Wisconsin. But hard winters and tough economic times drove many to consider a different place to live.

Reverend Saugstad was embroiled in religious doctrinal disputes within his Norwegian Lutheran Church in Crookston, Minnesota. At one point, a faction of his congregation locked him out and padlocked the doors of his church shut. From Jacobsen's articles, Saugstad learned about the isolated Bella Coola Valley with its fjords, snow-capped mountains, forests of giant trees and strong agricultural potential. In 1893, he made a reconnaissance trip out to British Columbia to assess the suitability of Bella Coola for himself, and he was duly impressed. He returned to Minnesota enthused, like Moses, at the prospect of leading an exodus of his congregation to the Promised Land on the west coast of Canada.

Christian Saugstad, founder of the Norwegian colony in Bella Coola at his farm in Hagensborg. Courtesy Peter Solhjell from Simon Bangen original prints.

Before they left Crookston, the enthusiastic group ratified a constitution on September 11, 1894, for the new settlement, which they called the Bella Coola Colony, British Columbia. The document outlined a strict set of bylaws. "The purpose of this colony shall be to induce moral, industrious and loyal Norwegian farmers, mechanics and businessmen to come to Bella Coola and make their homes there under the laws of British Columbia," the constitution read. It stated that members of the colony must be of good moral character, be hard working, and have sufficient resources for travel and provisions for a year. It also specified that colonists abstain from intoxicants like alcohol, except for sacramental or medicinal purposes.

The British Columbia government got behind the new colony, offering the settlers free land under its Homesteading Act. Each settler would receive 160 acres after making improvements to the land for five years. The government also promised to pay for a road and school for the new settlement. On their way up the coast in the SS *Princess Louise*, Saugstad had the colonists draw lots to determine which 160-acre parcel they would receive.

A year earlier the government had hired Filip Jacobsen and his father-in-law, Thor Thorsen, to build a twenty-kilometre trail up the valley from tidewater. However, when the colonists arrived with winter coming on, nothing could have prepared them for the harsh reality of hacking out a homestead in the Central Coast rainforest

First dock built by Norwegian colonists in Bella Coola. Courtesy Peter Solhjell from Simon Bangen original prints.

of British Columbia. Five of the eighty-four colonists returned on the next southbound steamer.

The remaining Norwegians followed the new trail up the valley and quickly established a tent encampment at Hagensborg. They began building their cabins hewn from the giant trees and created small clearings in the thick forest.

In the spring, another ship brought the wives and children of the original settlers. Guro Nordschow described her experiences coming to the new land. "I was 12 years old when we came on May 6, 1895. The Indians brought us ashore with our luggage. I slept on a pile of grain sacks with my sisters. The next day we trekked up the trail to Hagensborg. Torger Olsen carried my youngest sister, Ruth. The children thought it was all fun, but I remember my mother with tears in her eyes asking my father what had he been thinking, to bring five young girls into such a wilderness."

Torliev Viken sits reading beside first large home built in the Saloomt by Norwegian colonists. Courtesy Peter Solhjell from Simon Bangen original prints.

Funeral for Reverend Christian Saugstad, founder of the Norwegian colony. Courtesy Peter Solhjell from Simon Bangen original prints.

Guro said their cabin was just one room with a rough plank floor. "Right away we got down to business, grubbing up the earth around the huge stumps and clearing out the roots. Within a week we had potatoes in. We planted a fairly good vegetable garden that first year."

Torger Olsen was 26 when he came with the first group of Norwegians in 1894. He said they worked all winter building cabins and roads and trying to get some land cleared for gardens. "The women and children came in May and they planted gardens around the stumps and it soon looked quite nice around the cabins," he said. "One or two of the women had flower seeds with them and they put boxes on top of the stumps. That looked real cheery, full of pansies and nasturtiums."

A third ship arrived in the fall on 1895 bringing more settlers from Minnesota, swelling the Norwegian ranks to 200 members.

After leading his flock to the promised land of Bella Coola Valley, Reverend Christian Saugstad died unexpectedly in March 1897. He wasn't yet 60 years old. Though he was the undisputed leader of the colony, the constitution was written in such a way that the community could carry on. By 1910, the legal organization of the Bella Coola Colony had served its purpose and the constitution was dissolved.

Over thirty Norwegian settlers were given title to their 160 acres in the valley after fulfilling their obligations to improve their landholdings into farms within five years. Of course, nobody sought the Nuxalk approval in this divvying up of their homeland. But that is a different story.

Norwegian colonists build a road to the waterfront. Courtesy Peter Solhjell from Simon Banjen original prints.

It quickly became apparent to the settlers that they couldn't make a living solely as farmers. Many Norwegians also became fishermen. "After the fishing season was over, the men worked on the roads," wrote Georgia Bangen, who was only 7 years old when she came with the third group of colonists in the fall of 1895. "The first year they built a road which on one side had the steep mountain and on the other side the ocean dashing against it. They also built a wharf extending some three or four hundred feet out into the ocean, and here steamships landed."

Torger Olsen was the last surviving member of the 1894 Norwegian colonists. He established his farm near the mouth of the Salloomt River on the sunny side of the valley and used oxen to plough his fields and haul his lumber to town.

Other Norwegians migrated out of the Bella Coola Valley and established ranches "up top" in the high country of the Chilcotin Plateau.

Jacob Lunas

Norwegian Settlers in the Chilcotin

There's a ramshackle log barn on the side of the road at Towdystan in the West Chilcotin that defies the laws of physics. It was a landmark forty years ago and still stands tall today, teetering with an obvious lean to the south—yet remains upright. A host of other great structures across the Cariboo Chilcotin Coast landscape have succumbed to gravity, but not Fred Engebretson's barn.

It was only after a conversation with Fred that the secret of the building's mysterious longevity was explained. The roof is held upright by cables and triangular bracing, he told me. The wood, more than a century old, has been well-seasoned by the drying winds on the lee side of the Coast Mountains. Gravity be damned!

Though it's been more than a quarter century since Fred's passing, the old barn and homestead at Towdystan remain a legacy to the Norwegians who spilled out of the Bella Coola Valley to the Chilcotin high country in the early 1900s.

Before the Bella Coola Road was built through the Coast Mountains in 1953, the only land access to the Chilcotin was by trail. There were a dozen different trails out of the valley to the plateau, and one of these historical routes from the Precipice to Nimpo Lake was the Lunas Trail, named after Fred's grandfather, Jacob Lunas.

Lunas was a member of the first group of Norwegian settlers who arrived in Bella Coola with Reverend Christian Saugstad on October 30, 1894, aboard the *Princess Louise* steamship. Born in Norway in 1848, Lunas had immigrated to the United States with his wife Ingri around 1880 and settled in Climax, Minnesota. They had four children—Annie (1882), Johan (1883), Fred (1885) and Karen (1887)—when tragedy struck. Ingri and her three youngest children died from tuberculosis, leaving Jacob and Annie on their own.

Annie also suffered from TB, but she managed to survive. She was 13 years old when she arrived in Bella Coola with the second boatload of colonists in May 1895, to be reunited with her father. "I walked up the valley with a pack on my back for ten miles," she wrote in her memoirs. "There were no houses, no road, just a trail."

The trail went as far as Snootli Creek, where her father and two other men had built a house. "That's as far as the trail went. My Uncle Ole Gaarden lived in the house the men had built, and we all had to stay in his house." She said the men worked on the road all summer, then she and her father got a house farther up the valley, beyond Nusatsum River. "It didn't have a stove, so Father hired some Nuxalk men to bring one up the river by canoe to our place. They took that stove up the valley against the stream for sixteen miles, and charged my dad twenty dollars."

Fred Engebretson's derelict barn defying gravity. Photo Kris Andrews.

Annie, who had never cooked before, was immediately thrust into the role of homemaker. "I learned quickly," she said. "We mostly lived on beans. We had rolled oats and canned milk in the morning, then beans and pork and rice in the afternoon for I don't know how many years."

Homesteads in the narrow, steep-sided valley were subject to the whims of the ever-changing terrain and unpredictability of the weather. "One winter we had a bad flood and the water came into our house. Father went out to rescue our cow and calf, but the calf had drowned. We had to go up the hill to Iver Vestmoe's house to stay."

A year or so after Annie joined her father in Bella Coola, two Norwegian brothers, Tom and Ole Engebretson, arrived from North Dakota and established a homestead farther up the valley at Firvale. Ole Engebretson wasn't impressed with the primitive living conditions of the Central Coast wilderness and soon returned to North Dakota, but Tom Engebretson was drawn to life back in the bush. Besides that, he was smitten by the young Annie Lunas.

Jacob Lunas hired Nuxalk paddlers to bring his wood stove up the Bella Coola River to his Hagensborg homested. Courtesy Peter Solhjell from the Simon Bangen original prints.

Annie Engebretson at Towdystan.
Photo courtesy Engebretson family.

Maybe getting flooded out and losing his calf had something to do with Jacob Lunas deciding to explore the high country to the east. One day, in the company of his daughter, Annie, and future son-in-law Tom Engebretson, he took the trail up the valley and followed the Atnarko River and its tributary, the Hotnarko River, to the Precipice Valley. From there they cut a trail to Nimpo Lake, which historically became known as the Lunas Trail.

In 1901, Lunas, Annie and Tom pre-empted land at Towdystan, near the headwaters of the Dean River, which was known as the Salmon River in those days.

Another Norwegian colonist from Bella Coola, Ole Nygaard, built the first sod-roofed cabin at Towdystan for them. Then Nygaard headed east along the old Chilanko Trail to establish his own ranch at Chilanko Forks. Nygaard's Norwegian axe work at Towdystan was so precise it would have been impossible to fit a piece of paper between the dovetail notches.

Annie and Tom got married and had five children. Their first-born was Ida Josephine, whose birth date is unclear. Fred came next in 1910, followed by Harold in 1912, Lorena in 1920 and Thelma in 1924. "Thelma and I were kind of an afterthought,"

Tom Engebretson at his cabin at Towdystan. Photo courtesy the King family collection.

Working the land in the Bella Coola Valley. Photo courtesy Central Coast Archives.

joked Lorena Draney, who still lives in her own apartment in the Bella Coola seniors' residence. "I'm eight years younger than my youngest brother, Harold."

By the time Lorena and Thelma were born, the Engebretson family had moved back to Bella Coola so the older children could attend school. Jacob Lunas died in 1920, so neither Lorena nor Thelma ever met him. "I was 13 going on 14 when we moved back up top to Towdystan in 1934," Lorena said. "My sister and I lived up there until we got married. Then we moved out to where we were going to live on our own."

Lorena married Tim Draney and ranched up behind Nimpo Lake at Mud Lake, and Thelma married Earl McInroy, who ran a garage in Anahim Lake. Then both sisters retired with their husbands to the Bella Coola Valley.

Thelma said her mother loved the high plateau country. "She liked the space and freedom and always felt sorry for kids in the city because they didn't have any place to play in those little lots. She wanted acres for her kids to play in—a free life."

Despite suffering as a child from the tuberculosis that claimed the lives of her mother and siblings, Annie Lunas Engebretson lived a long life. "She was supposed to die," Thelma said, "but she fooled them and lived to be 99. It made her strong coming to Bella Coola and grubbing for survival between the stumps."

Fred Engebretson inherited the Towdystan Ranch and remained a bachelor all his days, becoming a colourful character in that country until he passed away in 1990 at the age of 80.

Chief Domas Squinas

Chief Domas Squinas of Anahim Lake was the patriarch of a large extended family on the western edge of the Chilcotin Plateau. His parents were Dakelh from Ulkatcho Village, and he spoke at least five languages, Dakelh, Nuxalk, Tsilhqot'in, Chinook and English. He could also communicate in the universal sign language.

Domas saw many changes in his lifetime. When he was born in 1854, his family would still have been knowledgeable about the traditional Dakelh skills like flint-knapping obsidian, hunting with bows and spears, and living in underground houses. When he died in the mid 1930s over 80 years old, airplanes were landing in Bella Coola Harbour.

Domas is described as a man who sat tall in his saddle "like a policeman" and always dressed elegantly. He had a passion for raising hot-blooded horses and racing them like the wind. In his prime, few people could beat him in a horse race.

For many years, Old Squinas and his family were the only occupants of Anahim Lake. Then in 1916, the government created a reserve of his property and sectioned it off to resettle the whole Ulkatcho community there.

Domas was born eight years before the "Great Darkening" of the smallpox epidemic of 1862 wiped out thousands of Indigenous people across the province. He would have witnessed the demographic change in nearby Bella Coola Valley, where the Nuxalk population was reduced to 400 souls from around 3,000 people in less than a year, and the many villages that once occupied the Central Coast fjords from South Bentinck Arm to Kimsquit and Stuie to Kwatna were forced to consolidate their numbers at Q'umk'uts at the mouth of the Bella Coola River just to survive.

On the Chilcotin Plateau, the Tsilhqot'in people suffered similar losses, while the Dakelh weren't hit quite so hard. They lived in more isolated locations off the beaten track of the Bentinck Road Trail that linked Bella Coola to the Cariboo goldfields where smallpox was introduced.

Domas was a boy of 10 when the Chilcotin War erupted in 1864, and would have witnessed the aftermath of the bloody turmoil inflicted on Alex McDonald's pack train near Sutless by Chief Lha Tŝ'aŝʔin. According to Domas's family, the bodies of those killed were buried beside the Dean River close to the where the RCMP detachment sits today in the community of Anahim Lake.

For sixteen years, Domas Squinas was Chief of the Ulkatcho people. Though his ranch, trapline and hunting territory was sixty kilometres south of Ulkatcho Village, his living remotely from the village was no different than other Ulkatcho families with households spread in isolated locations across the broad landscape. Each Ulkatcho family had its own territory to hunt, trap and fish and reap the bounty from the land. Like their Tsilhqot'in neighbours to the south, the Ulkatcho people lived in large extended family groups and occupied a number of seasonal homes and campsites across their territory as they moved about with the seasons, hunting, fishing and gathering.

Since ancient times, Ulkatcho Village on the shore of Gatcho Lake was unoccupied most of the year. It was an important gathering site and trading centre where people from hundreds of kilometres across the region would converge on special occasions. Before European contact, the only permanent structure at Ulkatcho Village

Domas Squinas portrait by Harlan I. Smith, Image 62147, courtesy Canadian Museum of History.

was the coastal-style Culla Culla House. Those who gathered there would stay in temporary brush shelters or tents. In the early 1900s, Oblate priest Father Thomas convinced the Ulkatcho people to build a church to replace the aging Culla Culla House, and soon each family had constructed their own European-style log houses in a village setting.

Domas established a prosperous ranch at Anahim Lake, where he raised horses, cattle and sheep. He trapped and hunted in the Ilgachuz and Itcha mountains to the east and in the Little Rainbow Mountains to the west. One of his favourite seasonal camps was at Stuie along the Atnarko River in the Bella Coola Valley.

Every spring he would head down through the Precipice Valley to Stuie to fish for salmon and pick berries. He had smokehouses there for drying salmon and spent many weeks with his extended family harvesting resources in the coastal valley. In the early 1920s, ethnographer Harlan Ingersoll Smith took a group photograph of the Squinas clan at Stuie. Domas stands out as the elder statesman of the group.

There were only horse trails through the mountains from Anahim Lake on the high Chilcotin Plateau to the Bella Coola Valley in those days, so Domas kept a wagon at the foot of the Precipice trail. He would use his team horses for packing supplies through the mountains, then hitch them up to his wagon at Stuie and travel in comfort down the eighty-kilometre wagon road to Bella Coola. There he could sell his fur, buy supplies and trade with the Nuxalk.

Domas's second wife, Christine, born in 1879 at Chezlatta, was considerably younger than he was. She was the mother of his two younger children, Thomas and Belonic. His two older sons, Donald and Louie, were the offspring of his first wife.

Domas Squinas house in Anahim Lake. Courtesy Peter Solhjell.

Nuxalk grizzly bear guide and storyteller Clayton Mack once described Anahim Lake as the place where Indigenous people from different cultural traditions mixed and lived.

Clayton himself was a good example. He was a Nuxalk man from Bella Coola, but as a teen was drawn to the high country of Anahim Lake. After mentoring with Domas Squinas for several years, he married Cecilia "Doll" Capoose, an Ulkatcho woman from Abuntlet Lake, a dozen kilometres north of the Squinas Ranch. Doll's sister, Josephine, married Domas's son, Louie Squinas.

Before the Squinas family got established at Anahim Lake, the country was the domain of the powerful Tŝilhqot'in Chief Nits'il?in ?Anahim. Like many Ulkatcho families, ?Anahim had family ties in the Bella Coola Valley. Both Domas and ?Anahim traced their origin to the Nuxalk village of Noosgulch (Nus'qulst). ?Anahim's main headquarters was Nagwentl'un, a village located on the south shore of Anahim Lake. The Ulkatcho name for this village was Nagwuntl'oo.

The smallpox epidemic of 1862 killed many people at Nagwentl'un, and in the aftermath of the Chilcotin War two years later, Chief ?Anahim moved his people east to Alexis Creek.

The community of Anahim Lake and nearby Anahim Peak (known by the Ulkatcho people as Besbut'a), were named after Chief ?Anahim. So were Anaham Flats, Anaham Meadows, Anaham Creek and Anaham Reserve (spelled with an "a") near Alexis Creek, some 200 kilometres farther east. It is one of the curious anomalies of the Chilcotin to have different spellings for the same man, etched on official maps of the region. In Bella Coola, Chief ?Anahim is known as Anuxim.

Christine Squinas, wife of Domas, with granddaughter Minnie Alexis and adopted son, Little Thomas Jack at their home in Anahim Lake. Little Thomas was hunting with Old Domas when Domas was attacked by a moose and mortally wounded. Photo taken in 1934 by Cliff Kopas.

Following pages: Domas Squinas and his extended family at their summer camp in Stuie. Taken in 1922 by Harlan I. Smith. Image 62183 courtesy Canadian Museum of History.

After Chief ?Anahim left Nagwentl'un for Alexis Creek country, it made room for Domas Squinas to become established at Anahim Lake.

The Tŝilhqot'in consider Anahim Peak (Besbut'a), located about thirty kilometres north of Anahim Lake, as the northwestern corner post of their territory, so Domas Squinas got established well within traditional Tŝilhqot'in domain.

But as Clayton Mack reminds us, the hard lines of culture seemed to soften along the western fringe of the Chilcotin Plateau. Over time, intermarriage between the Dakelh, Tŝilhqot'in and Nuxalk continued this cultural blending and bridging of differences.

Domas and Christine's youngest son, Thomas Squinas, married a Tŝilhqot'in woman, Celestine Dagg Guichon. Ellie Stillas, a Dakelh from Ulkatcho married Old Sulin, a Tŝilhqot'in from Fish Trap. Their son, Sam Sulin, married Mary, a Secwepemc woman from the Cariboo. Their daughter Susan married Gus Cahoose, a Dakelh from Ulkatcho, and so the process of cultural blending unfolded.

One of the names given to the Ulkatcho people by their Dakelh neighbours in Lhoosk'uz and Nazko was Nechowt'en. This roughly translates to "Dakelh people mixed with Tŝilhqot'in."

In his prime, Domas Squinas was a superb trapper and fearless horse rider. Clayton Mack shared a story his mother told him about Old Squinas.

> In 1920 the whole of Ulkatcho was down in the Bella Coola Valley for the sports day. Horse races and foot races on the 24th of May. The Tŝilhqot'in all came this way. The track was about a mile long on the other side of the river where the old village was.
>
> Old Man Squinas was pretty well off all the time. He had a good trapline, I guess. One year in March he was out on his trapline near Anahim Lake. The snow was pretty deep, and he saw a fresh fox track. There was a big price for fox furs that year, so Old Squinas, he followed that fox track. A little ways on, he found the fox dead on the trail. A lynx had killed it, but Old Man Squinas couldn't see that lynx. He yelled like hell, then suddenly a lynx jumped out of the bushes and ran away. Old Squinas jumped on his horse, chased that lynx up a tree and shot it.
>
> Old Squinas got $1,800 for that fox fur and that lynx fur. That was a lot of money in them days. With the money, he bought a new racehorse, a new stiff-brimmed hat, a new coat and a new saddle.
>
> On the 24th of May, Old Squinas came down to Bella Coola for the horse races. He was all dressed up, riding his new horse with his new saddle. He had his new coat on.
>
> The spectators sat down on long benches beside the track. My mother was there, sitting on the bench watching the races when Old Man Squinas rode past her on his fancy horse. Then my mother saw him pull a bottle of whisky out of his coat and take a drink. "Squinas!" my mother said. "Don't show off that bottle, the policeman's right there."

But Chief Squinas didn't care. "Today's the day! Shit!" he yelled.

By then it was too late. The policeman came. "Squinas, give me that bottle! Give it to me."

"It's my bottle, I buy it," Old Squinas argued, and he took another drink.

"Where you get that bottle from?" the policeman asked.

"I get it from a Chinese cannery worker down at the wharf."

The policeman said, "Okay, we look for that Chinese man tomorrow. You come with me right now to the jailhouse by the police station. I'm going to lock you up for the night."

Old Squinas went with the policeman, then he pulled his wallet out. "I give you $150 if you let me stay to watch my racehorse. They're going to run pretty soon now."

The policeman wouldn't go for it. "No, I'm going to take you to jail. Tomorrow if you show me which man sold you that bottle, I'll let you go after that."

Old Squinas had to miss his horse race. The next morning the policeman took him down to the wharf.

One Chinese man was washing his clothes in the river. "Squinas, is that the guy washing his clothes that sell you the bottle?" the policeman asked.

"No, not that one."

"Is it that guy down there working in his garden? Is that the guy?"

"No."

Another old Chinese man walked by them fast, carrying his groceries home from the store. "Is that the one?" the policeman asked again.

"No, not that one either."

"I'm going to get all the Chinese workers and line them up and I want you to pick which one sell you that whisky," the policeman says to Squinas.

In them days, there was over one hundred Chinese workers in the cannery. They got the contract to do the whole works of the salmon that summer. The policeman told the Chinese foreman, "Get all your men lined up so Old Squinas can look them over and tell which one sell him the whisky."

Soon all the cannery workers were lined up.

"Now, Squinas, which one of them sell you that bottle?"

Old Squinas walked up to that line. He bent over and looked carefully at each man. For the longest time he squinted, looking back and forth. Finally, he turned around and shook his head.

"Funny, Mr. Policeman," he said. "Them Chinese men all look the same to me. Every one of them looks like the other guy. Same kind of eyes, same kind of face. I don't know which one sell me that whisky."

"Okay, Squinas. Ten dollar fine!"

D'Arcy Christensen remembered Old Squinas vaguely from when he was a young kid growing up at Cless Pocket Ranch in Anahim Lake. D'Arcy's father had a store at the ranch and one day Old Squinas came in to do some shopping. D'Arcy had been given an old repeater .22 and he said it was a pretty dangerous rifle—especially for a young kid. "You take the shells out and sometimes one would stick in the magazine. Old Squinas sat down beside me and I figured this gun was empty. I was just a kid and I pulled the trigger and the damn thing went off and shot right beside him. He said, 'You just about shoot my ass that time!' It was pretty close. If I had it pointed up I could have killed the old guy."

CHIEF DOMAS SQUINAS KILLED BY A MOOSE

Clayton Mack was living with Domas Squinas in Anahim Lake when the old man died after getting attacked by a moose. He said Domas went hunting with his 8-year-old grandson, Little Thomas, in the Ilgatchas Mountains when they spotted a moose.

Domas aimed his .25-35 rifle at the animal and fired once, and the moose went right down in the thick deadfall. Old Squinas, thinking he killed it, leaned his rifle against a tree and took out his knife to cut its throat.

The animal was only stunned by the bullet and suddenly stood up as Domas approached him. The moose knocked the old man down and started attacking him with its front feet. "He opened his toes and kept hitting him," Clayton recalled, describing the severe cuts and bruises and broken ribs the old man suffered. After the moose ran off, Little Thomas managed to get his grandfather back on his horse and led him home.

Old Squinas only lived a month after that, Clayton says. "I helped look after him the best I can. I don't know why he didn't want to go down to Bella Coola to see the doctor. He was an old man when he died."

Domas Squinas is still fondly remembered by his family and the Ulkatcho community of Anahim Lake. He was a distinguished leader who left a strong legacy that remains to this day. He has many descendants who proudly continue his bloodline. In fact, you need look no further than his great-great-grandson Carey Price, goaltender for the Montreal Canadiens in the National Hockey League.

Benny Franklin

First Settler at Tatla Lake

I first learned of Benny Franklin from Tom Chignell, the noted telephone lineman who took up land near Tatla Lake in the late 1920s and named it Halfway Ranch (because it's halfway between Williams Lake and Bella Coola). Benny was an old man when Tom came to the Chilcotin from England as a 19-year-old to work for R. C. Cotton at Riske Creek in 1922. Benny had been the first settler to take up land at Tatla Lake in 1886. He came with his wife, Augustine, and their 2-year-old son, Albert. Benny's name is emblazoned across the Chilcotin landscape in significant ways. Franklin Arm on Chilko Lake is named after him. So is Franklin Glacier, which cuts a swath from Mount Waddington to the Klinaklini River. And then there are the Franklin Meadows on the old trail between Alexis Creek and Nazko.

Benny was born in Maine in 1842 and Augustine, considerably younger, was born in Brantford, Ontario, in 1866. They eloped and headed west in1882 when Augustine was just 16 and Benny was 40. Albert was born two years later in a logging camp on the Skykomish River in Washington State.

Saddle horse and pack horse were the primary modes of travel in the Chilcotin when Benny Franklin and his wife, Augustine, and their young son, Albert, arrived in 1886. Photo Joseph William collection.

Settlers and Tŝilhqo'tin family at a fish camp in the Chilcotin. Photo courtesy George Robson.

Now fate handed Benny a twisted hand. After working all winter falling trees and booming his logs in the Skykomish River, he lost every log he cut when the spring freshets broke his booms loose.

Undaunted, Benny took his family to Sumas Prairie on the Canada–US border and went into partnership with another man on a dairy farm. It was there that he learned from a passing surveyor about the bunch grass of the Chilcotin Plateau "up to a horse's knees" on the sidehills around Tatla Lake. The surveyor was fresh from spending two years surveying a route from Bute Inlet through the Chilcotin for the Grand Trunk Pacific Railway.

Benny sold his share in the dairy farm and took his wife and son to the Chilcotin. They pitched their tent at Hanceville and Benny rode to Tatla Lake to size up the country for ranching. He liked what he saw and immediately started building a wagon road west from Alexis Creek.

Benny staked his pre-emption on the big sprawling meadows on the west end of Tatla Lake and offered a caddy of tobacco as a peace offering to Guichon, the head of a Tŝilhqot'in family who lived in the area. Then he bought ten head of Polangus heifers and a bull to start his herd.

On their first trip into Tatla Lake, he and Augustine met Guichon at the junction of Chilanko Creek and the Chilcotin River, and the Tŝilhqot'in man asked, "Mika teke mowich?" (You want venison?) Benny answered, "Newitka!" (Yes, indeed!) Guichon headed off down the road, and just before Redstone Flats, he was waiting for them with a deer. He described how he had crawled up to it while it was sleeping and stabbed it with his knife.

Tsilhqot'in men hauling loose hay on a wagon. Photo Joseph William collection.

Albert Franklin, who grew up at Tatla Lake from the time he was 2 years old, said Guichon regularly hunted only with a sheath knife. Bullets were expensive and hard to come by. "When I was young, I remember there were only two muskets in the area," Albert wrote in his memoir. "Nemiah owned one, and Qaqeẑ (Ka-kus) had the other." He said most of the Tŝilhqot'in people still hunted with bows and arrows, spears and knives when the Franklins first arrived. One day Benny asked Guichon how they killed bear. Guichon replied, "Oh sometime man ketchum bear; sometime bear ketchum man." Within a few years, more Tŝilhqot'in people acquired firearms for hunting.

One day Benny asked a Tŝilhqot'in man by the name of Gilpin to guide him to the coast at Bute Inlet. "Dad had heard so much about Bute Inlet," Albert recalled. "They travelled by way of Chilko Lake and down Franklin Arm to the Southgate River and returned the same way."

Gilpin led the way up an old trading trail over the peak of a steep mountain to the headwaters of the Southgate River. It was hard going because the ice was slippery and the unbroken whiteness of the glacier made it difficult to see.

Gilpin broke off a lot of twigs before they started climbing and handed a bundle to Benny. "This place no talk," he said in his broken English dialect. "Spose talk, wind will come and blow us away. You throw one stick. Spose you see stick, you step. Spose no see stick, stop." Good advice when traversing a glacier with deep crevasses.

From the top of the mountain Benny could feel winds blowing from every direction up the mountainside. He said it was a funny feeling standing on a peak and feeling as if you were being lifted straight up.

They returned safely to Tatla Lake just in time for Benny to take his wife, Augustine, to Hanceville for the birth of their second son, Major, on May 17, 1892. They left Tatla Lake on May 1 with Benny rowing Augustine the twenty-seven-kilometre length of Tatla Lake in a rowboat while 8-year-old Albert brought the horses along the trail. They met at Bearhead Flat at the outflow of the lake, and continued by horseback from there.

Benny's infatuation with Bute Inlet continued after Major was born, and he made several trips back and forth following the Southgate River. He even managed to bring horses along this route, but one time he ran out of food when his horse slid off a bluff and was killed. "Dad was so hungry he had to eat the horse meat," Albert recalled. "He said the hardest thing he ever had to do was eat Charlie."

The only route into the Chilcotin from the Cariboo Road when Benny Franklin arrived was William Swanson's ferry across the Fraser River at the mouth of Chimney Creek. Government offices were in Clinton, so Benny decided to build a more direct route through Gang Ranch, crossing the Fraser River at Dog Creek.

In 1902, Benny sold his Tatla Lake ranch to Bob Graham and George Dagg for $1,700 and hired Gilpin to help him build a road from Alexis Creek to Nazko. He settled at Franklin Meadows along the Nazko River and spent the rest of his days roaming the Chilcotin.

Tom Chignell was still a young man when he came upon Benny Franklin's Democrat buggy and team of horses standing in the shallow water of Doc English Lake near Riske Creek. Benny's lifeless body lay in the water below them. He had apparently been watering his horses when he had a heart attack and fell off the buggy and drowned in a foot of water. Well into his 80s by that time, Benny's roving days were done. But not before he left his mark across a broad and rugged swath of the Chilcotin landscape.

Gerald Dester

First Postmaster at Riske Creek

It's not easy tracing genealogy back through time. The Indigenous people were very good at keeping track of who was related to who along that jagged line of cultural coupling that occurred between Caucasian men and Indigenous women at the time of first contact in the 1800s. The Catholic priests did their bit to help sort out the bloodlines in the juxtapositions that occurred. Later on, the internet turned up a few surprises that families on both sides of the racial divide are quite delighted with.

The history and background of men who grew up in London, Edinburgh, Stockholm or Paris would have been unperceivable to Indigenous people who grew up dipnetting salmon along the Chilcotin and Fraser rivers. Similarly, it would have been difficult for these outriders from "Mother Europe" to fully appreciate the sanctity of a people content with living subsistence lifestyles in harmony with the land.

Baptiste Dester and Clarence Mackill with a grizzly trophy at Kleena Kleene. Photo courtesy the Dester family.

Lottie Dester (Mrs. Johnny Chell) was raised as a Tŝilhqot'in by her mother's family. Veera Bonner photo.

Yet with an abundance of single white men and few European women to choose from, it didn't take long for the gene pool on the frontier to become mixed.

The Catholic Church can be thanked for keeping the genealogical record straight. Oblate priests went to great lengths to track down the paternity of white fathers responsible for Tŝilhqot'in and Secwepemc children and listing them on baptismal records. That was the case with Gerald Dester, sire of Baptiste Dester of Kleena Kleene, Lottie Dester Chell of Tl'etinqox, Isabel Davis of Australia, and Evelyn Dester of Vancouver.

Gerald Dester was a sea captain who came to Canada from Bath, England, in 1883 to work on the Canadian Pacific Railway. Some speculate that his image can be spotted in the series of photographs recording the pounding of the last spike at Craigellachie in 1885.

Gerald got established at Riske Creek where he operated a store and trading post in partnership with Fred Becher. In March 1892, he became the first postmaster of the "Chilcoten" Post Office at Riske Creek and held that position for two years.

It is easy to surmise that Gerald was homesick for the niceties of his English upbringing. His feet were in two worlds as he got established at Riske Creek, and he adapted to his circumstances by taking Jessie Peltwashaata, a Tsilhqot'in woman from Tl'etinqox, as his "country bride." They had two daughters together, Isabel, born in 1889, and Lottie, born in 1894. Then Gerald left Jessie to marry a woman who shared his own English background, but their union was short-lived.

Caroline Magee was the daughter of British immigrants who had settled in New Westminster in 1861. She and Gerald were married in 1897, and she joined him in Riske Creek. But life on the frontier didn't agree with Caroline. She moved back to Vancouver for the birth of their daughter, Evelyn, on January 31, 1898, and never returned.

Isabel Dester Davis was brought to England by her father when she was 11 years old and she never returned to the land of her birth. Photo courtesy Veera Bonner.

Now Gerald was determined to do right by his Tsilhqot'in daughters, Isabel and Lottie. At the very least he wanted to give them a "proper" English education, so in November 1900, he took 11-year-old Isabel back to England and left her with his family in Bath. He returned to Canada a year later with the intention of retrieving Lottie and taking her to England as well, but that never came about. On November 8, 1902, Gerald died of pneumonia and was buried at Alkali Lake.

Shortly before Gerald left for England with Isabel, however, he conceived a son with Yeleucy, a young Tsilhqot'in woman from Nemiah Valley. Unknown to Gerald, Baptiste Dester was born in August 1901, while he and Isabel were in England. Despite the Chilcotin's expansive landscape and sparsely populated community, few secrets were kept and word-of-mouth travelled like wildfire. That made it easy for Oblate priest Father François Marie Thomas to trace the identity of Baptiste's father. He entered G. Dester's name as the father on Baptiste's baptismal record. This led to further confusion later on.

Throughout his lifetime, Baptiste Dester was a greatly respected patriarch who put down roots in the West Chilcotin area of Kleena Kleene and Anahim Lake. He accomplished much in his eight decades, trapping all the way down the Klinaklini

Babtiste Dester's daughter Josephine Gregg with her aunt Maggie Baptiste. Josephine knew her grandfather was the postmaster at Riske Creek, but she knew very little else about him. Photo Gregg family collection.

River to Knight Inlet with his father-in-law, Old George Turner, and raising a family of seven children with Lucy Dagg.

Though Baptiste was partly white, culturally he was Tŝilhqot'in. His Indigenous status wasn't registered, however. Whether he voluntarily gave up his status or never received it because his father was white was never clear, but he was legally enfranchised and had "white rights." That meant he could own title to deeded property, buy alcohol if he wished, and vote in elections. Over the years, Baptiste owned a couple of ranches: one at Clearwater Lake and another down the Dean River near Cless Pocket Ranch north of Anahim Lake.

When Baptiste passed away in the 1980s, his family knew his father was an Englishman at Riske Creek, but otherwise knew very little about the man. That all changed in November 2007 when the Dester family held a family reunion in Williams Lake, and new light was shed on the family's genealogical past.

In their book, *Chilcotin: Preserving Pioneer Memories*, the Witte sisters tell the amazing story of how the two full sisters, Isabel and Lottie Dester, were raised in separate cultures two worlds apart. Isabel got her "proper" British education, as Gerald had intended, but she never married and never returned to the Chilcotin. Lottie grew up with their mother's people in the Chilcotin, got married at a young age to Johnny Chell, and raised a large Tsilhqot'in family. Lottie never learned to read or write.

Isabel corresponded regularly over the years with her childhood friends, Hattie Hance Witte of Big Creek and Hattie's brother, René Hance of Hanceville. They had grown up together at Hanceville where Gerald often left his daughters to play with the children of Tom and Nellie Hance.

In her letters, Isabel always remembered to ask about Lottie and would send her love and greetings. Sometimes she'd enclose a handkerchief which Hattie always conscientiously delivered. Occasionally Lottie would come to the Wittes seeking news of Isabel and took pride in looking at her latest snapshots.

After the First World War, Isabel changed her last name to Davis and immigrated to Australia. Though she dreamt of returning to the land of her birth to visit her sister and childhood friends, she never managed to do so. She remained "down under" the rest of her life.

At the 2007 Dester family reunion, the families of Baptiste Dester and Lottie Johnny Chell finally met up with the family members of Evelyn Dester, who they previously didn't know existed. By that time, Gerald Dester had more than 500 living descendants in the Chilcotin. Meanwhile, Evelyn had only one child, Valery Chambers, who arrived at the reunion with her son and daughter. "I came from a family of two," she told the gathering of 200 who assembled for the event. "I didn't have a dad and never knew I had so many relatives. I just love finding all you people I'm related to." It was Valery's son-in-law, John MacDonald, whose sleuthing through the internet triggered the reunion.

Josephine Gregg, daughter of Baptiste Dester, grew up knowing her Auntie Lottie and her large extended family. She also knew about her Aunt Isabel in Australia, though she never met her. But her biggest surprise was meeting her cousin, Valery Chambers, and learning about her Aunt Evelyn for the first time. "I never knew I had another aunt," she said. "It was pretty interesting learning so much more about my grandfather."

What made tracing the descendants of Gerald Dester difficult, was the "G. Dester" inscribed on Baptiste's birth certificate as his father. Historians, including the authors of *The Chilcotin: Preserving Pioneer Memories*, mistakenly assumed the "G" stood for "George," and this stymied John MacDonald's internet research. "I kept running into dead ends," he said. Then he tracked down Baptiste's grandson, Elliot Dester in Bella Coola. Elliot and John put the missing pieces of the genealogical puzzle together, and the dilemma was resolved.

Chilcotin Mud Pup

R. C. Cotton

Robert Cecil (R. C.) Cotton was a "mud pup" who brought elegance, class and forward-thinking to the ranching community of the Cariboo Chilcotin. In 1897, this eldest son of an English aristocratic family from Hampton Court, England, was sent to British Columbia to work for Mortimer Drummond of Riske Creek. He was only 18 years old.

"Mud pup" was a common expression referring to an agricultural apprentice who paid a farmer or rancher for the opportunity to work for them and learn the ropes of the profession. In R. C. Cotton's case, he paid Drummond $500 for his first year of employment, then volunteered to work for free the following summer. Finally Drummond paid him $25 per month as a bona fide ranch hand.

In 1899, Drummond let it be known he wanted to sell his Riske Creek Ranch, and R. C. Cotton was interested. He returned home to England that year to visit his family and managed to secure the funds to buy the ranch.

Though R. C. Cotton was the eldest son of a viscount, he was a nobleman without a title. His great-grandfather, Sir Stapleton Stapleton-Cotton, was given the title in 1827, being promoted from Baron Combermere to Viscount Combermere after a distinguished military and diplomatic career. When he died in 1865, his only son, Wellington Henry Stapleton-Cotton, inherited the title as the 2nd Viscount Combermere.

Robert Cecil (R. C.) Cotton in 1895. Photo courtesy Penny Hutchinson.

R. C. Cotton's father, Robert Wellington Stapleton-Cotton, became the 3rd Viscount Combermere upon Wellington Henry's death in 1891, but unfortunately for R. C. Cotton, that's where the peerage ended. Robert Cecil and his older sister, Madeline, were both illegitimate.

Their parents, Robert Wellington and Isabel Marian Chetwynd were both married to other people when they eloped in 1876. Before they had time to get divorced from their respective spouses, at the time a long and tortuous process, they had two children—Madeline in1877 and Robert Cecil in 1878.

Robert Wellington and Isabel finally married in 1880, but that wasn't soon enough to redeem their two oldest children's status under Britain's strict laws of primogeniture where title and inheritance descends to the oldest legitimate son. Their youngest son, Francis Lynch Stapleton-Cotton, born in 1887 and called Peter by the family, became the 4th Viscount Combermere when Robert Wellington died in 1898.

Non-inheriting sons like R. C. Cotton had three choices: they could go into the army, join the religious life, or head off to seek their fortune in the far reaches of the British Empire. R. C. Cotton made the latter choice and the Cotton and Drummond families made arrangements to send R. C. to Canada to work as a mud pup for Mortimer Percy George Douglas Drummond in British Columbia.

It was a pernicious twist of fate beyond his control that deprived R. C. from becoming a titled aristocrat, but he still received a share of the family fortunes. It was possibly an inheritance from his mother's family that provided him with the $40,000 needed to purchase the Riske Creek Ranch from Drummond.

R. C. Cotton also had an endowment, which gave him an advantage over many settlers trying to eke out a living in the Chilcotin. He was able to afford household servants, hire ranching staff and invest in significant improvements to his property over the years.

R. C. Cotton in his riding leather, 1899. Photo courtesy Penny Hutchinson.

After returning to British Columbia in 1900 and taking over ownership of the ranch, R. C. Cotton immediately started developing his holdings. He pre-empted further land grants to expand his ranch, bought stock from Douglas Lake Ranch, and registered his own "W" brand.

He also renamed Riske Creek Ranch, which had been pre-empted by Ludwig William Riske in 1873 on the west side of the Fraser River upstream from the mouth of the Chilcotin River. It became officially known as The Cotton Ranche—spelled with an "e."

In 1906, Maud Waller, a young woman from Tasmania, arrived in the Cariboo to work as a governess for the six kids of Field Yolland's family in 150 Mile House. Field Yolland had come to British Columbia in 1894 as a Church of England priest. He later became chief li-

Cotton House on the Cotton Ranche near Riske Creek. Photo Penny Hutchinson.

cence inspector for 150 Mile House and Soda Creek. It didn't take long for Maud Waller and R. C. Cotton to become acquainted, and friendship turned to romance. They became engaged in 1908, and the next year they were married in Vancouver in February 1909.

The *Vancouver Sun* reported a quiet Saturday wedding in St. Paul's Church in Vancouver: "Archdeacon Pentreath united in wedlock Mr. R. Cecil Cotton of Chilcoten [*sic*] to Miss Waller who is well known in the Cariboo having resided for several months at the 150 Mile House. Mr. Skinner, an old Caribooite, gave the bride away and Mr. A.H.T. Chetwynd acted as best man…"

Less than a year later, on January 8, 1910, Maud gave birth to their daughter, Sylvia Isabel. She would be the couple's only child. It is said R. C. rode sixty-five kilometres on his saddle horse to 150 Mile House as his wife went into labour to get a doctor to attend the birth.

Shortly after Sylvia was born, 20-year-old Madeline "Queenie" Wheeler from Liverpool was hired as her nanny. Not only did she care for the baby but she became a close intergenerational family friend. In 1912, Queenie moved to Farwell Canyon on the Chilcotin River to work as a housekeeper for Gordon Farwell. Two years later she married Farwell's partner, Gerald Blenkinsop, an Englishman from Warwickshire. Young Sylvia, known to all as "Baby," was the flower girl at their wedding.

Like R. C. Cotton, Farwell was a mud pup from a well-to-do English family. He arrived in the Chilcotin from Leicestershire in 1903 to work for Fred Beaumont on the River Ranch. Once he gained sufficient experience and competence in the ranching profession, he bought his own place along the Chilcotin River from Louis Vedan.

Farwell Canyon, which now immortalizes Gordon Farwell's name, is known as Nagwentl'ed by the Tŝilhqot'in people. There are ancient pictographs on rocks above the rushing water marking this site as one of the most important Indigenous dipnet fishing stations in the region. Before the Great Darkening, as some people call the smallpox epidemic of 1862, this canyon was Secwepemc territory. The disease wiped out the Canyon Shuswap and the few survivors migrated to the east side of the Fraser River to Alkali Lake and Dog Creek.

Maud Cotton and "Baby" (Sylvia). Photo courtesy Penny Hutchinson.

This tiny plot of fertile ground, surrounded by towering hoodoos and crowned by the largest sand dune in British Columbia, is one of the most significant microclimates of the Chilcotin. It supports the largest herd of California bighorn sheep in North America and marks the northern extent of the great arid and semi-arid expanse that stretches up the continent from Mexico. From the earliest days, a bridge was built over the narrow canyon.

In 1912, R. C. and Maude went to England to meet R. C.'s family. Peter, the 4th Viscount Combermere, now 25 years old, sailed back to North America with them on the *Empress of Britain* to visit the ranch and see British Columbia for the first time.

Sylvia's next nanny was an Irish girl, Chris Riley, nicknamed "Weenie." Once her term of employment was complete, she too left to take up housekeeping duties for Gordon Farwell. She and Farwell were later married. According to Veera Bonner, the two couples called their isolated hideaway "Happy Valley." The roads leading out of the canyon on both sides of the river were very narrow and treacherous and the two wives, Queenie and Weenie, seldom left home.

In 1919, Farwell and Blenkinsop sold their oasis to Gang Ranch and moved to Sugar Cane Jacks Meadow in Big Creek, a much higher and cooler location. The old farm in the canyon remains a significant camping and fishing site for Tŝilhqot'in and Secwepemc people, who still dipnet salmon there every year.

Like many aristocratic British ex-pats, R. C. Cotton introduced a few old-world customs to his ranch. He raised pheasant and grouse for weekend shoots and hosted polo matches on his hayfields. When Williams Lake became a bigger settlement with the coming of the Pacific Great Eastern railway in 1919, R. C. Cotton became a patron of the Williams Lake Stampede and a racing judge. His brother Peter, 4th Viscount Combermere, was visiting in 1923 when Jo Flieger won the Stampede's second-ever mountain race on Grey Eagle, one of R. C. Cotton's horses. Two years later Flieger won the fourth stampede mountain race on Grey Eagle. The horse later died at the ranch in 1928.

The railway provided a means to get Cariboo Chilcotin cattle to market in Vancouver. Three or four weeks before the sale, R. C. and the cowboys would drive 300 or 400 head of cattle from the ranch to the stockyards in Williams Lake. R. C. favoured raising shorthorns and carried between 1,400 and 1,500 animals on his almost-6,000 hectare (14,000 acres) spread. For many years, he was president of the Cariboo Cattlemen's Association. Maud had her own herd of shorthorns, sired by a bull she bought from the Prince of Wales.

A 1937 Vancouver *Province* newspaper article describes R. C. Cotton as a man of decided opinion who was hard to convince of anything he was not certain of. "He is able to say 'no' quicker and more often than any other man in the whole Cariboo," quipped the writer.

Caricature of R. C. Cotton. Penny Hutchinson collection.

R. C. Cotton was loved and respected by his neighbours and those who worked for him. "He was called 'Daddy' by everybody and he treated us all kindly and caring like family," said his granddaughter Carole Hutchinson, who was raised by R. C. and Maud as a child at the Cotton Ranche.

There is one rumour that R. C. Cotton's biographer, Antoinette Danaher, wants to dispel. There was talk around the country that R. C. Cotton lived with a Tŝilhqot'in woman from Toosey in the early days and may have had children with her. Speculation that he might have had other children besides Sylvia was fuelled by the custom of everyone at nearby Toosey also referring to him as "Daddy." Danaher said she found no evidence that R. C. Cotton had a "summer wife," as many early settlers did. "In my opinion he had no illegitimate children because he knew first-hand the pain that illegitimacy can bring."

In 1945, the Cotton Ranche was sold to John Wade of Chilco Ranch and R. C. and Maud spent their remaining years at the west end of Williams Lake, where they continued to raise a smaller herd of 75 shorthorns. Maud passed away in 1954, followed by R. C. two years later.

The fertile flat at the west end of Williams Lake is still referred to as the Cotton Site.

Jim Robertson of Nemiah Valley

Jim Robertson was the first member of a large Scottish family to come to Canada in the late 1890s. He made his way around Cape Horn to British Columbia and continued up the coast to Bella Coola, where he got a job in a fish cannery.

"There was quite a big age difference between Uncle Jim and my dad, Sandy Robertson," said Phil Robertson, who was born in Alexis Creek in 1927. "I never knew Uncle Jim, but I heard lots of stories about him." He said his uncle was the foreman in charge of a crew of Chinese workers when they got into a big fight and started throwing salmon cans around. "My uncle got nailed on the side of his head by a can of salmon and it pretty near killed him," Phil said.

Jim quit his job and headed for the high country of the Chilcotin Plateau. Eventually he made his way to Nemiah Valley, which he took an immediate liking to. He took out a pre-emption on a flat piece of ground near the mouth of Nemiah Creek and started raising some cattle and horses there. His letters home to his family fondly described Nemiah Valley as being very much like Scotland.

Sandy and Margaret Robertson settled in Alexis Creek after Jim Robertson's death. Photo courtesy Phil Robertson.

Ollie Nukalow (Johnny Robertson) was Jim Robertson's son. Photo courtesy Al Elsey.

In 1906, Jim's younger sister Margaret gave birth to her first child, Alexina, in an Edinburgh hospital the same day her husband, Alex Reay, got killed in a threshing machine accident. "He got caught in the belt and it killed him," Phil said. Margaret was devastated and worried about how she was going to support herself and her young daughter. Soon she lapsed into a bad bout of depression. "The doctor told her she should get out of Scotland and go someplace else," Phil said. "Go over to Canada where her brother was, and stay there a while."

So that's what Margaret did. She left Alexina in the care of some relatives and headed for Canada to keep house for her brother in Nemiah Valley.

"Uncle Jim had a little Indian gal too," Phil said. "And they had a son together, but he kept this a secret from the family." The priest baptized Jim's son Johnny Robertson, though everyone called him Ollie Nukalow. The baby's mother, Loosap, had a number of other children over the years, all fathered by different white men. Her oldest daughter, Lilly Skinner, also known as Chiwid, later became a Chilcotin legend, living outdoors by herself for fifty years. Margaret Reay likely didn't know her brother Jim had a young son when he brought her to his isolated ranch in Nemiah Valley. The baby would have been in the care of Loosap and her extended family.

There was a noticeable absence of single white women in the Chilcotin when Margaret showed up to visit her brother. The country was flooded with single white men, and her presence as an unmarried woman of European extraction didn't go unnoticed. It didn't take long for eligible suitors to get wind that she was there. George Dagg and Bob Graham, ranching partners in Tatla Lake, were soon competing for her affections.

Margaret wasn't ready to jump into a relationship so soon after losing her husband, but eventually she came to terms with her loss. After two years, she felt strong enough to return home to Scotland to see her daughter and family, and she was on her way to Ashcroft to catch the train to Halifax when Bob Graham intercepted her and convinced her to marry him. They said their vows and returned to Tatla Lake.

By the time Margaret departed for Scotland to retrieve Alexina, she was pregnant with Bob Graham's first child. Their daughter, Betty, was born in Edinburgh in 1911. The following year Margaret returned to Canada with both daughters, accompanied by two of her sisters and two brothers. On June 11, 1912, just two months after the sinking of the *Titanic*, they set sail for Canada on a twelve-day voyage across the Atlantic.

For Alexina, the experience aboard the ship was very unpleasant. "Everyone on the ship was terribly seasick," she said. "I don't remember what we ate on the ship, but I do remember eating an awful lot of oranges. To this day, I still don't like oranges."

There weren't a lot of other children on the boat and Alexina didn't have much to do. "I did have a doll and baby carriage which I played with, but when we were about to arrive in Halifax, my two uncles threw them overboard because they would be too much trouble on the train. To this day, I have not forgiven them for doing that."

After a rough ocean voyage, they arrived in Halifax and took the train across the country. Bob Graham was waiting in Ashcroft to meet them with his wagon and horses.

Phil's dad, Sandy Robertson, accompanied Margaret to Canada, and when they got to the Chilcotin he went to Nemiah Valley to visit their brother Jim. He worked for Bob Graham in Tatla Lake until the war broke out in 1914, then he joined the Seaforth Highlanders and went overseas.

It was while Sandy Robertson was on the battlefields of Europe in 1916 that he learned the tragic news of his brother Jim Robertson's death in Nemiah Valley. "He died of a gunshot to the brain," said Phil. "The police ruled it was suicide, but he was shot in the back of the head with his own gun."

After the war, Sandy Robertson met his future wife, Margaret Thomson, in Aberdeenshire, before returning to the Chilcotin. Margaret came out to meet him in 1921 and they got married and settled at Alexis Creek and started raising their family. Phil was born in 1927, the third of eleven children.

"I never believed my uncle, Jim Robertson, took his own life," Phil said. "I was talking to the chief in Nemiah Valley about how Jim died. He looked into it and told me Jim didn't commit suicide, some other joker shot him. A lot of stuff went on in those days, but you couldn't prove nothing."

The best-kept family secret was Ollie Nukalow. "Casimile Lulua told me I had a cousin in Anahim Lake," Phil said. "I was heading up there for stampede and he says, 'You gonna see your cousin, eh?' I said, what cousin? 'You got half-breed cousin. His name is Robertson too. Must be your cousin.'

"I told him he was full of you-know-what, and he laughed and said, 'You just high tone. You don't want talk to your cousin.'

"I never did meet Ollie Nukalow. I thought Casimile was kidding so I put it off and never thought any more about it. Ollie died in a logging accident in Bella Coola in 1960 before I had a chance to meet him."

Phil said his brother-in-law, Al Elsey, knew Ollie Nukalow well. "He said he was a powerful man and a tremendous worker. He packed the powder and diesel fuel across the rockslide on his back when they were building the road to Bella Coola."

It is a fact that many of the first white settlers had Indigenous wives when they first came to the country. Some abandoned their Indigenous families when they got their imported white brides. Some pretended they didn't exist. "These old-timers didn't want to tell their kids that the first ones in the country had Indian wives," Phil said. "When they got their white wives and families, they didn't want to tell. But the Indians knew."

Al Elsey had a story about Ollie Nukalow, Jim Robertson's son.

> When I came to Bella Coola in September 1951, the Ulkatcho people used to camp in the trees next to the Cedar Inn where the Bella Coola townsite is today. That's where I met Ollie Nukalow.
>
> Not long after I was there, Ollie came over to the house and asked if there was any work he could do. He said he needed enough money to buy a box of snuff, a comb and a pair of gloves. The total cost was just over two bucks.
>
> I didn't have any work for him to do, but I loaned him the money. Two or three dollars was half a day's pay in those days.
>
> He said, "When I come down in the springtime I'll pay you."
>
> I just trusted the guy.
>
> In the spring of 1952, there was a shortage of hay in Anahim Lake, and Ollie brought a bunch of his horses down to the valley. That was fairly common in those days. The first thing he did, when they camped and made their fire over in the big spruce trees across from the co-op store, Ollie came over and paid me.
>
> "I owe you," he said.
>
> We became really good friends after that. As the years went by he worked for me quite a bit. When we got Talchako Lodge, he came and split fence posts for me one year. Ollie was a tremendous worker. When he said something, he meant it.
>
> A year later at Red Hill Cabin at the top of the Bella Coola Hill, Ollie took me moose hunting for the first time. That was the year the Bella Coola Road was being built, and it wasn't finished yet. We drove from Bella Coola to the top of the first set of switchbacks and back-packed about two and a half miles the rest of the way to Red Hill. Ollie and his wife, Aggie Sill, were camped there at Young Creek.
>
> Ollie smelled our smoke and came down and offered to rent us horses and take us hunting.
>
> The next day we started out, and rode four horses up the mountain. We took a shortcut up the West Branch through a schmozzle of deadfall and didn't get to the East Fork until 2:30 in the afternoon. We got up to just below timberline and shot two moose. By the time we got them gutted, it was about 5 o'clock. It was about eleven miles back to Red Hill camp. We got home about 10 o'clock.
>
> The next day we got the pack horses and went back up. But they were slow. We were slow getting going in the morning, and didn't get

Phil and Joyce Robertson at McLeese Lake. Phil regrets he never got the chance to meet his cousin Ollie Nukalow. Photo Sage Birchwater.

there until about 3 o'clock. Then Ollie said—I'll never forget this—"Well, tea time!"

We had no tea. We didn't have anything with us. I thought he was joking. We were at timberline and all there was to burn is some short scrub willow brush and a few balsams. So Ollie breaks off a bunch of dead sticks and pretty soon he's got a little fire going. Just a tiny little fire.

He's got this little sack, a grey-looking flour sack tied on behind his saddle. He takes it out and he's got four bully beef cans, with lids not quite cut right off.

"Cup?" he says.

Also in the sack he's got a can of tobacco, half a pound of Players tobacco. So he takes his bandana off his neck, spreads it on the grass, takes his tobacco, dumps it in the bandana, and ties it up so it won't spill.

Then he goes down to this little tiny creek and washes out the tin can, fills it with water, and sticks it on the fire. Pretty soon it's boiling.

Then he reaches into his shirt pocket and takes a handful of loose tea. Throws it in there.

"Tea time," he says.

So we have a cup of tea. Then he says, "Soogar?"

I says, "You're kidding!"

Then he laughed, and over on the other side in his shirt pocket, he's got some lumped sugar.

Bob and Margaret Graham

Robert "Bob" Graham was 20 years old when he arrived in the Chilcotin from County Antrim, Ireland, in 1891. His older brother, Alex, had come to Canada five years earlier and had settled near Alexis Creek with his wife, Anna.

Bob pre-empted some land where the village of Alexis Creek is today, then headed to the Klondike to seek his fortune in the gold rush. In 1901, he returned to the Chilcotin and handed his Alexis Creek pre-emption over to Alex and went into a partnership with George Dagg to purchase Benny Franklin's ranch at Tatla Lake. In 1902, Bob Graham was 31 years old.

After Bob successfully won Margaret Reay's affections and convinced her to become his bride, his ranching partnership with George Dagg quickly dissolved. Dagg eventually returned to England, but left behind a strong legacy of offspring he had conceived with various Tsilhqot'in women. His children included Billy Dagg, Lucy Dagg, Celestine Dagg and Casimil Dagg, and there may have been others.

When Bob Graham met Margaret at the Ashcroft train station on her return from Scotland with their infant daughter, Betty, in June 1912, she arrived with two sisters, two brothers, and her 6-year-old daughter, Alexina Reay. Margaret decided to let Alexina stay on the train to New Westminster with one of her sisters because the weather was very hot and the bugs were so bad.

Bob Graham. Photo courtesy the Graham family.

Margaret and Betty and two of her brothers went to the Chilcotin with Bob. In the fall, when it was cooler, Alexina came with her aunt to Ashcroft and took the stagecoach to Alexis Creek. From there they travelled in a two-horse cart to Tatla Lake. "It was very rough and the roads were very bad," Alexina remembered.

In 1914, Margaret Graham opened the first post office in Tatla Lake. Before that, the mail only got delivered as far west as Redstone.

In 1915, Margaret gave birth to her first son in the brand-new hospital in Alexis Creek. William Robert Graham or W. R., as he was known as an adult, was the first baby born in the new hospital. Four years later, on October 27, 1919, Margaret gave birth to a second son, Alex, completing their family.

Margaret Graham. Photo courtesy the Graham family.

Over the years, Margaret and Bob developed Tatla Lake Ranch into one of the great establishments of the West Chilcotin.

Alexina said there was an Australian doctor in Alexis Creek by the name of Dr. Wright who invariably prescribed iodine as a remedy for every ill. She remembered the time a cowboy at Tatla Lake cut the ball of his foot very badly and came into the ranch house late one night with his riding boot almost full of blood. The weather was very cold and his foot was frozen. By four in the morning, his foot had thawed out and it was bleeding profusely.

"The blood was running along the living room floor," Alexina remembered. "Everyone was frantic about what to do, so we phoned Dr. Wright. Needless to say, he said put a little iodine on it."

Finally Bob resorted to extreme measures to stop the bleeding. He took a fire poker, cleaned it well, put it into the red-hot coals of the fire, and seared the cut closed. "It took a lot of courage to do that," Alexina said, "but that's the only thing my stepfather could have done to save that man's life. Otherwise he would have bled to death."

She said the injured cowboy was none other than 21-year-old Lester Dorsey. "It was the middle of winter and would have taken three days to get to Alexis Creek at that time of year," Alexina recalled, noting that Bob Graham had quite a bit of medical training before he left Ireland. "He could sew up cuts and wounds very well, and kept drugs on hand in case of an accident."

As with most pioneering and ranching families, the children helped with the chores as soon as they were able. When Betty was 8 years old, she'd ride the hay mower all day long.

"I would ride the hay rake because I was bigger," Alexina said. "I fit the rake better than Betty did. The men folk would harness the horses in the morning and take care of them in the evening, but this was an all-day job for us girls during hay season."

One fall, Bob Graham returned home from the beef drive to Williams Lake driving an Overland car. He went in with the beef drive and someone talked him into buying the car. He had never driven a vehicle before but was determined to drive it home himself. He got someone else to bring the horses and chuckwagon back to Tatla Lake and drove the car as far as Lees Corner. He wondered why the car seemed to be running a bit hot, then it was discovered that he had covered the whole 100-kilometre distance in second gear.

In 1930, big changes were about to happen at the Graham ranch. Bob and Margaret decided to build a stopping house at Tatla Lake. Bob purchased a steam tractor and hired Tom Chignell to drive it from Ashcroft. It broke down halfway across the Gang Ranch and repairs had to be made before Tom could complete the journey to Tatla Lake.

The steam tractor was used to power a sawmill to cut lumber for the ambitious new project. Though Bob oversaw the construction of the "Big House," as it became known, the vision of the mansion belonged to Margaret Graham. The building was completed in 1932.

"Ever since I can remember, Mrs. Graham was putting up guests," her daughter-in-law, Joy Graham, recalled. "She didn't call it an inn or anything like that, just a stopping house."

It was built during the Depression when there were many travellers who were looking for work, and many stayed and worked on the construction project, crafting Margaret's vision of a perfect house. Originally there were six bedrooms upstairs and the master bedroom and big dining room downstairs. Each bed in the house had two handmade quilts sewn by Margaret and Betty and stuffed with wool from their own sheep. The place was heated by a factory-made furnace that took four-foot long pieces of firewood.

Lee Butler described the Grahams' Big House as the nicest building in the country. He said they had one dining room for special guests and another for family, ranch workers and friends who were visiting. He remembered dining with the family. "We were invited in for lunch and that was quite a thing. There were big oak tables, linoleum flooring, real silverware cutlery, and delicate china plates."

The Graham Big House was the only house in Tatla Lake with electric lights. They were powered by one of the first light plants in the Chilcotin. Margaret Graham's nephew, Phil Robertson, said Bill Graham got the light plant and wired

Hay crew finds a cool place on the Graham ranch to have lunch. Photo courtesy the Graham family.

the house himself. The Big House was also one of the first dwellings to have running water. Upstairs there were hardwood floors, brass fittings on the doors, and cedar cupboards.

The Grahams were well known for their hospitality and if no one was home, the back door was always open and the coffeepot was always on. A truck driver once described how if nobody was in the building and you needed a place to sleep, you would go upstairs and any room with the door open was a free room. He said if you were hungry you could just make yourself something to eat if nobody was there to cook for you.

As the Graham children grew up, they each found their place in the family dynamic.

Alexina was 6 years old when she first came to the ranch in fall 1912. Because there were no schools, she ended up boarding with an aunt in Alberta when she was 10 years old to get her schooling. "I came home by train every second summer through the Rockies to Ashcroft, then by stagecoach to Alexis Creek where someone would meet me," she said.

It was clear to Alexina that she didn't want to chase cows the rest of her life, so she took teachers' training in Vancouver. In 1925 a school was started in Tatla Lake and Alexina became its first teacher. Classes were held in a little warehouse on the ranch at the beginning of the year, but in the spring a small log building was constructed for the school.

Children at Tatla Lake School. Tommy Holte, Alice Holte (Engebretson), Illa Holte (Graham), Alex Graham and Bill Graham. Photo courtesy the Graham family.

Tatla Lake storekeeper Betty Graham.
Photo courtesy the Graham family.

Alexina taught one year at Tatla Lake, then the following year got a job teaching at Meldrum Creek. From there, her teaching career took her to Prince George where she taught for several years. She never moved back to Tatla Lake permanently.

"We always wore dresses," Alexina recalled. "My stepfather would never allow us to wear pants. We were allowed to wear riding skirts, which our mother made from heavy denim. My sister, when she was 16, put on a pair of pants and my stepfather told her to take those things off!"

She said they would order material from the Eaton's catalogue to make clothes. "Then Mother would cut them out and sew them up. This is where we got all our clothes because there was no store in the Chilcotin that had that kind of thing."

Betty was 14 years old the year Alexina taught school at Tatla Lake. There wasn't a lot for a young woman to do in the outback of the West Chilcotin, so Margaret Graham encouraged Betty to start a store and run the post office as a way of keeping her daughter at home.

It was common for the big ranches in the Chilcotin to have a store where extra items could be sold to people who lived nearby. In the early days, ranchers would make big supply runs to Ashcroft twice a year, using six-horse teams pulling two wagons. They would purchase bulk supplies of food, hardware and building materials needed for the ranch. It only made sense to haul extra flour, beans, sugar, dried fruit, hardware and other staples that could be sold in smaller quantities at a mark-up to help pay the shipping costs. People were always coming to the ranch for extra supplies anyway.

By the time Betty started her store, the Chilcotin was well served by trucker Tommy Hodgson, who brought supplies and mail every week from Williams Lake. In time, Betty became the backbone of the Tatla Lake community.

She started her store in a small log building next to the old Graham ranch house. Then once the Big House was finished, she relocated her store to a small log building next door. In 1939 a newer and larger store was built, which Betty ran for the next forty years.

Jim Mackill and Bob Graham visit on the back stairs of the Graham Big House. Photo courtesy the Graham family.

Betty had a reputation for kindness and helping others. In particular, she is remembered for the way she took care of Chiwid, the iconic Tŝilhqot'in recluse who lived outdoors in the outback of the Chilcotin for fifty years after receiving a severe beating from her husband.

Betty managed to secure a small government pension for Chiwid, then would track her down in her obscure camping places and deliver boxes of food and staples to keep her alive.

Betty married Fred Linder in the 1940s, and he is also remembered for his genial manner. When it came to emergencies, he was just the man to have with you. He seemed to always know just what to do.

Bill and Alex Graham took over separate aspects of the Tatla Lake ranching operation. Bill became a mechanic and built a shop and looked after the machinery and farming on the ranch. Alex was responsible for the animals. Bill had the first Caterpillar in the country and built roads across the region from Chilanko Forks to the Bella Coola Hill.

Phil Robertson said Tatla Lake was a good ranch. Some ranches were more piecemeal and spread out with hayfields miles away from the headquarters, but Tatla Lake ranch had everything right there. "They could be haying or working with the cattle, then come in for lunch. They did everything right from the house."

Because the fields flooded every year, they never had to be fertilized. "They got good crops year after year."

Phil was born in Alexis Creek in 1927 and spent several summers at the Graham ranch as a young boy. He remembered the big haying crews when everything was done with horses. "There were two or three mowers and two or three rakes and four or five hay slips hauling the hay to the stack yards." He said there was a big table set up in the basement of the bunkhouse to feed the hay crew, and extra room above the boiler in the shop for the men to sleep. "It was full of men and Aunt Margaret was a damn good cook. In the early morning, Ben Wilson would go and get the horses."

Chiwid next to her brush house near Tatla Lake. Joy Graham would often take supplies and food to Chiwid to help her survive the winter. Photo courtesy the Graham family.

He said the horses were only used a couple of months of the year during haying time, then gradually the ranch became more mechanized. "Gradually they got more machinery and they disposed of the horses. Now two or three people can cut the whole hay crop."

Bob Graham died in 1952, followed by Margaret Graham in 1958. Fred Linder died in 1969, followed by Alex Graham in 1973. Betty married Hugh McDonald and continued to run the Tatla Lake General Store until her death in 1980.

In 1976, the Graham family sold the ranch, but held on to the Big House and the store. The Big House became known as the Graham Inn and was sold to Bruno and Jutta Krawzik in the early 1980s. After Bill Graham died in 1983, his wife Joy sold the last vestige of the Graham family landholdings, which had once dominated the community of Tatla Lake.

Over the years, the Graham Inn has gone through a number of owners, but it remains one of the great icons of the West Chilcotin and a lasting legacy to the vision and memory of Bob and Margaret Graham.

Tommy Hodgson

Chilcotin Trucking Pioneer

Tommy Hodgson made a name for himself as a pioneer trucker in the Chilcotin. Born in Yorkshire, England, in 1885, he came to Canada with his parents in 1897 and moved to 150 Mile House in 1912 to take a job driving the weekly mail run to Alexis Creek. He drove for the Inland Express Company.

With the outbreak of the First World War in 1914, Tommy dutifully enlisted for service in the Canadian army but was turned down because of varicose veins. He took over the Alexis Creek mail contract on his own and continued trucking into the Chilcotin for the rest of his life until his death in 1945.

The Hodgson trucks drove through the Chilcotin in all kinds of weather. Photo courtesy Sage Birchwater collection.

Tommy married Edyth Paxton in 1915, and the couple had six children. There were three sons—Jack, Wilfred and Patrick (Cookie)—and three daughters—Phyllis, Marjorie and Betty Jean.

The Hodgson sons all drove for their father as soon as they were big enough to reach the pedals. When Tommy died in 1945, his son Wilf Hodgson and Wilf's brother-in-law Joe Gillis took over the freight line until they sold the business in 1962.

Wilf Hodgson recalled accompanying his father into the Chilcotin when he was 6 or 7 years old. "It was around 1926 and we stayed overnight with Old Bob Pyper at Chilanko Forks. He had quite a big store, and Arthur Haddock, the fur buyer, was there. It was Easter time and the priest was coming. When the priest came in those days, there was big excitement."

Chilanko Forks was just west of Redstone Flats where Father François Marie Thomas was holding the big gathering known as Priest Time. Tŝilhqot'in families converged on Pyper's store to sell their winter catch of furs before heading for the religious and social celebration.

"They came with their horses, packhorses and wagons," Wilf remembered. "Nobody came in cars. It was big excitement. I remember at night they played lahal right by Pyper's store. All night long you'd hear these Indians wailing away there.

Bob Pyper (top right) began his career in the Chilcotin as a provincial policeman. He later ran a store at Chilanko Forks for many years until it was set on fire by a disgruntled neighbour. Photo courtesy Wilf Hodgson.

When you're a small kid it's kind of an eerie sort of feeling. I guess they had a bit of homebrew, I don't know. By daylight it kind of quietened right down."

Hank Law rode a bicycle to the Chilcotin from Vancouver in the early 1930s. At Riske Creek he traded his bicycle for a horse. Photo courtesy the Law family.

By the time he was 17, Wilf was driving regularly for his dad. One very cold winter day in 1937, he arrived at Chilanko Forks with the mail and a few groceries for Bob Pyper. The place was strangely silent. "Old Pyper was the only one living between Redstone and Tatla Lake in those days," Wilf said. "The old fellow had a store there for years, then somebody burned the store down. I guess he didn't have any insurance, so he went broke.

"I knocked at the door and he wouldn't answer," Wilf continued. "There was no smoke coming out of the chimney so I went around to the side of the house and looked through the window. There was Old Pyper sitting in his chair staring at me out the window. He didn't move. Then I realized he was dead. I had to get into the house and phone Andy Stuart at Redstone."

Eventually a provincial police officer, Bill Broughten, who was stationed at Alexis Creek, showed up to retrieve Pyper's body. He hired Hank Law to help him. "He paid me $3.20 to be a policeman for a day," Hank grimaced. "They could shoot at you for that. We had to go in and get Old Pyper. He was in his underwear froze stiff as a board across the table in his old shack on the road before you get to Pyper Lake."

K. B. Moore

Tatlayoko's First Rancher

Kennon Beverly (K. B.) Moore was the first rancher in Tatlayoko Valley. Born to a wealthy family in Massachusetts in 1891, he could trace his lineage back to the *Mayflower* and the founding of the city of Boston.

K. B. was educated at home by personal tutors, then in 1908, at 17 years old, he left home to explore the world and seek his fortune. He rode the rods of freight trains across North America, eventually arriving in British Columbia. He found his way to the Chilcotin and got a job as a ranch hand for Norman Lee at Hanceville.

After working for a year or two for Norman Lee, K. B. decided to look for his own piece of land. Taking the saddle horse he received for wages, he and two young friends from New Mexico travelled west across the Chilcotin to Chezacut, where he had heard there was an expanse of broad meadows that could be staked for homesteads. He found a nice meadow, later named Moore Flats, and spent a year there proving up the land. An unfortunate tragedy shattered his enthusiasm for that country, though, when one of his young friends drowned.

In April 1914, K. B. started searching for a new place to live. He rode horseback west and then south to Tatlayoko Valley, where he was impressed by the spectacular mountain scenery, and the much warmer growing climate. Chezacut was still icebound with snow while Tatlayoko was sprouting green shoots. He found enough natural feed to stake out his horse overnight on a forty-foot rope and not have to restake him in the morning.

K. B. was still an American citizen when Canada entered the First World War in August 1914, but he felt a patriotic duty to defend his adopted land. He enlisted with the Royal Canadian Engineers and was sent to the front laying track for munitions cars.

Before K. B. left the Chilcotin for the Great War, he proposed to a young woman, Dolly Church, whose brother, Dick Church, owned a ranch at Big Creek. Unfortunately, once he got overseas, K. B. received a "Dear John" letter from Dolly, telling him she had met someone else she wanted to marry.

K. B.'s whole company was gassed in the trenches and most of them died, but K. B. was lucky. He was sent to Scotland to recuperate, and for a whole year he lived with a family who owned a distillery and happened to produce some of the country's finest Scotch whiskey. Each day K. B. received a dram of the "medicine," which he claimed restored his health.

After the war, K. B. returned to the Chilcotin with renewed vigour. He promptly took out a pre-emption in Tatlayoko Valley, staking the Circle X Ranch at the north end of Tatlayoko Lake. He also discovered that his old flame, Dolly Church, had not married after all, and one day he received a love letter from her begging him to take her back. The couple married and had two children, Isobel, born in 1920, and Beverly Kennon, born in 1922.

It was a Moore family tradition in Boston to reverse the order of the names, "Beverly" and "Kennon," with each succeeding generation of oldest males. K. B.'s father was Beverly Kennon and his grandfather was Kennon Beverly.

K. B. Moore was an American but joined the Royal Canadian Engineers in 1914. He served in World War I but was injured in a gas attack. Photo courtesy the Bracewell family.

When K. B. established his ranch, the provincial range officer suggested that he apply for the grazing rights for the whole Tatlayoko Valley because no one else had pre-empted the land there. K. B. declined, saying he wanted neighbours. "Then we can round up our cattle together, brand our animals together, and take our beef to market together," he told the grazing inspector. The future, as far as he was concerned, was to have a community of people supporting one another.

Soon more people moved into Tatlayoko Valley, and by the mid-1920s there were several ranching families, including the McGhees, Belameys and Purjues. To a fault, K. B. Moore was conciliatory and generous. When one rancher ranging cattle down the west side of Tatlayoko Lake experienced bear problems, K. B. agreed to share his range on the north end of the Potato Mountain Range, even though it meant he would have to run fewer cattle there himself.

K. B.'s fortunes with his wife, Dolly, were short-lived. When he returned home from the annual beef drive to Williams Lake one fall, Dolly and the two children were gone. "The kids were 7 or 8 years old," said K. B.'s grandson, Barry Moore. "She took the cookstove, the wagon and horses, twenty head of cattle, and went to Anahim Lake. She cleaned him out. When he came back from the beef drive, he had nothing."

Despite the setback, K. B.'s kind nature prevailed.

"Grandpa never spoke badly about Dolly," said Gerry Bracewell, K. B.'s daughter-in-law. "He fed her horses and cattle every winter, sold her calves in the fall, and sent her the money. He never cut her down or complained about what she did. He was in love with that woman right to the end."

K. B. became one of country's first game guides, apprenticing with the legendary Ralph Edwards of Lonesome Lake.

K. B. Moore (far right) on the shore of Tatlayoko Lake where he established his Circle X ranch. Photo courtesy Gerry Bracewell.

Gerry Bracewell came to Tatlayoko Valley to work for K. B. Moore in 1940. With K. B.'s encouragement, she married his son, Beverly, and they had two sons, Marty and Barry. Unfortunately, Gerry and Bev's marriage didn't last. Bev pulled out and left Gerry and the kids on his father's ranch when the boys were still toddlers.

Gerry, who had lost her own dad when she was 5 years old, said K. B. became the father-figure she had never known. Likewise, Gerry, Marty and Barry became the family K. B. had always wished he had, ever since his own wife and kids had left so many years earlier.

K. B. handed over his guide-outfitting business to Gerry after mentoring her in the ways of big game hunting. She went on to become one of the province's most notable registered female game guides—with a career that spanned five decades.

When K. B. was on his deathbed in 1954, Gerry was at his side. She said, "Granddad had an expression of awe and wonder on his face." She figured he was consoled because his fondest dream of having his family carry on the traditions he had started was being realized.

"When I am but a speck of dust in the giant arms of dust… some blood of mine will yet be warm; some heart will echo my old cares and happiness," was his favourite quote.

Eagle Lake Henry

Eagle Lake Henry was one of those individuals who lived large upon the landscape of the Chilcotin. Henry's Crossing near the outflow of Chilko Lake was named after him. There's a bridge there now, but in Henry's day, it was a wide, shallow section of the Chilko River where able horsemen could ford the river on a saddle horse or drive teams of sturdy workhorses through stream pulling big-wheeled wagons. Henry lived on the east side of the Chilko River, where he established his Mountain House ranch.

He was born Alexis Sill around 1886 in the country north of Chilko Lake known to the Tŝilhqot'in people as Neghatalhchuẑ (Neg-a-tal-chuz). Henry's mother, Agenis (Aga-nees), was Tŝilhqot'in and his father, Thomas Sill, was Dakelh from Ulkatcho, some 200 kilometres to the northwest.

What made Henry unique is that he opted for his white rights. That meant he voluntarily gave up his Indian status so he could buy crown land, vote in elections and legally consume alcohol, just like any other non-Indigenous citizen. These things were denied Indigenous people with Indian status, who were considered wards of the federal government. Giving up his status didn't make Henry any less Tŝilhqot'in in that he still practised the cultural traditions of his people, like hunting, trapping, fishing and digging wild potatoes, but having his own deeded land and independent source of wealth gave him a leg up in his dealings with others, and equality under the law.

Henry never went to school and didn't know how to read or write, but he knew how to get things done. Andy Stuart had the only store west of Alexis Creek, and Henry trusted him implicitly to advise him on legal matters and in dealings with government.

Eagle Lake Henry on his wedding day with his first wife Alyetta. On the left is Eagle Lake Henry's dad, Thomas Sill. Also with them is Alyetta's daughter from a previous relationship, who died from TB at a young age. Photo courtesy Cassidy Sill.

Henry was the oldest of several children born to his mother, who had offspring from several different men. He was also his father Thomas Sill's oldest child. Thomas later had five sons with Aggie Bouchie Sill.

Thomas Sill and Agenis didn't live together very long and Henry spent his early years with his mother's family in Neghatalhchuẑ until he was about 12 years old. Then the man living with his mother kicked him out of the household to fend for himself. Despite the distances that separated them, Thomas Sill took an

Bob and June Draney in Bella Coola. June was Eagle Lake Henry and Alyetta's granddaughter and grew up with them at Mountain House. Photo Sage Birchwater.

active role in raising his son and later on mentoring him as an adult.

"There was nothing for Thomas Sill down at Chilko Lake," said Henry's granddaughter, June Draney. "I guess that's why he left. I guess Henry's mom, Agenis, didn't want to move to Anahim Lake. They were both pretty young when Henry was born."

Thomas Sill would purchase supplies for his store in Bella Coola, then bring them up the steep trails to the plateau by horseback. When Henry was old enough to work, his father would go and get him to help with the pack train and store.

"I guess Grandpa Henry was getting into his teens one of the last times he helped his dad with the pack train from Bella Coola. He said he had a horse to ride going down the mountain, but on the way back he had to walk, because his horse would be loaded with supplies for the store.

"He was eating huckleberries one time, hanging back as the pack train went up the hill. Then he looked over and saw a grizzly bear eating berries on the other side of the same bush he was picking from. He said he sure got out of there in a hurry."

Working with his father, Henry became an expert horseman and astute businessman. Despite having no formal education, he had a wealth of practical skills. He was a crack shot with his rifle, an excellent hunter and trapper, a successful rancher, and a leader among men. He always had the best equipment, which he kept in top running order, and raised the best horses in the country. Perhaps what set him apart from other people most was his astute business sense where he always drove a hard bargain. Henry hired many people around Neghatalhchuẑ to work for him.

"He always paid cash for everything," remembered June Draney. "There was no such thing as taking anything from the government. He took out hunters in the fall and always tried to hire the locals." She said that Doris and Madeline Lulua worked for Henry when they were young. "I remember him telling them, you better have cattle of your own. Sure, your uncle Lashaway Lulua is the chief at Nemiah, but he's not going to be worrying about you guys. So you guys have to make it on your own. Be independent. Have something of your own."

June remembered when she was still a young child growing up with her grandparents, that Henry's half-brother, Joe Sill, had come by with their 12-year-old younger brother, Edward. Thomas Sill had died and Eagle Lake Henry and his wife, Alyetta, welcomed Edward into their household and raised him.

When Henry was born, the reserve system, which set aside tiny plots of land for Indigenous people, was still in its infancy in the Chilcotin. The long tentacles of bureaucracy hadn't become embedded in the remote back country of Nemiah Valley or Neghatalhchuẑ yet, so that part of the Chilcotin was mostly like it always had been with Tŝilhqot'in people living off the land and occupying the whole of the landscape.

Memories of the Chilcotin War, which had happened twenty-two years before Henry's birth, and the smallpox epidemic two years before that, which wiped out three-quarters of the Tŝilhqot'in population, were still fresh in the minds of Henry's kinfolk as he grew up.

It is said Henry made his grubstake to start ranching by his success as a trapper.

Veera Bonner wrote in her book *Chilcotin: Preserving Pioneer Memories* that Henry and Alyetta were picking huckleberries one summer in the Potato Mountains when they discovered a den of silver foxes. The price for silver foxes was very high and Henry returned that winter and trapped five of these animals and got $500 a piece for the pelts. He saved the money and in the spring he and Alyetta rode to Anahim Lake and bought twenty head of cattle from rancher Antone Capoose.

One of the earliest written accounts of Eagle Lake Henry can be found in *Pack Horse Tracks: The Recollections of a Geologist's Life in British Columbia and the Yukon, 1924–1954*, written by Hugh Samuel Bostock. Henry and Alyetta were hired to pack for the geological survey from Tatlayoko Valley to Bella Coola for the 1925 field season headed by Dr. Victor Dolmage. Bostock was a graduate of McGill University in his first season with the Geological Survey of Canada.

In his memoir, Bostock gave a revealing snapshot of life in the Chilcotin at that time, describing Henry as amazingly observant of every little detail—which he admitted was sometimes embarrassing. He said Henry was about 5 feet 9 inches tall, weighed 160 pounds and was around 37 years old. "He was reputedly the wealthiest man in the country bar none," wrote Bostock, "and he trusted no one but Redstone storekeeper Andy Stuart." He said when Henry took the job to pack the survey, the conditions of his job had to be written out in detail and submitted to Andy Stuart before Henry accepted it "because Henry could not read, write or sign his name."

Bostock described Henry and Alyetta as living at Mountain House with Henry's half-brother, Billy Dagg, who was still in his early 20s, and Billy's wife and two children.

> They had 200 head of cattle and many horses including a thoroughbred Texas saddle stallion, a Percheron stallion and several good brood mares. It was commonly known around Tatla Lake that Henry had the best horses in the country. "During the fall Henry and Billy would take out hunting parties with their pack trains, then in winter once the snow fell, they would go out trapping and hunting coyotes. In the spring they would work at the ranch branding the calves and

Cattle were forced to swim across the rivers in the Chilcotin before bridges were constructed. Photo Joseph William collection.

> repairing fences. In the summers when Henry and Alyetta took out survey parties, Billy would stay home putting up the hay.

That's how it was in July of 1925 when Henry and Alyetta were guiding the Dolmage survey party down the West Branch of the Homathko River at Bluff Lake. They were six weeks into the survey, when Henry and Alyetta got word that tragedy had struck back home at Mountain House. Billy's wife and infant son had died from the flu, and Billy and his 2-year-old daughter, Mary Jane, were very ill. Henry and Alyetta returned home immediately to deal with the crisis. By the end of the summer Billy Dagg and young Mary Jane had recovered from their illness, but Billy was no longer able to care for his daughter.

Henry and Alyetta, with no children of their own, readily adopted Mary Jane and raised her as their own child. A few years later they were given a second child, Dona Elkins, and they had a ready-made family.

His apparent inability to procreate his own offspring often bothered Henry. He would profess, "I try and I try, but I just can't make it."

Eagle Lake Henry Started Young Providing for his Family

June Draney was Mary Jane's oldest child, and she grew up with her mother and younger siblings at Mountain House with Eagle Lake Henry and Alyetta. "Even though our mother was there too, everybody, including my sister, brother and I, called Alyetta, 'Momma'."

Billy Dagg on horseback. Photo courtesy June Draney.

She said her grandfather had been forced to become the main provider for his family at a young age. "He was the oldest of quite a few children. Grandpa Henry went out and hunted when he was still a young boy," June said. "He always told us, don't waste your food."

She remembered a story Henry told to emphasize this point. His family had run out of food early one spring, and his mother went out to gather kinikinnick berries and gave Henry a hook to go ice-fishing and the last piece of dried fish skin to use as bait. "He was chewing on that fish skin to soften it so he could put it on his hook. Ooooh, how I wanted to swallow it, he told us, but I needed it. I had to use it to bait my hook."

Henry watched closely, hoping a fish would take the hook. Finally, a big Dolly Varden swallowed it. The fish line cut into his hands, but he held on. "He said he had that fish out of there so fast," June said. "After that he could use a fish eye or gills for bait and he caught a lot of fish after that. His mother was so proud of him."

As Henry was growing up, the first ranches were starting to come into the West Chilcotin country. He was around 12 years old when he started working as a ranch hand for the Newtons and Bayliffs downstream from Mountain House near the confluence of the Chilko and Chilcotin rivers.

There are many stories about how Alexis Sill got the name Eagle Lake Henry. June told me her version.

> He had never gone to school and couldn't speak much English. When the rancher asked him his name, he couldn't understand what Grandpa told him. When he said his name, Alexis Sill, it might have sounded more like Alexeesill. Then the rancher asked where he was from, and he told him Eagle Lake.
>
> "Well, you look like a little Eagle Lake Henry to me," the rancher said. "I think we better call you Eagle Lake Henry."
>
> That's how he got his name. He liked the name so he kept it. It sounded kind of strong to him, I guess. A powerful name.

Henry and Alyetta Get Married

As a young man, Henry had an eye for a young woman, Alyetta, who once lived in Eagle Lake country, but had moved with her mother and stepfather, Alex Humm, to Tl'etinqox (Anaham Reserve) near Alexis Creek.

Henry was packing freight for his dad, Thomas Sill, at Anahim Lake when Thomas suggested he ought to think about getting married. Then his father picked out a woman for him. "Of course, as Henry tells it, it sounds like this woman was quite big," recalled June. "They called her Big Millie."

Alyetta and Eagle Lake Henry in their prime. Photo courtesy Harry Haynes.

She said that Henry went down to the waterhole one day to get some water, and there was Millie waiting for him on the trail. "He said he went way around her. The next day I saddled my horse and went to find your grandma, he told me."

Tl'etinqox, where Alyetta lived with her mother and Alex Humm, was more than 200 kilometres to the east across the Chilcotin Plateau. June said the community was starting to get ahead. "Someone showed them how to grow wheat and they were raising lots of pigs," she recalled.

When Eagle Lake Henry started courting Alyetta, he decided if he was going to live at Tl'etinqox he should put in a garden. He dug a long ditch to bring water from a nearby creek, but by the time everyone else started "T-ing" off from his ditch, not much water reached his garden site.

Henry felt discouraged.

Alex Humm had a freight wagon and team and he hired Henry and Alyetta to go to Ashcroft to bring back supplies. After freighting for his father-in-law all spring and summer, Henry was disappointed with the small amount of money Alex Humm offered him as wages in the fall. "I don't know about you, but I'm going back to Chilko Lake to go trapping," Henry told Alyetta.

Alex Humm came out and tried to intervene. "You're not taking my daughter back there." But Alyetta was determined. "I'm going with him," she said.

They headed west, each riding their own saddle horse and leading one pack horse. Henry only had $7 in his pocket when they reached Pete Stuart's store at Redstone. They decided to stay around Redstone and trapped until Christmas. "They made quite a bit of money," June said.

Then Eagle Lake Henry and Alyetta went back to Tl'etinqox to get married. Their wedding picture with Thomas Sill and Alyetta's young daughter shows them decked out in fancy attire. "Thomas Sill must have bought the outfit for them," June figured. "The wedding photo was on the Mountain House wall for years."

Alyetta's young daughter was born before she met Henry, and was quite sickly when they got married. Unfortunately, she died soon after the wedding. "I think she must have had TB," June said. "I don't remember asking Granny her name, but I think it might have been Christine."

Though Eagle Lake Henry always regretted he couldn't have any biological children of his own and blamed himself for it, June figured it was likely a condition inherited by Alyetta. "The women in Granny's family only had one child," she explained. "So after Christine, there were no more children for her. Henry thought it was his fault all the time, but Granny talked about other aunts who only had one child."

Henry Becomes a White Man and a Rancher

Trapping was a mainstay of the Chilcotin economy as Henry grew up and he soon learned to become very proficient at it. Henry and Alyetta continued trapping every winter, and then in the spring they would go to work on various ranches. One winter they made $1,400 before Christmas, which was good money in those days. That's when Henry decided to use the money he made from trapping to start a ranch of his own.

In 1919 Andy Stuart was the new owner of Redstone Store. He had taken over from his brother Pete, who had been killed in a car crash in Vancouver. Andy quickly became Eagle Lake Henry's most trusted friend and advisor in his business dealings and with government paperwork.

When Henry told Andy he wanted to go ranching, Andy asked where he planned to do it. "At my mother's place at Mountain House," Henry replied. Andy asked if he had title to the place, and Henry said, no. He didn't know anything about paper to own the land.

Andy warned he would need to own his own land and have a piece of property in his name because a lot of people were coming into the country after the First World War and buying up all the places. "They'll buy it right from under you. The buildings and everything you own, you won't own it anymore."

Andy explained that Henry would need to get his white rights if he wanted to own deeded land. "Okay, we'll do that," Henry replied, "because I want to own it myself."

Andy Stuart helped Henry with the paperwork to get enfranchised. This meant he voluntarily had to give up his Indian status.

Henry got title to his place at Mountain House, and true to Andy Stuart's prediction, other settlers armed with soldier's homesteading grants were flooding into the country. Most of the good places close to Mountain House had already been taken. Andy told Henry if he found a good meadow he liked, he could pre-empt it, and he explained how a pre-emption worked. "You have to put up a cabin and a barn and fences and stuff like that, and get it passed by the land inspector."

There weren't any meadows close to Mountain House, so Henry staked Far Meadow, about fifteen kilometres away, and chopped an access road to it from Mountain House. Over the years, he took up more pre-emptions, and acquired places abandoned by other settlers. In one instance, he drained a lake.

"When Grandpa got Timothy Meadow, he got a bunch of guys to dig a ditch and drain it," June said. "He asked what kind of grass he should plant and they said timothy. That's how it got its name. I guess with all the dead fish they got quite a crop." Unfortunately the ground was too soft and spongy to hold up a team of horses pulling a mower, so he got his crew to cut it with scythes.

Eagle Lake Henry at Far Meadow with his favourite hunting dog, Gyp. Photo courtesy June Draney.

From the very beginning, Henry established a reputation for honesty. He would always pay his debts, and June gave an example of his dealings when he first started ranching.

"He told Alex Graham, owner of the C1 Ranch in Alexis Creek, he didn't have enough money to put up his hay. Alex Graham asked how much he needed and Grandpa said six or seven hundred dollars to pay for his haying crew, food and other expenses. Well, I can loan that to you, Alex said, and they shook hands over it. In those days, a handshake was like a contract.

"Alex said, as soon as you ship your cattle and have them sold, then you can pay me back. So that's what he did. Right away after selling his cattle, Grandpa gave him back his $700."

Alyetta and Eagle Lake Henry Are Given a Second Daughter to Raise as their Own

June Draney said that a year or two after Eagle Lake Henry and Alyetta adopted her mother, Mary Jane, Joe and Matilda Elkins gave them a second daughter, Dona. "I guess way back, when Joe Elkins was still in the basket, his mother left to go partying, and she left him hanging in his basket from the branch of a tree. Granny found him there along the trail and brought him home and looked after him. That was before she and Grampa Henry were together.

"Joe was just a baby so she had to make some white sauce because they didn't have any milk to feed him, and he became part of the family. When Alyetta and Grampa Henry got married they would take Joe Elkins with them quite a bit when he was still a young boy.

"Eventually Joe Elkins married Matilda and they had a big family. I guess there was a party some place and Matilda left her baby Dona behind. When Dona needed some attention, Granny, being the motherly type, took the baby and was looking after her."

That's when Joe Elkins surprised them.

"You know, you raised me. If it wasn't for you, I might not be here today. You love babies and Mary Jane needs a sister. How about we give you Dona to raise?"

So that's how it went.

When the girls were old enough for school, Henry made sure he boarded them out so they could get an education. One year he boarded them out with a family at Riske Creek. After that, he paid the Bellamy family and others in Tatlayoko Valley to board the girls there so they could go to school. Both girls graduated from Grade 8, the highest grade available in the valley. Later they married two brothers from ʔEsdilagh (Alexandria), Pete and Gabby Baptiste.

Black Beauty

When Mary Jane and Dona were small, Henry was out checking his traps on horseback late one winter when he came upon a bunch of wild horses. They had a little foal with them that had just been born. As Henry got closer with his dogs, the wild bunch spooked and took off, leaving the newborn filly behind. The young horse sprinted over next to Henry's horse and just stuck to its side. Henry thought he better take the little foal home with him because with the wild bunch gone, it was too young to leave by itself in the wild. The little filly just stuck to the side of his saddle horse all the way home to Mountain House.

Dona was little and grew attached to the young filly, and it became her horse. They even had it in the house a few times. As the little horse grew up, it was obvious she had come from a good strain. Maybe the Newtons had lost some of their hot-blooded Arabians, because she could really run. Dona trained her to ride and named her Black Beauty.

A year or two later, Eagle Lake Henry took his family to the annual gathering in the Potato Mountains to dig wild potatoes and celebrate with other Tsilhqot'in families who would arrive from near and far. People would come from Nemiah Valley, Redstone, Redbrush, Anaham, Stone, Riske Creek and even from Anahim Lake. They'd stay up on the mountain for a week or two hunting deer, digging mountain potatoes, picking berries and playing lahal. One of the big highlights of these social and cultural events was horse-racing.

Dona, left, Alyetta, Eliza Quilt and Mary Jane. Photo courtesy Harry Haynes.

Soon after Eagle Lake Henry and Alyetta had set up camp, Dona and Mary Jane jumped on their horses and headed down the mountain to pick up the mail in Tatlayoko. This was a four-hour ride down the mountain and back up again, a drop of 1,200 metres (3,600 feet) in elevation. Dona rode her spirited Black Beauty.

June said that soon after they left some people from Nemiah Valley arrived and they began to argue about who had the fastest horse. "They put up some money and were waiting for Dona's little Black Beauty to get back to the camp. The minute Dona and Mary Jane returned, they pulled off Dona's saddle and put their own saddle on Black Beauty's back. They were going to race her. Dona was worried her horse would be too tired, but she won the quarter-mile race despite going all the way down the mountain and back that same day."

Eugene Sammy William Finds His Own Place

Boise Williams said Eagle Lake Henry was his father's uncle. "We used to call him Grandpa," Boise said.

Boise's father, Eugene Sammy William, was the son of Eagle Lake Henry's sister, Annie, and he grew up in the Nemiah Valley and Eagle Lake country. Boise's mother, Mabel Williams, was from K'l Deldel (Redbrush) north of Redstone.

"Before I was born, my family lived in my mother's country around K'l Deldel for twelve years hunting squirrels and going back and forth between Redstone and

Francis, Eddie, Euphrasia, Mabel Williams and Eugene William, with kids Julianna and Agnes. Photo courtesy Euphrasia Williams.

Nemiah Valley," Boise said. "My dad would hunt squirrels all the time. He'd go by every tree and look for squirrels in the winter time, poke with a stick and out they're coming. Shoot them. Then they'd move to Nemiah Valley for maybe a month to visit with my dad's parents. Then my mother wanted to go back to Redstone and they all moved back to K'l Deldel."

Travelling back and forth, they'd always stay with Eagle Lake Henry and Alyetta at Mountain House. One day Henry said to Eugene, "You're moving around just like a coyote. Coyote move his family around to catch rabbits or squirrels until he run out, then he move to another spot." Henry urged Eugene to consider settling down. "There's a nice place by a creek down here along the river where you could build a ranch. Tomorrow we go look at it."

The next day, Henry and Eugene rode down to where Brittany Creek runs into the Chilko River. The place had previously been settled by a man named Chaucer but was now abandoned. At the Chaucer place, Eugene found a bucket strategically placed in the creek to catch the water so he renamed it Nuŝay Bighinlin (Noos-ae-bay-leen) which means "water running into a bucket."

The next day, Henry said Mabel and the kids could stay with Alyetta at Mountain House while he took Eugene to the government office several days' travel away to get title to the property. There were no government offices in Williams Lake in those days, just a few houses, so they had to go farther. Maybe to 150 Mile House or Clinton. When they got there, Henry explained to Eugene, "This is a government office. This is where you do business."

Eagle Lake Henry and Alyetta socialize with Tex Hanson, a rancher and guide-outfitter from Clearwater Lake. Photo courtesy Katie Schuk.

Boise's father didn't know very much English at all. "My dad and Grandpa Henry were in the office talking to two guys for a couple of hours. Every once in a while, Eagle Lake Henry asked my dad, 'You understand what they're talking about?' Dad said, 'No'.

"When they were done, Eagle Lake Henry told Dad, 'Now you've got some land. You've got a place now.' That's when my dad settled down and got a little ranch and raised some cattle, horses and his family."

June Draney said that at one point the negotiations for the Chaucer place weren't going very well. "They weren't going to let Eugene buy it. Then Grandpa Henry stood up and said, 'Well. Eugene, I guess we'll go to Ottawa and see…' Then the guy finally changed his tune and let him have it."

This story illustrates the sharp divide that separated the Indigenous and settler realities in the Cariboo Chilcotin. Eugene Sammy William spoke no English and lived hunting and gathering off the land in the back country that stretched over 100 kilometres between K'l Deldel and Nemiah Valley. He was living like his ancestors had for centuries before him. But times were changing and Eagle Lake Henry could see it coming.

The intrusion of newcomers, harbingers of a whole different way of life based on private land ownership, was quite foreign to Eugene and his family when Boise was born in July 1948 at his parents' camp beside the Chilcotin Road near Redstone.

"I was born in a little meadow near Stuart's store," Boise said. "My folks were camping there, waiting for the Siwash fish to come up the Chilcotin River. The day after I was born they took me to Redstone Flats. Father Hennessy was there, and I was baptized the next day. It was Priest Time, my dad used to call it. The people come from all over the country. Dad was saying sometimes people were baptized at 20 years old."

Boise said when his parents brought him back to their camp, his Uncle Casimer, the head of the family, asked what they named him. When they told him "John," Casimer was outraged. He said, take him back the next day and get the priest to change his name to Boise. "So they took me back and had my name changed. That's why my birth certificate says Boise John. Whoever went with my mom must have told the priest my name was John."

Boise said if his dad had wanted it, Eagle Lake Henry probably would have helped him be a white guy. But he never took it that far. But Eugene managed to avoid sending his kids to St. Joseph's Mission residential school in Williams Lake. Like Henry, Eugene got his children educated in the public school system in Tatlayoko Valley.

June Draney Goes to School in Tatlayoko

June Draney said she and her sisters and brother did most of their schooling at the public school in Tatlayoko Valley, just like their mother Mary Jane had done. June actually spent her first year of school at St. Joseph's Mission because there was no school in Tatlayoko that year. The same thing had happened to her mother when she started school.

"It was okay with me," June said. "I had a big sister to look after me at the mission. All the first graders at the mission were given a big sister to show them around. It was lonely at first being away from my family. All these little beds we had to sleep in. My little sister was too young to go to school there but they sent her anyway. My big sister was kind of harum-scarum, but she was okay. I made it through the year okay. The teacher had a big class. I think I came second in math anyway. The next year the school opened in Tatlayoko so we went there."

The common theme running through Eagle Lake Henry's life was his sense of empowerment. Where many Indigenous people were run roughshod over by the church and the government, Henry wouldn't allow people in authority to push him around. The power of being enfranchised and having white rights, along with his own strong will, allowed him to put his children into residential school then pull them out again with impunity.

June Draney gave an example of how Eagle Lake Henry held on to his dignity and inner authority when government officials tried to boss him around.

"Grandpa Henry got this letter saying he had to renew his guiding licence. That meant he had to get in his vehicle and drive all the way to Alexis Creek about three hours away where the game warden always helped him fill it all out. This time there was a new guy in there. Grandpa walked in and there didn't seem to be anybody around and the office door was kind of open so he walked in.

"I don't know if he startled the guy or he was asleep, but he told Grandpa to go way back down there and then you come back and knock on the door. Grandpa said he just kept walking and drove back home. He said he wrote a letter to Victoria explaining what happened to him.

"The game warden was trying to find out who wrote the letter for Henry because he couldn't write. He got a hold of my uncle and he was kind of quizzing him. My uncle said, I don't know. He's got lots of friends and neighbours. He's got an ex-cop, Johnny Blatchford, for a neighbour. Anybody could have written the letter for him. Maybe next time you'll treat him a little different.

"The game warden got quite a scolding from Victoria. Henry said the roads were rough and the way he treated me, go way back and knock on the door… He liked people to be honest with him and treat him like a human, I guess."

Going to school in Tatlayoko, June said that she and her sister had to board out with the Purjue family until October while her parents Mary Jane and Pete, grandparents Eagle Lake Henry and Alyetta, and her brother Marvin finished haying. "When we first started school, we stayed in a tent for a month. Then Johnny and Edith Henderson said we might as well move down to their place. They had an old house so we moved there."

She said they had a pet wether (castrated) billy goat called Willie at Mountain House before they started school.

"We also had a dog and one pig and we were just like gypsies. My stepdad Pete Baptiste made a thing for Willie to ride in the back of the wagon. We had to cross the Chilko River and it was getting quite late. Of course, the dog had to swim. The little kids were crying because there was no room for Willie in the wagon, so he had to swim along with the dog. The kids were crying, 'Willie.' Pete was hoping Willie would keep going down the river because he was always getting into mischief.

"We crossed the river and there were three channels. We got to the other side and were waiting. The kids were crying because they thought their goat got washed down the river. Then the dog came and was shaking himself off. Then all of a sudden we heard this Baaaaah! There was Willie just a-coming. He didn't have time to shake himself off until he got to the wagon, then he shook himself off.

"We got our goat and took him all the way to Tatlayoko. Then once we moved closer to neighbours we had to give him away because he was getting into mischief."

Policeman Johnny Blatchford Throws Henry into the Slammer

Johnny Blatchford was a member of the British Columbia Provincial Police Force in Williams Lake in 1937 when he met Eagle Lake Henry for the first time. "Eagle Lake Henry was in town shipping cattle and he got drunk and was raising hell with his family, so they had me arrest him and put him in the coop. When he sobered up, he was a pretty good guy. And he was pretty sorry he was in the coop. So I helped him get organized and he paid his $10 fine."

Before the bridge was built at Henry's Crossing this is how June Draney and her family crossed the river to go to school in Tatlayoko. Photo courtesy Joseph William.

Johnny Blatchford, Dr. Hallows, Cheeta Johnny, Rene Hance and Dan Weir. Photo courtesy Johnny Blatchford.

In 1940, Johnny got posted to the provincial police detachment in Alexis Creek and he met Henry again when he came in to buy his trapping licence. "I told him, Henry, I want to buy a place, and he told me about Tsuniah Lake. The country was wide open, so I leased it right away." Tsuniah Lake was sixteen kilometres from Mountain House and Johnny was Henry's neighbour for twenty-five years.

Johnny said, "We used to go to Tatla Lake for groceries. In the winter we'd cross the Chilko River with a team and sleigh, but we couldn't cross in high water. Then we'd take a boat and swim our horses across the river. We left a wagon on each side of the river so we could pick up our mail in Tatla Lake then go back home again. I lived there seven years before they put a bridge across at Henry's Crossing."

June Draney remembered it was 1956 when the neighbours got together and put the bridge in at Henry's Crossing. "The government must have put up some money, but the local people did all the work. Grandpa Henry didn't want just anybody to use his horses, so he got Alex Mattheson to skid the logs in. He knew Alex was good with horses."

June said her Grandfather Henry's white rights meant he could legally buy alcohol for himself, but he wasn't allowed to give it to other Indigenous people. "He bought liquor for native people who didn't have the right, and he went to jail for three months over that," June recalled. "I remember that because Granny and I had to come back home. I guess Grampa hired Harold Stuart to take us back to Chilko Lake with the car. He could have paid his fine but he wanted to see what Oakalla looked like."

Eagle Lake Henry's Idea of a Good Business Deal

Back in 1925, when Eagle Lake Henry and Alyetta returned to Mountain House to take care of Billy Dagg and his daughter, Mary Jane, when they were recovering from the flu, Henry got his friend Neganie Guichon to take his place guiding the survey party at Bluff Lake.

The young surveyor, Bostock, was a little unnerved when Henry brought Neganie into their camp. Six weeks earlier when the survey crew had passed through Williams Lake on their way to the Chilcotin, he had seen Neganie in police custody heading to Vancouver to stand trial for murder. Eagle Lake Henry assured Bostock that Neganie was innocent of the charges and had been falsely accused by his enemies. He said Neganie had been acquitted because the witnesses failed to show up at the court, then Eagle Lake Henry explained why Neganie's enemies were so sore at him.

Neganie was one of the best hunters in the Chilcotin and he had a love for fast horses. Horse racing was one of the great passions in the Chilcotin in those days, especially among the Tŝilhqot'in people, and Neganie was no exception.

Being a close friend of Eagle Lake Henry, Neganie asked if he could acquire a fast horse from him, but he had no money to pay for it. Henry, who had the best horses in the country, told Neganie he could have one if he did exactly what he instructed. He gave him one of his best horses along with ten dollars cash and told him to go to the fall round-up in Williams Lake and challenge a certain man that neither of them liked to a horse race.

"Bet this guy ten dollars you can beat him," Henry said. "Make like you beat your horse like hell and you let the other guy win, then pay him the ten dollars."

A few years earlier Henry had sold this other man a horse and somehow the deal went sour. Henry kept close track of all his bloodlines and he knew that Neganie's horse was the better animal.

Then he told Neganie to go to the spring round-up and challenge the man again. "This time tell him you fed your horse good all winter, and bet him again you can beat him. This time bet him everything you got against everything he has. He will think he can beat you again, but I know you can beat him easy. Your horse is much better than his horse. You get everything he's got including his horse, then come and pay me."

Henry warned him they couldn't bet their wives and children because the police wouldn't allow it. Neganie did what he was told and cleaned his rival out of everything, and he paid Henry handsomely for his horse. Henry thought this was a masterly way of doing business but Neganie's foes thought otherwise. So that's why they tried to frame him for a murder he didn't commit.

Alyetta Died in 1953

June Draney was 12 years old when her grandmother Alyetta died in 1953. It was a devastating blow. "I was lost and thought I won't be able to live anymore. We had our mother there too, but Alyetta was more like our mother."

Two or three years later, Henry married Millie West, the widow of Johnny Setah of Nemiah Valley. Millie had come from Anahim Lake. June said she was Charlie West's sister. After Johnny Setah died, Millie continued to live in Nemiah Valley.

June says when Alyetta was on her deathbed, she encouraged Henry to remarry. "I know you don't like being alone, so you better find another woman."

Millie lived with Henry for about ten years until her death in the mid-1960s.

Eagle Lake Henry's Last Days

Boise Williams was staying at his Aunt Lucy's place in Nemiah Valley on the shore of Chilko Lake when he got a sudden urge to go and see Eagle Lake Henry. It was early spring 1967, and there was still lots of snow on the ground. "I told Lucy, I've got to go see my grandfather Eagle Lake Henry, so I saddle up my horse and away I went."

It was a two-day journey from Nemiah Valley past Konni Lake, up Elkin Creek and through the back country to Mountain House. Henry had been living there alone since Millie had died and had actually sold his place to Tatlayoko Rancher Joe Schuk, who allowed him to keep living there as long as he needed to.

Boise rode all day to his grandparents Sam and Annie Bulyam's place on Upper Elkin Creek where his parents were staying. "The next day I told my mom and dad I'm going to see Eagle Lake Henry and away I went. I rode to Far Meadow, then to Burnt Stable, and I finally got to Mountain House about ten miles away. I walked into Eagle Lake Henry's kitchen, but there was nobody in it."

He went into the living room and saw Eagle Lake Henry lying on the couch. "You kind of saved my life, he told me. I could hardly believe what he said. There were a bunch of people talking to me, he said. The first bell went. When you hear three bells you die. Then the second bell went. I was just waiting for the third bell when you showed up."

What Eagle Lake Henry said next really floored Boise. "He said, when you left Nemiah, I was looking at you riding your horse. I was looking at you all the way. First you left Lucy's house and stopped at William Setah's house, then you went again. Then you stopped at Naghtaneqed (Konni Lake). You stayed there for a while then you took off again and rode all the way to Eddie's Upper Place. I was looking at you all the way, then you stayed overnight at your grandparents' place and then came to my house. You kind of saved my life because the third bell was going to ring."

Henry told Boise he couldn't eat anymore and was waiting to die. He urged him to cook himself some food and give his horse some grain, and offered to let him spend the night. "But I could die anytime, he said. It's up to you. You can stay overnight or go back and tell your parents."

Boise said when somebody tells you something like that, you don't feel right, and you think about it. "I told him I'd go back and tell my parents."

After preparing himself a quick meal, Boise jumped on his horse and rode the sixteen kilometres back to Upper Elkin Creek to tell his parents about Eagle Lake Henry. "That same night I got back, I said Henry's not doing too good. He told me he might not make it through the night."

Early the next morning, Eugene and Mabel saddled their horses and rode to Mountain House. Henry's neighbours, Jack and Diane Castleman, were already there. "Castleman and my dad drove off to Alexis Creek to get Dieter Kellinghusen with the airplane. My mom and Castleman's wife stayed at the house with Grandpa Henry."

A few hours later, Kellinghusen flew to Mountain House with his friend Gerhardt Wilder and they landed on skis in front of Eagle Lake Henry's cabin. Kellinghusen said Eagle Lake Henry was sitting at the front of his cabin by himself and was quite frail.

"Obviously, he knew it was his last trip," Kellinghusen said. "He said goodbye to Mrs. Castleman and Boise's mother who helped push him into the plane, then he told Gerhardt and me, this is my last trip, you don't have to bring me back. We radioed the police and the police notified the airport that there is a guy coming that needs a ride to the hospital. So we flew him to the airport in Williams Lake. When we got there, Eagle Lake Henry wanted to know how much it cost and he had the cash money. He paid us for what Gerhardt said we had used for fuel, he said goodbye boys and I will not see you again. They took him to the hospital and three days later he was dead."

Boise said after Henry lost his second wife, Millie, he appreciated having him stop by.

"I used to drop in lots of times and visit him. He liked that. After he lost his second wife, he liked having somebody to talk to. He was lonely by himself. He had his dog and two cats, a set of work horses and two saddle horses, that's all he had left.

"He was telling me a story when I dropped in one time. You're not in a hurry, are you? Nope. Stay overnight…"

Eagle Lake Henry and Millie at Mountain House. Photo Veera Bonner.

Boise Williams grew up around his great uncle Eagle Lake Henry, and thought of him as his grandpa. Photo Sage Birchwater.

June Draney said her Grandpa Henry was always helping people out, just as he helped Eugene Sammy get his land at the Chaucer Place.

"We had more people on the living room floor who had crossed the river and still had miles to go before they got home. If the weather was bad, then they stayed overnight and he fed their horses.

"Grandpa Henry had both worlds together. He never condemned anyone who came in our door, whether you were Indian, white, Chinese or whatever you were. I think he could tell a person's character. There are some people, if you have a good horse they want to get from you, they will come and give you a drink. He could tell those kinds of people if they weren't honest.

"Andy Stuart was a really important guy in Grandpa Henry's world. When his brothers and sisters decided to shop at Redstone, he chopped a road from Chilko Lake country all the way over to Stuart's. They used this road for years. It was the only road. The first one put in."

Bullshit Valleau

There's a creek that drains the western slopes of the Niut Mountains between Tatlayoko Valley and the West Branch of the Homathko River. Locally it is known as Deer Creek, but on government maps it's called Valleau Creek and it empties into the West Branch at the outflow of Bluff Lake. Today there's little known about Valleau, but in his day he was one of the more talked-about characters in the West Chilcotin.

When he came into the country from the United States sometime after the First World War, only the census-taker and postmaster knew his full name, Harvey Theodor Valleau. To everyone else, he was just Valleau, along with a number of descriptive appellatives folks cared to add. Bullshit Valleau was a favourite, or Bullshit Balloo in the local vernacular.

Valleau settled on the south shore of Bluff Lake about twenty kilometres south of Tatla Lake and was the last man down the trail beyond the end of the wagon road that ended at the north shore of the lake. He was protected from the world by high rocky bluffs that dropped abruptly to the lakeshore, accessed only by a narrow winding horse trail that picked its way over the bluffs.

Valleau liked it that way.

He didn't welcome strangers easily unless he invited them himself and even then a guest could quickly overstay his welcome. He had signs posted along the trail telling people to keep out. It was said Valleau couldn't bear another man's smoke across his sky.

South of Bluff Lake he had free run of the West Branch Valley all the way to its confluence with the main Homathko River, sixty kilometres downstream. Beyond there the ramparts of the Coast Range blocked easy access to the mouth of the river at Bute Inlet. He trapped animals for fur in wintertime, kept a herd of horses for packing supplies to his trap cabins, and always had a few goats because the goat milk soothed his often-irritated stomach. Like other men, he took work where he could get it on ranches around the country.

Hugh Samuel Bostock

Hugh Samuel Bostock shared some vivid insight into Valleau's character and behaviour in his memoir, *Pack Horse Tracks.* He was in his first field season with the Geological Survey of Canada in 1925, serving under Dr. Victor Dolmage, head of the geological survey in the Chilcotin that summer. Their task was to compile a topographical map and chart mineral formations from Tatlayoko Lake to Bella Coola, previously unmapped territory in British Columbia.

Dolmage hired Eagle Lake Henry with his string of pack horses and saddle horses to transport and guide the party. Henry's wife, Alyetta, helped out with the horses.

A view of Bluff Lake from the trail over the bluffs. Valleau's cabin can be seen on the distant southern shore. Photo Sage Birchwater.

They started the survey at K. B. Moore's ranch on Tatlayoko Lake at the end of May and by the end of June they had moved into the West Branch Valley, heading for Bluff Lake.

Valleau was the only settler in the valley, but as luck would have it, he was away working for rancher Arthur Knoll at Chilanko Forks when the surveyors arrived. Bostock describes the barrage of Valleau's unwelcome signs posted along the trail: "Keep out. This is my valley." "No one wanted." "Indians shot on sight." "Beware of man traps and spring guns." And so on.

The survey party camped near Valleau's small ranch. Things went as planned with Eagle Lake Henry and Alyetta guiding the surveyors to the high points of land where they could take their readings and measurements using a transit and plane-table to map the area.

They had been in Valleau's domain for about two weeks when Eagle Lake Henry received the tragic news that a flu epidemic had killed his sister-in-law and nephew, and left his half-brother, Billy Dagg and niece, Mary Jane, very ill. Billy Dagg was looking after their Mountain House Ranch while Henry and Alyetta were guiding the surveyors, so they headed home to Mountain House immediately, some fifty kilometres away. Before departing, Henry left his string of saddle horses and pack horses with his trusted friend, Neganie Guichon, and asked him to take over the guiding duties for the survey party. Neganie, a Tŝilhqot'in man from K'l Deldel (Redbrush), arrived in camp with his wife and 10-year-old son. He was an expert hunter and guide in his own right, but wasn't the invincible, powerful individual that Henry was.

Two days after Henry and Alyetta departed, Valleau showed up, accompanied by Arthur Knoll's 12-year-old son, Ollie Knoll. Soon all hell broke loose.

Bostock describes how Valleau pulled out his gun and immediately started raving at Neganie, telling him to get out of his valley or he would shoot him. Neganie responded that he was working for Dolmage and wasn't leaving. "You Hiyu bullshit Balloo," Neganie baited. "You scared to shoot me. You scared to shoot any man!"

Ollie Knoll witnessed the whole thing.

"I was 12 or 13 years old when I went down with Valleau to Bluff Lake. What the crazy bugger did, he walked up to Neganie and took his pistol and hit him over the head. Of course, you do something like that, you draw blood on him. He could have hurt him pretty bad.

"Old Valleau was dead against Indians. I guess they did go down there and poach on his trapline, so then he got pretty bitter with them. You couldn't blame him in a way."

This was the unfortunate fissure along the edge of the frontier where Indigenous people were becoming more and more marginalized in the land their ancestors had occupied for centuries. As more settlers moved into the country, there was less land for them to continue their traditional ways.

With Neganie cold-cocked on the ground, mayhem erupted.

Bostock described Mrs. Neganie flying into a rage at Valleau, and hitting him in the face. Then suddenly she was overcome by a seizure and fell to the ground, frothing at the mouth. "Neganie was still on the ground and bleeding profusely from the long cut Valleau made on his head, yet he managed to gather his wife in his arms while she continued to rave at Valleau until she became unconscious. Valleau stood over them brandishing his gun, and continued a stream of curses, threats and verbal abuse against them."

One member of the survey party, Osbourne, was very sick with the flu and Dolmage defused Valleau's tirade by telling him there was a sick man in the other tent. Valleau responded immediately, abruptly changing his demeanour and offering to cheer Osbourne up. He went into Osbourne's tent and spent an hour talking to him.

The next morning, to keep the peace, Dolmage convinced Neganie to leave the valley and head back to Tatla Lake to find a doctor to get his head sewn up. Neganie reluctantly complied and shortly after he and his family disappeared up the trail, Valleau offered his services to the survey party. "Seeing as I have fired your packer, I guess I better give you a hand," he said.

According to Bostock, sugar wouldn't have melted in Valleau's mouth after that. From then on, he was well behaved and did everything he could to be helpful. A few days later, when the work at Bluff Lake was complete, Valleau helped the surveyors pack up their horses and escorted them to the end of the trail beyond the bluffs and the road leading out of the West Branch Valley to Tatla Lake.

Valleau promised to return and help pack the survey party in a few more days, but said he had to head down the valley with his horses to supply his line of trapping cabins first. That was the last they saw of him, and Bostock said he was glad of it. A few days later, Neganie rejoined the party as their guide, and his hunting prowess was appreciated by the surveyors as he provided venison for their table. Bostock described Neganie's uncanny method of hunting.

> On July 20th we moved to Kleena Kleene Flats glad to have seen no more of Belloo. I rode beside Neganie whenever I had the opportunity. He was much quieter than Eagle Lake Henry, but now and then some little gem of interest came from him. On our way Neganie pointed out and described with glee, a place where his father and some other Indians one night had crept up to four sleeping white men and cut their throats. A little further on he suddenly sprang from his horse and drawing his battered old .22 rifle, shot into the bush across a creek, to no purpose as it seemed to us. He threw down his rifle and ran across a stream in his moccasins as a large buck wandered out of the bushes shaking its head. Drawing his hunting knife and holding the buck's horn in his left hand, he plunged the knife into its throat and jumped back. Blood gushed from the buck and in a moment it fell over. We thought this was a lucky shot until during the following days, we saw him repeat the whole performance exactly, a number of times. His rifle was an old single shot and fired nothing bigger than .22 "long" cartridges, not even "long rifle" cartridges, so there was no question he was a dead shot with it, hitting the bucks in exactly the right spot to stun them.

Ten days later, Billy Dagg rode into camp, replacing Neganie as the guide for the party, and Bostock said he was sorry to see him go. "We regretted Neganie's departure as we knew he was the best guide in the country, and he had also told us many interesting things."

Bostock concluded his account of Neganie, saying an article appeared in a Vancouver newspaper a year later, announcing Neganie's death. A short note in the August 24, 1926, edition of the *Province* stated that Neganie, after drinking homebrew, had beaten his wife unconscious. After sobering up and thinking he had killed his wife, he shot himself dead.

Randolph Mulvahill said the Tsilhqot'in people always told him that it was Eagle Lake Henry who shot Neganie.

"When Neganie got drunk he'd go crazy and fight his wife. She used to wear her hair braided down the back, and they said he was dragging her around by her hair. He had her hair wrapped around his saddle horn and was spinning his horse around and she was swinging around in the air. They figured he was going to kill her.

"That's when they say Eagle Lake Henry shot him, right on the horse. This is what the Indians told me. Shot him in the head and killed him. And they blamed it on a 12-year-old kid they called Sugar George. The officials said he was shot with a .22, but the Indians said, hell, it was no .22, it was a rifle. A .250-3000. It blew his head practically off.

"Eagle Lake Henry was a good shot. That kid, do you ever suppose he'd be able to hit him spinning around on a horse? It's not logical he would even hit him at all. Sugar George was the most cross-eyed man in the country. The Indians swore up and down that Eagle Lake Henry is the guy who shot him, and I imagine that's right."

June Draney, Eagle Lake Henry's granddaughter, said she heard the stories of Henry's involvement in Neganie's death, but she never believed them.

"People tried to point a finger at Grandpa Henry over Neganie's death, but he had lots of witnesses. They said Neganie shot himself, then somebody tried to blame Grandpa Henry.

"Surveyors were at the house and Neganie had a good horse he was going to race. Billy Dagg was there and all the surveyors were there and they were waiting for this racehorse to come from Burnt Stable. All of a sudden Lashaway Lulua showed up, his horse all lathered, and he said Neganie shot himself, so there'll be no racing.

"Grandpa Henry told Andy Stuart who was all there when this happened. He had a lot of witnesses so he wasn't worried."

Valleau's Disagreeable Nature

Valleau had a reputation—obstreperous one minute, then warm and agreeable the next. Ollie Knoll described him as the kind of man you didn't want to spend too much time with in any one stretch. "He was one of those guys if you knew him for four or five days, it was time to dissolve your partnership for a while."

He said Valleau regularly needed to get away from people. "He'd stay away so long, then he comes back and talk and talk and talk so you couldn't get a word in edgewise. That's how I remember him. I guess he always had trouble with his neighbours."

Ollie said it was Valleau who first took Jim Holt into Sapeye Lake in the West Branch Valley. At first he couldn't do enough to help Jim get started. He provided all the tools and equipment Jim Holt needed to build his cabin.

"Old Jim Holt was telling us everything was going fine, then all of a sudden Valleau took his saws and axes and tools and went home.

"That's how he was. At first Old Valleau would give you everything he's got. If he had it, you could take it. He was one of those guys. Jim said Valleau brought everything that you need to put up this building. Before they got finished, Valleau comes up one morning right on the war path. He wanted everything he brought, back out of there. After that Valleau and Jim Holt were at loggerheads. Valleau was good if you left him alone and didn't get into any kind of deal with him. If you just be friends."

Pete McCormick was a horse-freighter on the Cariboo Road between Ashcroft and Barkerville when the Pacific Great Eastern Railway and the internal combustion engine ended horse freighting on the province's great north–south corridor. He moved west to the Chilcotin where horse culture would still thrive for another half century and settled at Clearwater Lake. Bill Bliss said Pete McCormick and Valleau got into a fist fight in the middle of the Chilcotin Road one day. Both men jumped off their wagons in front of Bill's house at Willow Springs, and had it out. Bill claimed that Pete came out the better for it.

The Munday Mountaineering Expedition

Don and Phyllis Munday were famed mountaineers who made more than thirty first ascents in the Coast Mountains of British Columbia between 1920 and 1950. In his classic 1948 book, *The Unknown Mountain*, Don Munday describes how a chance meeting with mountaineer Henry S. Hall Jr. in Vancouver led to the couple taking part in a spur-of-the-moment 1933 expedition down the West Branch Valley to Mt. Waddington. Munday gives a lively account of the six-week trek. In particular, he reveals insight into Valleau's erratic behaviour and the pins-and-needles tension that existed between him and Pete McCormick.

The Mundays took the steamship to Squamish, the Pacific Great Eastern train to Williams Lake, and Hodgson's freight truck stage to Tatla Lake. From there they went by horseback for eighty kilometres down the West Branch Valley to Scimitar Creek. The mountaineers were met at Bluff Lake by chief guide and horse packer Pete McCormick, his assistant Valleau, and Pete Evjen. They supplied seventeen horses, nine of them belonging to Valleau, to transport the party down the valley to the Scimitar Glacier. Munday said Valleau was continually feuding with McCormick.

He also reported that Valleau was jinxed with misadventure. "Twice he nearly drowned two of his horses when they slipped off a rocky ledge into the fast moving waters of the West Branch River. Valleau couldn't swim, but somehow managed to retrieve the animals." He said Valleau's reckless manner predictably led to his daily dunking with his horses as they made their way along the rugged trail.

"Valleau revealed he slept with a sawn-off shotgun under his pillow," wrote Munday. "But gave no hint whether this resulted from known clashes with his nearest neighbours or a more remote tragedy in which the gossips believed." He recalled one incident where Valleau dropped his pipe, and then a loaded revolver he was carrying, into a black hole among the rocks. "The weapon stuck muzzle up, just out of Valleau's reach. Another packer with longer arms helping with the trek, Pete Evjen, hung head down and took the risk of getting it."

Despite Valleau's confrontational way with people, Munday observed Valleau's uncanny way with his animals. "It was always a remarkable sight to see Valleau come in with his horses. They had never been stabled and had not learned to eat oats, yet as he walked one with a rope, the others crowded for a chance to walk with noses beside his cheeks."

On their homeward journey, once the mountaineers had concluded their exploration of Mt. Waddington, Valleau and Pete McCormick got into a bitter argument

Mountaineers and packers pole a raft carrying their supplies across the West Branch River at Scimitar Creek, while their horses swim. Photo Sir Norman Watson.

over the terms of his employment. At his camp at the north end of Twist Lake, Valleau announced he was pulling out with his nine horses and would let the climbing party get out of the valley as best they could.

"Valleau shut himself inside his nearby trap cabin for the night, and woke us in the night by firing a shot," Munday wrote. "But we agreed not to mention it in the morning. He breakfasted alone in his cabin perhaps looking for an advance from us. Failing this he went out for his horses staked in the meadow, and saddled and loaded them as if nothing had happened."

When they finally got back to Bluff Lake at the end of July, Munday said the roses were still blooming and the paintbrush flamed in the meadows. "In Valleau's garden were strawberries, carrots and lettuce without stint."

After the Mundays boarded the mail stage at Tatla Lake for their return journey home, Munday said that Valleau renewed his dispute with Pete McCormick and his neighbours in the West Branch. Barely a month after the expedition returned safely to Tatla Lake, Valleau lost it and took a shot at Johnny Hamm with his .30-30 rifle. Some people speculate the bullet might have hit Johnny if he hadn't stepped down onto a log to cross a creek the moment Valleau fired his gun. Fortunately Valleau wasn't a very good shot, as Don Munday attests. "Four good-sized wolf whelps ran forward curiously within 40 yards of us on a gravel bar," he wrote. "Valleau knelt and got three shots, but all wide."

In early spring 1934, a second mountaineering group headed down the West Branch to Mt. Waddington, led by Sir Norman Watson. Pete McCormick was hired as the chief packer to transport the party along the same route he took the Munday expedition the previous summer.

Valleau was not part of Pete McCormick's entourage on this occasion, because he was cooling his heels in Oakalla Prison, after a dispute with his neighbours got too heated. Instead, McCormick hired Bob Nicholson and Leonard Butler to help with the outfit.

The Sir Norman Watson expedition was unique. It started down the West Branch into the wilderness in mid-March, earlier than usual, with snow and ice still thick on the land. Their plan was for half of the party to ascend the Scimitar Glacier to Fury Gap and ski down the Franklin Glacier to the Klinaklini River and Knight Inlet on the coast. The other half was to return the way they came to Tatla Lake, by horseback with Pete McCormick.

Don Munday said Sir Norman Watson told him that the mountaineers returning to Tatla Lake were nervous as they anticipated Valleau's imminent release from prison. "They told us they never sat on the same side of the campfire as Pete McCormick owing to the fear of Valleau, whom they believed was prowling around unseen. They never saw more than tracks which they believed were his."

Munday wrote that Valleau had long tried to exercise ownership of the whole valley down to the main river forks of the Homathko River, but his rule had been challenged too often. "Before long he moved hundreds of miles northward."

A SINISTER DEFENCE

Elora Alden, the daughter of Leonard and Hilda Butler, grew up at the family ranch in the West Branch Valley on the north side of Bluff Lake. She said Valleau took a shot at their neighbour Johnny Hamm one time, and she figures that's the reason he got run out of the West Branch Valley. "Johnny was going across this little field he made and Valleau was perched on the hillside watching him. Johnny jumped this little stream just as Valleau shot and he missed Johnny. The cops came in and Johnny was going to lay a charge against Valleau, but I guess he escaped and went out over the mountain and he never came back. He escaped out over the mountain and ended up at Hazelton and that's where he's buried."

Elora heard a story of a more sinister nature concerning Valleau's attempt to defend his coveted valley. Shortly after he arrived in the country, Old George Turner and his wife, Louisa One-Eye, and their two young children, Young George and Mary Ann, came down the West Branch to go trapping.

Opposite: Leonard Butler, who owned the ranch on the other side of Bluff Lake from Valleau, was hired by Pete McCormick to help pack the Sir Norman Watson mountaineering expedition in 1934. Valleau was unavailable because he was cooling his heels in Oakalla prison after firing his rifle at Johnny Hamm. Photo Frank Swannell. Image I-59517 courtesy of the Royal BC Museum and Archives.

"I guess the kids were pretty damn young. Turner regularly came into the West Branch to go trapping way down the valley some place. This was way before the Nicholsons ever showed up there, and way before my parents, Leonard and Hilda Butler, came to the country.

"All the old Indians packed dried salmon with them because that was their source of food, especially if they were moving. Louisa had left some salmon hanging up in the cabin when they were trapping there the year before.

"They got to the cabin late at night. I guess there was quite a bit of snow and the kids were played out and hungry as bears. The old woman took that sack of salmon down while Turner was trying to get a fire going in the stove. She wanted to give the kids something to chew on until she could fix something better. And Turner turned around and looked at that slab of salmon that she had in her hands, and he snatched that salmon out of her hand. He told Dad about this. He took a piece and he tasted it. All that fish was laced with strychnine. Valleau had poisoned it.

"I said to my brother Lee one time, I wonder why Old Turner didn't just kill old Valleau. But I don't think he wanted to get involved with the cops in Canada, because for years they were looking for parts of the Dalton Gang that had gone missing after their last bank hold-up in Coffeeville, Kansas. Old George was supposed to be a member of that outlaw gang before he headed north into Canada."

A Horse Deal Gone Bad with Scotty Shields

Shortly after Scotty Shields arrived in the Chilcotin and settled in Tatlayoko Valley in 1928, he purchased a young mare from Valleau for a saddle horse. There weren't a lot of fences in those days, and horses being herd animals, they have a natural instinct to head home to familiar ground and their equine families if they get separated. It wasn't uncommon for horse traders to sell animals to unsuspecting customers, knowing full well that as soon as the horses got loose, they would make their way back home. That's what happened to the horse Scotty bought from Valleau.

When Scotty noticed his horse was no longer in his pasture, word got back to him that she had returned to Bluff Lake, and was running with Valleau's herd. When Scotty happened to see Valleau in Tatla Lake sometime later, Valleau confirmed his horse was there. He also mentioned that he wanted to be paid for pasturing Scotty's animal.

It took Scotty about three years before he actually got around to retrieving his horse. By then she had given birth to two foals. Since Valleau had been using Scotty's mare as a pack animal, Scotty figured she'd paid her dues to her former owner and he wasn't too interested in paying Valleau for her keep. The even stickier question remained concerning the ownership of the mare's two offspring. Apparently Valleau had put his brand on the young horses, so a classic backwoods dispute was shaping up.

That's how the matter sat when Scotty took the back route through the mountains from Tatlayoko Valley to Valleau's place in the West Branch, riding up the Crazy Creek trail past Niut Mountain. From there he crossed the divide into the West Branch, and followed the trail down Deer Creek (Valleau Creek) to Bluff Lake.

Scotty said the wild horses that "polluted" the country in those days, kept the trails open through the mountains.

When Scotty got to Bluff Lake, Valleau wasn't home, but Bern Mullin, Valleau's young trapping partner, was there. According to the custom of the country, Bern welcomed Scotty inside and offered him a meal.

Scotty had been on the trail for a couple of nights and was quite ravenous. Bern went out behind the cabin and cut off a couple of thick moose steaks from a hind quarter hanging there, and opened up the draft of the heater to get the frying pan hot. Soon the steaks were sizzling.

All of a sudden a loud bang shook the cabin and both Scotty and Bern hit the floor. They both figured Valleau had returned and upon discovering Scotty in the neighbourhood, had fired a shot at the cabin. After a prolonged silence it slowly dawned on the two men that it wasn't gunfire that had rocked the cabin. A can of pine tar Valleau had heating up behind the heater to doctor his animals had suddenly exploded from the heat of the intense fire.

Both men laughed when they realized how they had been fooled. At the same time, they remained on edge in case Valleau actually did show up. Scotty said he wasted no time rounding up his mare and her two offspring, and heading back home with them the way he had come over the mountains.

Valleau Cools His Heels in Prison

It was no secret that Valleau spent some time in the "square-circle," as some people referred to prison. There are a few stories and rumours about how this happened. Some people figured it was over the burning of Bob Pyper's store, but most people agree that it came from a dispute he was having with his nearest neighbours, Bob Nicholson and Johnny Hamm.

The Hamm and Nicholson families were farming in Rosthern, Saskatchewan, when the Great Depression dust-bowl drought devastated the prairies. In fall 1931, after another failed crop, Bob Nicholson, Johnny Hamm and Charlie Godfrey, all brothers-in-law, headed west to look for new ground for their families. They made it as far as the Cariboo when they ran into Valleau at the Log Cabin Hotel in Williams Lake.

When Valleau learned of their predicament of drought and starvation, he bragged about his well-watered valley 225 kilometres west of there. It had an abundance of both water and raw land to be developed, he boasted. The three men from the scorched prairie needed little convincing to abandon their plans to go to Quesnel and instead to follow Valleau into the Chilcotin to check out this Promised Land for themselves.

Exactly why Valleau, a loner who guarded his privacy so intensely, would invite three strangers in search of land into his domain is anybody's guess. Maybe Valleau genuinely felt sorry for these desperate prairie farmers when he invited them to his personal paradise. Of course, there could have been a more nefarious reason for his generosity born out of feuds he was having with his neighbours James Lee Holt and

Leonard Butler. Once the three men saw the splendour of the West Branch Valley, there was no turning them back. They knew they had found what they were looking for and returned to Saskatchewan to make plans to bring their families west to take up land in Valleau's Shangri-La.

For Valleau, the situation was a powder keg waiting to ignite. These hardy newcomers from Saskatchewan were no strangers to hard work, and, to make matters worse, they were part of a large industrious extended family. It didn't take Valleau long to sour on the new arrivals once they showed up the following year to register and start developing their pre-emptions. Soon other members of the Hamm family followed, and Valleau's bad dream turned into a nightmare and hostilities grew. He did his best to run the settlers from Saskatchewan out of the valley, but they wouldn't be intimidated.

Annie Nicholson, Bob's wife, said it was gunfire from Valleau, aimed in the direction of her brother that finally tipped the scales. The law caught up with Valleau, and the Chilcotin court registry shows Harvey T. Valleau being charged with an indictable offence on September 14, 1933. Exactly a month later on October 14 in Williams Lake he was sentenced to five months in Oakalla Prison. This wasn't his first violent outburst, nor would it be his last, but it was the beginning of the end for this free-wheeling loner who liked to pretend he was a gunslinger.

The Last Chilcotin Shoot-out

Renowned grizzly bear guide Clayton Mack was working for Lester Dorsey near Anahim Lake one spring when word got out that there was going to be a party at the Graham Ranch in Tatla Lake. Lester wasn't too eager to interrupt the work on his ranch but his workers insisted.

"A bunch of us were building a fence for Lester," Clayton said. "Somebody come up from Tatla and said a big dance at Tatla Lake this weekend. Lester said it was too far away. We started talking. We've been invited. Come on boys, let's go. Finally Lester said he'd go too. So a bunch of us went down there on horseback."

It was a two-day, hundred-kilometre ride to Tatla Lake. Clayton said he went into the Graham ranch house and saw Valleau standing in a corner of the room.

"I sat down on a corner of the woodpile by the stove, then Jim Holt came in and sat beside me. Then Jim Holt and Valleau start arguing and calling each other names across the room.

"Then Valleau reached down in his shoes and pulled a knife out. Jim Holt stood up and he had nothing. Jim sat down on that woodpile again. He grabbed a piece of wood and got up again. Valleau had that knife pointed towards Jim. Then Jim hit Valleau's hand with the firewood and the knife went flying. Somebody yelled, Jim's got a handgun, and we all took off. I went out the back door and some guys went through the front door.

"When I came around to the front of the house I could see Shorty King walking kind of funny. There was blood on the back of his pants. Somebody yelled Jim

Holt shot Shorty King in the backside! Then Eddie Collett stuck his hand in Shorty King's back pocket and he feel a bunch of broken glass. I guess he slipped when he was running and broke the bottle of lemon extract he bought in the store. Bunch of crazy guys."

Randolph Mulvahill heard about the Last Chilcotin Shoot-out from Lester Dorsey, but it had a slightly different twist than Clayton Mack's version. That's the joy of storytelling.

"The Grahams had a dance at Tatla Lake and Valleau shows up," Randolph said. "Then Jim Holt comes to the dance. Old Jim was an easygoing bugger about half tough; a pretty good size man. Valleau walks up to Jim and says when you going to bring back that wagon you stole of mine? Jim says, I didn't steal no goddamn wagon of yours, and Valleau argues, by God, you did. You either bring it back or goddamn you, I'll take it out on your hide.

"Just outside the door they had a bunch of firewood piled up for the school. Valleau jumped back from the door of the dance hall and pulls a great big knife out, and he's going to tackle Old Jim. Jim picks up some stovewood in his hand and he says, 'Alright Valleau, start a-whittling!'

"Valleau makes a jab at him with his knife and Old Jim hit him over the head with the stovewood stick and laid him out. Lester would laugh about it when he told that story. Valleau start a-whittling!"

According to local legend, this was the last shootout in Tatla Lake, and not a single shot was fired.

Randolph Mulvahill's Positive Memories of Valleau

Randolph Mulvahill said Valleau came to stay with his family when his father, Charlie Mulvahill, was gone for a month on a beef drive to Ashcroft.

"Mom had to stay there at Chezacut Lake all alone with us kids, so Dad got Valleau to come and work around the ranch fixing stockyards and milking the cow.

"Our milk cow was wild and would fight you every time you wanted to milk her. The Old Man figured she was too much for our mother to handle. With three kids to look after, and all alone in the bush, anything could happen with a cow like that and she might get hurt. So he got Valleau.

"Mother told Valleau he'd have to catch the cow and tie her up to milk her, and he said don't worry about it, I'll handle her. So he got her in the corral the first time and milked her. After he milked her that one time, he'd just go out in the yard and milk this wild cow any old time, and she wouldn't move. He had this way with animals. The same with horses. Once he handled a horse just a little while, he could do anything with it. There was something uncanny about the bugger."

Randolph said when Valleau moved out of the country, he came up to Chezacut and worked for his dad some more. "He never pulled any of his old tricks when he was working for us. He had no reason to and he got along good with us. The Old Man liked him. He said he was a good old guy."

Valleau earning two dollars swimming his horse across the Chilko River at Lava Canyon. Photo courtesy Wilf Hodgson.

Randolph says Bern Mullin bought out Valleau when he left the country, and Randolph asked Bern one time if he thought Valleau was crazy. "He said, not really. He said that was just Valleau's way of holding the country. And it really was. He kept the Indians out of there, no doubt. And that was his objective, to run the Indians out. Most of it was bluff."

West Branch had become too crowded for Valleau, so he eventually left the country with his string of horses and goats and settled near Vanderhoof, where he spent the rest of his days.

The only photograph of Valleau shows him midstream in the turbulent waters of Chilko River after betting someone two dollars he could swim his horse across at Lava Canyon. The significance of this feat, in the boiling current of a river that has taken the lives of many people who have had the misfortune of falling in, is that Valleau could not swim.

Valleau left his mark in his old cabin on the south shore of Bluff Lake. In the 1980s, the building was renovated and incorporated into an elegant office for White Saddle Helicopter owner, Jen King. The hefty fir log walls were still pocked by gunshot and contained chunks of lead buried in them from Valleau's shooting rampages. Whether it was from taking shots at packrats or at phantom enemies he imagined were lurking about outside was never clear.

For Jen King, the bullet holes added to the mystique of the place, where she served afternoon tea on fine English china to her mountain-climbing clients, and stories were told of the wild and unpredictable Valleau.

James Lee Holt

Gunslinger from the American West

There's a cabin on the east end of Big Eagle (Choelquoit) Lake known as the Jim Holt Cabin. It's a range cabin for cowboys keeping track of cattle for the C-1 Ranch of Alexis Creek. It's called Jim Holt Cabin because James Lee "Jim" Holt was the first range rider to work for Duke Marten when cattle were first introduced to that country in the 1930s. It was likely Jim who built the cabin.

Jim arrived in the Chilcotin after the First World War, pushing fifty head of horses from Bonner's Ferry Idaho with his stepson, Leonard Butler. He was married to Leonard's mother, Ada, and the couple had two sons, Clay and Dean Holt.

Leonard took up land on the fertile flats between Bluff Lake and Sapeye Lake in the West Branch of the Homathko River. In 1928, he married Hilda McKill and they had three children, Lee, Jack and Elora (Eleanor). Jim and Ada homesteaded nearby at Sapeye Lake. After a few years, Jim and Ada split up, and she married a man by the name of Kurt Heiney.

"Lee is named after Jim Holt," said Elora. "It's from his middle name, James Lee Holt. Dad and Mom named Lee after Jim even if he was a gunslinger. Dad thought a lot of Jim."

Jim was an integral part of the American Wild West gun culture when he migrated north to Canada. Laurie Haynes, who arrived in Tatlayoko Valley as a 9-year-old with his mother and four brothers in 1929, remembered Jim Holt fondly. He spent time with Jim and Leonard Butler in the West Branch Valley while he was growing up, and said Jim still had chunks of lead bullets buried in his body from gun battles gone awry. Old Jim ultimately carried these remnants of the Wild West to his grave.

Lee Butler recalled a story told to him by his dad, Leonard Butler, about a set-to between Jim Holt and the infamous Harvey Theodor Valleau.

"Dad and Jim were riding their horses up from the lake when they met Valleau coming the other way along the road. There was some kind of argument over a hound dog and Valleau asked Jim to go for his gun. Valleau imagined he was some sort of gunslinger, and everyone knew that Jim was a real gunslinger. Jim didn't have a gun on him and Dad was packing a .30-30.

"Valleau kept pulling his pistol out of his shirt and poking it back in, and taunting Jim to go for it. Jim was edging over towards Dad and said, give me that gun. Dad kept moving away and wouldn't give it to him. He knew that Jim would have killed Valleau right there if he'd let him have that .30-30."

Elora Alden confirmed her father was carrying a rifle at the time and Jim Holt wasn't armed.

Del Naomi Haynes, Alex Paxton and Jim Holt on a beef drive. Photo courtesy Harry Haynes.

"Jim hardly went anywhere without his sidearm. Why he didn't have it that day is beyond me. I guess he figured if they encountered a bear, Dad had the rifle. When they met Valleau on the trail, Valleau must have noticed that Jim wasn't wearing his sidearm so he got a little cocky. He told Jim, go for your gun.

"Valleau knew damn well Jim didn't have a gun on him, and Jim tried his best to get the rifle in Dad's scabbard. Dad said there wasn't any doubt he'd have shot Valleau right then and there. You didn't confront an old gunslinger like that and get away with it."

Rumours and Truth

Grizzly bear guide and storyteller Clayton Mack said he spent one winter with Jim Holt near Anahim Lake. He said Old Jim had no money and nothing to eat and was trying to start a ranch at Pelican Lake, so Clayton moved in with him. "He told me he was pretty good with a handgun, so I said okay, I'll make a bull's-eye for you out on the side of the cabin. I'm getting a little bit old, Jim said, I'm shaking now. Bang, he hit the bull's-eye every time, the old bugger."

Now Clayton Mack was known to fabricate the truth a bit in his storytelling. But at times his portrayals of myth and magic were so richly sprinkled with truth it was difficult to separate fact from fiction. He told one story about Jim Holt shooting a policeman in Tatla Lake after getting caught up in a cattle-rustling scheme with Bullshit Valleau. The yarn defies belief but it was built around a truth few people knew about.

Clayton said Jim got paid $1,600 by Pat Burns to buy cattle in the Chilcotin for Burns Meatpacking Company in Vancouver. But instead of purchasing the animals, Clayton said Jim got Valleau to help him rustle cattle belonging to other people off the range and pocketing the money. "Bullshit Valleau was Jim's workman," Clayton insisted.

He elaborated how the two men would shoot the cattle, skin them and send the beef to Vancouver. They hid

Jim Holt was a gunslinger from the American Wild West. Photo courtesy Harry Haynes.

the hides marked with various people's brands in an abandoned cabin that Valleau was supposed to set on fire before anybody found out. But Clayton said Valleau took too long to dispose of the evidence and somebody did find out.

He said Old Jim had the $1,600 from Pat Burns burning a hole in his pocket when he walked into Bob Graham's ranch house in Tatla Lake and was surprised by the police officer hot on the trail of the cattle thieves. "The policeman catch up to them now. Jim walk in the front door and the policeman come up behind him. Stick 'em up, Jim! And Jim was pretty good with a hand gun. Oldtimers. Bang! He shot the policeman right there. Get away."

Clayton said Jim Holt claimed self-defence in the killing, telling the judge the policeman had no business to say "stick 'em up" when he had that $1,600 in his pocket. "That's a lot of money, and that's what he told the judge. He thought he was being robbed, and he got off. He killed a lot of men in the States before he came to the Chilcotin."

Clayton's yarn, of course, was not believable to anyone who spent much time in the Chilcotin. If a police officer had been killed at Tatla Lake by Jim Holt or anyone else, it would have become the lore of local legend. But no such stories exist.

The other red flag of disbelief was associating Jim with cattle-rustling. This was a hanging offence in the United States where Jim had come from and didn't fit his character. He might have been a gunslinger, but he wasn't a thief.

So Clayton's story of Jim Holt rustling cattle and shooting a policeman in Tatla Lake didn't pass the credibility test. It was a story not worth mentioning until Elora Alden said something shocking. "Jim Holt actually did kill a cop one time when he was working for Pat Burns," she said. "But it wasn't in the Chilcotin."

Elora said the killing occurred in Alberta, a long time before Jim and her grandmother got together. Jim was a young man then and went to Alberta looking for a job. Pat Burns, who owned a cattle empire and meat processing company, found out that Jim was good with a gun.

"I guess Pat Burns was having a hell of a time. He'd send one of the cowboys in every month to get the payroll from the bank. The guy would pick up the money then get held up on the trail and the payroll would go missing. They couldn't find the guy who was doing the stealing so they hired Jim to pack the payroll because he was pretty fast with the gun.

"So this one time when he was coming back from town with the payroll, it was getting kind of dusk towards evening and this rider stepped out of the bushes beside the trail and told Jim to halt. Well, Jim whipped out his six-shooter and shot him. It turned out to be a Northwest Mounted Police officer that Jim had shot. Jim went on the run, high-balling it back across the border. Then they found out later that it had been the police officer who had been stealing the payroll all along. Jim fixed that."

Elora also laid to rest any suggestion that Jim Holt was involved in a cattle-rustling scheme with Valleau. "Jim Holt was never a cattle rustler in his life. He wouldn't steal off anybody."

Jim's Last Days

Randolph Mulvahill described Jim Holt as a "tough old cowboy from across the line," who in his prime was one of the top bronc riders in the world. "He was a hell of a good rodeo rider in his time. A wild horse man." He says Jim Holt rode the range at Big Eagle Lake and helped with the annual beef drives into Williams Lake until old age caught up to him.

"Old Jim was an easy-going old bugger about half tough," Randolph said. "Then he went across the line to his sister's place and died there when he was about 90. Those chunks of lead still in his body."

Packer Pete McCormick

One of the more dynamic characters in the Chilcotin during the early 1900s was horse freighter and packer Pete McCormick. Originally from the United States, he drove freight wagons on the Cariboo Road between Ashcroft and Barkerville for several years before moving west in 1916 and settling at Clearwater Lake just west of Kleena Kleene. (Clearwater Lake was known as McCormick Lake during Pete's time, but its name was changed after he was gone.)

It took skill to drive tandem teams of horses hauling heavy loads of goods and supplies rounding hairpin turns where Pete first made his living on the Cariboo Road. An error of just a few centimetres could mean a plunge to the death down the sheer sides of a ravine to the rocks below.

There was one story Pete told of a man who was driving a particularly stubborn team of mules. He couldn't get them to go so he built a fire underneath the animals. He got them to move alright, one wagonload forward, and the fire consumed the wagon and all its contents.

The coming of the internal combustion engine and the building of Pacific Great Eastern Railway put an end to horse freighting along the Cariboo Road, so Pete headed west to the Chilcotin where his horsemanship skills were still valued.

A couple of books by distinguished mountaineers shed some insight into the life and times of Pete McCormick. Don Munday described Pete's horsemanship and prowess in his 1948 book, *Unknown Mountain*. Pete took the mountaineers through the impenetrable wilderness of the West Branch River to Scimitar Glacier at the base of Mt. Waddington in 1933. Munday said Pete was unflappable despite contending with his arch-rival, the notorious Bullshit Valleau, who threatened to sabotage the expedition before they safely made it back to civilization.

Then, a year later, Pete took the Sir Norman Watson ski mountaineering expedition down the same route to Scimitar Glacier, where half the party ascended Fury Gap and skied down the Franklin Glacier to Knight Inlet at the mouth of the Klinaklini River. Of course, Valleau was not on this trip because he was behind bars for taking rifle shots at his neighbours a few months earlier.

"Pete's confidence in himself and his outfit was completely infectious," wrote E. J. King, recounting the epic slog into the wilderness in the 1934 book *Round Mystery Mountain*. "He inspired faith, performing miracles hourly, getting the pack-train through. In his company, we forgot all about our aches and discomfort, listening eagerly to all he had to say, describing a region that has no written history."

There could be no greater social gap than the one that may have existed between the aristocratic British mountain climbers and the rough-and-ready backwoodsman, Pete McCormick. Yet there was a nobility they shared and recognized in each other.

Alcohol greased the wheels of Old Chilcotin in those days, and Pete McCormick was no exception to this practice. Whenever he made his way to Williams Lake for business or pleasure, it was only natural to rendezvous with old friends at the Lakeview Hotel or other watering holes like the Log Cabin Hotel or the Maple Leaf. When his money ran out, he would extricate himself from whatever unseemly situation he was in, and retreat home to the safety of the West Chilcotin.

That's how it was when Sir Norman Watson sent Pete advance payment for his outfitting services, with the understanding that he would meet the expedition members in Vancouver to acquire what they needed for the trip. They were naturally concerned when Pete didn't show up at the appointed time in Vancouver as had been arranged.

As E. J. King described it, Pete's celebrations with his friends had been on a royal scale when he reached Williams Lake on his way to Vancouver. The festivities continued for a week until his friends placed him on the southbound Pacific Great Eastern train for Vancouver in the care of a perfect stranger, a Mr. Campbell.

Pete made it to Vancouver okay, but Mr. Campbell lost track of him in the "stews of the seaport," and feeling a sense of duty, contacted the mountaineers. He was worried because, as he put it, "Pete was an infant-in-arms when away from his familiar mountains."

Packer Pete McCormick was at home riding his horses in the mountains. Photo courtesy Sir Norman Watson.

Pete eventually showed up none the worse for wear, and proved his worth to the expedition. Once back in his familiar territory in the wilds of the Chilcotin, he guided them to their destination and safely brought them back to Tatla Lake again. He provided them with an adventure of their lives, notwithstanding their lurking fear of Valleau.

Back safely at Tatla Lake, Pete stated his intention to accompany the expedition members on their return trip to Vancouver. He gave the excuse that he needed to see a dentist, but E. J. King admitted he felt some misgivings. To start with, King was concerned that Pete might get waylaid by his legion of friends in Williams Lake and never make it out of the Cariboo. "Our stay in Williams Lake was very brief," wrote King. "We transacted our business with the bank as quickly as we could and furtively slunk out of the town before the news of our arrival could reach Pete's many friends who would, we knew, have formed themselves at a moment's notice into an active committee of welcome."

In their haste to leave Williams Lake, they forgot to stock up with sufficient food for the journey, trusting they'd find an open roadhouse along the way. They were very hungry by the time they found an establishment at Lac La Hache, only to be quite shocked when greeted at the door by two girls in beach pyjamas. "We thought we were thoroughly inured to shocks," writes King. "The shanty was a fishing lodge run by our hostess and her husband. They quickly fixed for us an ample lunch, but Pete had to be coaxed back into the car."

Pete enriched their journey down the old Gold Rush Road by telling tales at every bend in the trail where he had once driven the stagecoach. "Pete was happy as

Pete McCormick leads the Sir Norman Watson mountaineering expedition through the shallows at Twist Lake on their way to Mount Waddington. Photo courtesy Sir Norman Watson.

a child as we drove along, reliving parts of his life," recalled King. "Wild orgies and old-timer bottle parties figured largely in Pete's stories of those strenuous days. It's a wonder anyone survived at all."

When they reached Vancouver, King notes that Pete suddenly disappeared without saying goodbye. King and other members of the party were transferring their luggage into a taxi when they noticed Pete was gone. A few months later, now back in England, King got a letter from Pete, postmarked Kleena Kleene: "Sorry I could not see you off. I was getting married in Vancouver. I now have someone to comb my hair."

Pete's Domestic Life

Pete McCormick returned safely to Clearwater Lake from Vancouver with his new "bride" in the early summer of 1934.

Hank Law, a young man who had bicycled to the Chilcotin on his own epic journey up the Cariboo Road from Vancouver a couple of years earlier, was staying in a cabin on the opposite shore of Clearwater Lake from Pete. He remembered Pete's triumphant return from the big city with his wallet flush from his horse-packing ventures and a woman by his side. "With the money Pete got from packing these guys into Mystery Mountain, he went down to the coast and came back with this lady," Hank recalled. "The talk was that she was an elderly madam. I met her and you couldn't wish for a better person."

Hank said "Missus Pete," as he referred to her, was an avid fisherman. "She was getting on in years and was quite rotund. She just loved to get out there and go fly-fishing."

One day Hank got a message from Missus Pete that she needed his help with Pete, who got roughed up trying to break some horses. "I went over there and she had Pete lying in his bunk. He had broken some ribs but wasn't spitting blood, so I figured it wasn't too bad." Hank got an old truck inner tube and used it to make a rubber bandage. "I took a big piece and slid it around him and sewed it to keep it firm. He was lying on his back with his head here and his feet there, and was pretty immobile."

Pete never did see a dentist in Vancouver and his teeth were in pretty bad shape. Before Hank took leave of the cabin, Missus Pete asked him if he knew anything about pulling teeth. "All he had left in his head were four wonky old teeth. He had pyorrhea real bad and these four snags that stuck up interfered with him smoking his pipe. She said, while we've got him down, let's take his teeth out."

Hank agreed to do it and asked if they had any pliers handy. Missus Pete rustled around and produced a pair of forge tongs, and they got down to business. "I got hold of each tooth with the jaws of the pliers and hit my hand once, and it just popped out. Pete couldn't do much. He was kind of a baby lying there moaning, but he realized it was a good thing."

As Hank was leaving, he overheard Missus Pete say, "While Dr. Law is here, you wouldn't want to be castrated, would you?" Then he heard her let loose a roar

Hank Law was a young bachelor living at Clearwater Lake when he met packer Pete McCormick. Photo courtesy the Law family.

of laughter. "I can hear her laugh yet. It would echo off the trees and all around about the mountain. She was one of the nicest old women—real on the button, no fooling around, not wanting caviar every day. She could make a meal out of nothing. That's the sign of a good cook when they can make a meal out of nothing."

A few weeks later, Hank headed down the Klinaklini River on a raft, looking for some land to homestead on. The water was high and the raft tipped and he lost everything he owned, including his shoes, and had to walk back to Pete's place barefoot. "All I had left was my saddle and my gun. I borrowed a saddle horse and some boots from Pete and rode into Tatla Lake just as the stage was pulling in."

He arrived just in time to see Pete McCormick's old nemesis, Harvey Theodor Valleau, get off the stage. "Valleau was a loudmouth type, and started bragging that he got himself a new .30-30 and was going to square up a few bills. He said he'd done his schooling—meaning he was just coming out of the pen for burning Bob Pyper's store. Old Pete might have had something to do with it, but this was their feud."

When Hank got back to Clearwater Lake, he called Pete outside because he didn't want to alarm his missus, and told him that Valleau was back. "He went into his shack and put a shell into the barrel of his .30-30 right now, put it on safety, and stood it there by the door."

Hank spent a fitful night at Pete's place. "That night I camped at Pete's because I was going to get another horse from him the next day and go down the river and try and find some of my stuff. I guess a deer jumped in the bush in the night, and old Pete went outside, flattened against the building and yelled, 'Come out wherever you are!' Then Pow! Pow! Pow! Pow! He fired off a few rounds, shooting into the bush. These old buggers were tough."

One day Pete showed Hank a place up on the hillside underneath a big fir tree where he suspected Valleau had been spying on him. "Pete took the trouble to catch his saddle horse and take me up there. There was a little milking stool under this tree and cigarette butts all around—tailor-mades too—and boot marks in the sand. You could sit there and see Pete's cabin down below. I think it was just a psychological thing Old Valleau was doing to scare the shit out of him. This was the game they played. In that country, if you didn't yell out coming into someone's camp, you'd better be ready to duck."

Finding Pete's Body

Provincial policeman Johnny Blatchford was new to the Chilcotin. He had been assigned to the police detachment in Alexis Creek in 1940 for only a few months when he got the call that Pete McCormick was missing down the Klinaklini Valley.

It was September, and Pete was taking a party of Americans by horseback into the mountains. They were about thirty kilometres down the valley when he told his clients to wait while he looked for an easier route around some bad windfall. He never came back. The clients were afraid they'd get lost if they went looking for him, so they headed back up the trail to Kleena Kleene and called the police station in Alexis Creek.

Blatchford said, after getting the call, "I drove right out to Kleena Kleene and borrowed some horses from Jim Mackill at One Eye Lake and got Baptiste Dester and Dave Wilson to go with me to show me the way. I'd never been down the Klinaklini Valley before, and Baptiste and Dave knew the country."

Eventually they found Pete McCormick's horse tied up to a tree. "I was riding ahead and stopped my horse to wait for the others and thought I heard a horse whinny farther down the trail, but I wasn't sure. Then my horse's head went up. When Baptiste and Dave caught up to me, Pete McCormick's horse whinnied again, and this time we all heard her.

"My horse whinnied back at her, so we rode right over and Pete had her tied to a tree at the top of a ravine. She'd been there a couple of days and had all the ground beat up and dusty. Pete had left her there and had gone down to get a drink at the bottom of the gully. He got his drink and died about half-way coming back up the ravine. He was on his hands and knees and had a heart attack and it killed him."

Johnny had packed a canvas tarpaulin along and they used it to wrap up Pete's body. "His nose and mouth were all full of fly eggs and he stunk like hell, so we rolled him in the tarp and tied it good and put him on the packhorse and hauled him out of there."

Before the men could tie Pete's stiffened body onto the packhorse, they had to adjust his shape so he didn't catch on branches and trees along the narrow trail. He had been dead for several days lying flat on the ground, and rigor mortis had left his body rigid. To remedy this, the searchers positioned his corpse still wrapped in a tarp, over a fallen windfall log and left it overnight. By morning it had neatly folded into a shape that made it possible to tie onto the pack horse.

Trapper Annie Nicholson

Wilds of the West Branch

A friend and I responded to a newspaper ad in 1975 and bought a trapline in the wilds of the Chilcotin. We were living in Williams Lake at the time and neither of us knew a thing about trapping. Our ambition was to move to the bush and get out of the urban environment we had known all our lives. We knew a couple of guys with a trapline near Tatla Lake who had built a barn and were raising goats there, so we figured a trapline would afford us the chance to get established on the land.

When I showed a map of this trapping area to a friend working for forestry, his eyes rolled and he pointed to the concentration of topographic lines. "This is steep mountain country," he commented. Our trapline lay in one of the wildest parts of British Columbia, some sixty kilometres down the West Branch Valley south of Tatla Lake. It was indeed in the shadow of some of the highest mountain peaks in the province.

One of the first people we met in the West Branch was Trapper Annie Nicholson. She was a heavy-set woman in her early 70s. She had known better days and her arthritis was getting to her. In her prime, she had been strong and invincible and would spend weeks at a time alone in the rugged wilderness trapping. Becoming infirm came as a shock to her. She'd led a remarkable life.

Annie lived in a ramshackle lumber-frame house halfway down the valley that she shared with her long-time friend, Bern Mullin. They weren't a married couple but had been inseparable friends and business partners for more than forty years. They owned adjacent ranches a couple of kilometres apart and had hayed, irrigated and cultivated their fields together, and run their cattle as a single herd for several decades. They kept their own brands and knew each animal by name.

Annie took care of the business end of things, like dealing with the outside world and government paperwork, shipping their cattle to market and buying replacement bulls at the stockyards. She made marathon shopping excursions into Williams Lake a couple of times a year while Bern was content to remain in the valley and keep the home fires burning. He rarely ventured out to Tatla Lake for the weekly mail run and grocery shopping because Annie took care of all that too.

As they got older, they found it more practical to share accommodations in Bern's big lumber-frame house that he had built on Burnt Creek rather than live separately. Annie had her own cozy log cabin three or four kilometres up the valley and was sensitive about being "shacked up" with a man she wasn't married to. "What would the neighbours say?" she would fret. But she and Bern occupied opposite corners of Bern's big house, and they each had their own assortment of dogs and personal belongings cordoned off by plywood dividers.

Annie had once owned our trapline, another thirty kilometres down the valley, though she hadn't trapped it for a decade or more. We often consulted her on trapping matters and how to survive in the raw wilderness. She always came up with a gem of wisdom to share. "Keep track of the time of day," she'd caution. "Get a pocket watch and set it so you know what time it will get dark. Setting it to the proper time doesn't matter. Just be sure you don't get stuck on the trail at night."

Annie Hamm and Bob Nicholson on their wedding day. Photo courtesy Lorie Wilson.

Annie was a single mother of five after her husband, Bob Nicholson, pulled out of the country in 1936 and left them to fend for themselves. Once her children were old enough to stay on their own, Annie would head off down the valley and spend a month or two trapping marten and squirrels to earn a cash income to put food on the table. In those years trapping was the mainstay of the Chilcotin economy.

When Annie arrived in the Chilcotin from Saskatchewan in October 1932 with her husband and five children, the whole country was in the grip of the Great Depression. She came from hardy Mennonite stock. Her grandparents had emigrated from Odessa in southern Russia in the late 1870s to escape religious persecution. They found political asylum in Canada in a German-speaking Mennonite reserve in Stanley Township, Manitoba. Her father David Hamm was born in Odessa in 1871, but came to Manitoba as a young child. Her mother Sara was born in Stanley Township in 1879.

Sara was in her late teens when she and David got married, and their first two children, Sarah and Lizzy, were born in Manitoba. Then, around the turn of the century, they homesteaded in Rosthern, Saskatchewan, where they pre-empted a quarter section of land. They were about twenty kilometres from Batoche, where Louis Riel fought his last battle during the Northwest Rebellion of 1885. Annie was born in 1904, the fifth of twelve children, and she and the rest of her siblings were born in Rosthern.

Annie met her husband, Bob Nicholson, at a dance in Prince Albert, Saskatchewan. In 1923 they eloped because Annie's parents didn't approve of their union. Bob was a rough-and-tumble cowboy from Oregon who was neither Mennonite nor

Annie Nicholson, Bert Hamm and Nellie Frasier. Photo courtesy Lorie Wilson.

Bern Mullin. Photo courtesy Lorie Wilson.

of German extraction. Despite the disapproval of her family, Annie and Bob settled in Rosthern where most of her siblings resided, and she gave birth to five children in quick succession.

When the Great Depression began in 1929 and money became scarce, farmers in the prairies couldn't sell their wheat. Compounding this was several years of drought where farmers were lucky to recover the seed they had planted in spring. In fall 1931, after another crop failure had turned their prairie breadbasket into a dust bowl, Annie's husband, her brother Johnny Hamm, and their brother-in-law Charlie Godfrey, headed for British Columbia to look for new land to settle. As mentioned earlier, they got as far as Williams Lake when they ran into Harvey Theodor Valleau at the Log Cabin Hotel and he enticed them to follow him to the Chilcotin to check out the potential of the West Branch Valley.

It didn't take much convincing for the men to realize they had found what they were looking for. They returned to Saskatchewan to sell their land and bring their families west. In October 1932, Bob and Annie Nicholson arrived in Tatla Lake with their five children in a convoy of two vehicles that also included Johnny Hamm, Charlie Godfrey and his wife Matilda, known as Tildy, who was Annie and Johnny's sister. They packed as many belongings as they could fit into a car and a pickup truck and drove west, crossing the Rockies through the Crowsnest Pass and following the better roads into the United States before swinging north up the Okanagan Valley to the Cariboo. When they arrived in Tatla Lake, they sold their two automobiles and bought wagons and horses.

Annie Nicholson and Bern Mullin outside Bern's lumber frame house in the West Branch. They spent their last years together there living in opposite corners of the building with their own assortment of dogs. Photo courtesy Lorie Wilson.

Annie and her children spent the winter in Tatla Lake while Bob, Johnny, Charlie and Tildy headed down into the West Branch to work at improving their quarter-section pre-emptions down the valley below Valleau's headquarters at Bluff Lake. The people of Tatla Lake welcomed Annie and the children: the community needed four more children to qualify for a government-paid schoolteacher, and three of the five Nicholson kids were school age. Needing one more child to reach the required quota meant registering two-year-old Terry, who was very good at amusing himself at the back of the classroom while the other children did their schoolwork. By spring, Bob, Johnny, Charlie and Tildy had built accommodations for three families.

Bern Mullin and August Schnarr

Bern Mullin was living at Bluff Lake with Valleau when Annie and her family moved into the valley in 1932. He was just 22 years old when he rode the rails from Bathurst, New Brunswick, to British Columbia at the start of the Great Depression and somehow found his way to the Chilcotin. That's where Valleau befriended him and invited him into the West Branch.

Bern's quiet demeanour allowed him to co-exist with Valleau longer than the usual shelf-life of friendships afforded the erratic Bluff Lake renegade. When Valleau left the country, he sold his assets and property to Bern.

Just how far Valleau trapped down the West Branch Valley is not clear and how he shared the territory with Bute Inlet trapper August Schnarr is a bit of a mystery. Trapping domains were largely defined by might of will in those days.

Schnarr was a mythical figure to folks living in the West Branch, and they spoke of him in awe. It was said he trapped up the Homathko River from the coast as far up the West Branch Valley as Twist Lake. Then he crossed over the divide into the Klinaklini Valley and trapped his way back to the coast at Knight Inlet.

He would pack his food and traps with him and work short sections of the river at a time. He'd make his sets in one area for a few weeks, then pull his traps and move on to a different area. After two or three months moving over the landscape, he'd return home with his fur catch. Somehow he got past Murderer's Bar and Waddington Canyon carrying his heavy pack loads. Asked how her father got past these impenetrable barricades, his daughter Pearl said he simply followed the game trails.

Through a curious twist of fate, Johnny Hamm purchased Schnarr's trapping rights in the lower West Branch Valley. Shortly after Valleau had left the country, Schnarr showed up at Johnny's place on a cold winter day, saying he was on his way to sell his trapline to Leonard Butler. Johnny offered to buy the line, so Schnarr sold it to him instead.

Bern Mullin said Schnarr stopped by his cabin on his trapping rounds one winter but refused his invitation to come inside and spend the night. Schnarr told him he was used to sleeping outdoors and had built up a natural resistance to the elements. He said he'd get sick if he stayed in a heated cabin. Bern said Schnarr spent the night in his woodshed.

Johnny Hamm Goes Trapping

It was a rugged two-day hike down the trail from Johnny Hamm's homestead to the start of his new trapping area at Twist Lake. From there, it was another three days of hard bushwhacking to the forks of the Homathko River. The trail crossed several rockslides and numerous robust side creeks; as well, it required crossing the main river itself several times.

For one crossing, Johnny stretched a steel cable over the rushing water and used a pulley to go from side to side. In another place, where the river boiled through a long, narrow canyon, he felled a tree from one lip of the rocky gorge to the other, and walked or crawled over the boiling torrent thirty metres below. Trapping in the Lower Homathko was a young man's game. One false step or a slip with a sharp axe could spell a person's doom.

Over the next few years, Johnny built a network of log cabins located a winter's day travel apart. Unlike Schnarr, he equipped his shelters with heaters or stoves so he could warm up and dry out after a hard day snowshoeing. A few years later, after Johnny Hamm left the valley, Annie Nicholson inherited the trapline from her brother.

Bob Nicholson Pulls Up Stakes

Life in the West Branch Valley wasn't easy for Annie Nicholson. Her husband Bob had a love of horses. He was always buying, selling or trading them, and if there was a horse he particularly wanted that he couldn't buy or trade for, he simply took it.

One day Bob came home to the West Branch with a white horse and proceeded to paint black spots on its coat to make it a pinto. Then he turned it out into the pasture across the river. The children were told not to say anything about it, but soon the horse's owner, Jim Mackill, arrived with the law.

Mackill knew Bob Nicholson had wanted that horse, and when it went missing he was sure he knew where to find it. Sure enough the pinto across the river turned out to be his missing white horse.

On July 2, 1935, Bob Nicholson appeared before Justice of the Peace Gabriel Thomas Lane Bayliff in the Graham family's Big House in Tatla Lake to face charges of stealing a horse and illegally branding it.

Lorie Wilson says her mother, Lorna, was only 9 years old when she and her younger brother, Terry, and younger sister, Ulah, were brought to the trial with their mother as character witnesses for Bob Nicholson. "They were there to generate sympathy for the horse thief," Lorie says. "You can't send this man away; he has a wife and a bunch of kids to support. It seemed to have worked. This time he didn't go to jail."

Bert Hamm gets ready to leave Rosthern, Saskatchewan, with his parents, David and Sara Hamm, three siblings, Edgar, David Jr., and Wanda, and nephew Joe Schuk in April 1936. Photo courtesy Bert Hamm.

The court threw out the horse-stealing charge for lack of evidence, but convicted Nicholson of illegally branding someone else's animal and gave him a one-year suspended sentence with no obligation to pay court costs.

Things never did go right for Bob Nicholson in the Chilcotin after that, and within a year he pulled up stakes and left Annie and their five children behind in the West Branch to fend for themselves. "My mother was 10 years old when he took all the horses and left," Lorie says.

After Bob Nicholson was gone, Lorie says her family remained good friends with the other families who were involved in the horse-stealing incident. "In fact the whole Chilcotin must have known about it, but never once did I hear anyone say anything about my grandfather. His crime did not seem to have been visited upon my grandmother and her children."

More Hamm Family Members Arrive

On May 9, 1936, the next wave of Hamm family members arrived from Saskatchewan. Annie's younger brother Bert brought their parents, David and Sara Hamm, and their three youngest children, David Jr., Wanda and Edgar to settle in the West Branch. Also stuffed into Bert's 1928 Plymouth sedan was his 18-year-old nephew Joe Schuk and a border collie dog. A few years later, Joe established a successful ranching operation in Tatlayoko Valley, which he ran until he was 93 years old.

The following year another contingent of the Hamm family settled at Bluff Lake when Lena Hamm Bittner, her husband, Gustaf, and their three children, Rosella, Alan and Leona made the trek from Rosthern.

Johnny Hamm married schoolteacher Yolande Pemberton when she came to teach the Hamm, Nicholson and Butler children in the early West Branch School built by the community on Johnny's property. With the start of the Second World War, Johnny and Yolande moved away and changed their last name to Hamilton to avoid discrimination during that conflict with Germany.

Besides trapping down the West Branch for many years in the rugged wilderness, Annie Nicholson worked as a cook for a geological survey party that traversed the country on horseback for several years. She grew a large garden in the temperate climate of the West Branch Valley and sold her excess produce to Betty Graham Linder at Tatla Lake General Store.

Annie and Bern lived close to the land, scratching out a living with their small cattle herd, doing things by hand the old-time way. Inseparable companions, they both died in the fall of 1981. Annie was the first to go in September, followed by Bern two months later.

Old George Turner

A Chilcotin Mystery: Bank Robber or Lawman?

One of the true characters of the Chilcotin that people still talk about is Old George Turner of Kleena Kleene.

He was reputed to have been an outlaw from the American West. Some said he had been a member of the infamous Dalton Gang, and had picked up and fled across the border into Canada in the 1890s before the law could catch up to him. At least that's how the story goes, fed by kitchen table chatter and conversations around the campfire.

It was rumoured he was the one member of the Dalton Gang who got away after the foiled double-bank holdup attempt in Coffeyville, Kansas, on October 5, 1892. Four members of the gang were killed in the gun battle that erupted after they brashly tried to rob two banks at the same time. Only one gang member, Emmett Dalton, was captured alive, after surviving twenty-three gunshot wounds. He was sentenced to life imprisonment and served fourteen years before being pardoned. A sixth member of the party tending the horses, was never accounted for, and the identity of the horse wrangler remained a mystery.

It was speculated that George Turner might have been this man.

One story is that Turner reached the Cariboo Chilcotin Coast by steamship sailing from Vancouver to Bella Coola. From there he headed to the wilderness of the mountains and the high plateau. The Chilcotin was an ideal refuge for a desperado seeking anonymity because it was the custom in that country not to pry into an individual's personal business. More than a few Americans with a questionable past made their way into the Chilcotin, after crossing the border into Canada just ahead of a posse and a cloud of dust.

George Turner commanded respect from anyone who crossed his trail. He was a first-rate trapper, frontiersman, and dog tough. He was a man you didn't dare cross.

He took a Tŝilhqot'in wife, Louisa One-Eye, the daughter of Chief One-Eye Charlie of One Eye Lake, and they settled at Kleena Kleene. Despite having an infirm right arm, Louisa capably performed the tasks expected of a woman at the time.

Before George met Louisa, she had two children with other men, Timothy Stillas and Lucy Dagg. Old Turner and Louisa had two children together, George Junior and Mary Ann (Ross).

Old Turner trapped down the Klinaklini River as far as Knight Inlet with his stepson-in-law, Baptiste Dester.

It was an incident that happened at Towdystan sometime around the beginning of the First World War that fuelled speculation that Old Turner might have been connected to the Dalton Gang.

Old George Turner (circa 1930). Photo courtesy Al Elsey.

Turner was good friends with Annie and Tom Engebretson, who had a ranch at Towdystan. Their son Fred, born in 1910, was just a kid when he witnessed a bizarre confrontation between Old Turner and two strangers who tracked him down to Towdystan.

Shortly after Emmett Dalton was released from jail, a man and a woman arrived on horseback, having ridden all the way up from the United States. Thanks to the single-strand telephone line, attached to trees in some places, that stretched from Williams Lake to Bella Coola, Old Turner knew they were coming. It's said he hung around the Engebretson ranch house because it had a phone.

Fred remembered Old Turner being pretty fidgety when he saw the pair cross the creek at Towdystan. He said Turner grabbed a double-bitted axe and went out to talk to them. Fred couldn't hear what was being said, but he figured the strangers were looking for their share of the loot accrued from long-ago bank heists and train robberies. "The man had a six-gun pointed at Old Turner, and Turner was swirling his double-bitted axe around," Fred recalled. "There were a few tense moments."

Fred said his parents had shotguns pointing out the windows of the old house, and the visitors knew they were outnumbered. Finally they just turned around and left. "They must have figured they weren't going to get the money," Fred continued. "They had to leave or get riddled with bullets. Then Old Turner got scared and figured the cops might be following him, so he got some grub and took off across the mountains."

Old George Turner lived to be an old man. Some say he was over 90 years old when he died at Kleena Kleene around 1955. The summer before he died, Old Turner showed his friends Elora Alden and Grace Kellogg the grave of Chief One-Eye Charlie on the shore of One Eye Lake. His last wish was to be buried next to his father-in-law. That winter, Tom Chignell performed the eulogy as the body of Old Turner was laid to rest. Despite his passing, the mystery of the Dalton Gang outlaw continued to live on.

Some Bizarre Twists to the Story

The question of whether Old Turner was a gunslinger or not continued to be debated long after he was gone. To all appearances, he was someone from south of the border who slipped into Canada to get out of rifle range of whoever might be pursuing him.

But, as Paul St. Pierre liked to say, the chatter of country gossip never really sleeps. Old Turner's reputation had taken on a life of its own because he was so reclusive and private about his personal business. People speculated that he had something to hide.

A twist in Old Turner's story was introduced in 1958, three years after his death, when W. H. Turnbull published a beekeeping journal for British Columbia's Centennial. In its pages, he revealed a side of Old George Turner no one had heard much about.

According to Turnbull, Old Turner entered the annals of beekeeping history when he decided to rob a bee tree one day. He procured enough honey to satisfy his sweet tooth for a year, then got busy and found a hollow cedar tree with a shell about two inches thick.

"He cut the tree into fourteen-inch blocks which he cleaned out and set with cross sticks to carry honey combs," Turnbull said. "Then he located a swarm of bees and established an apiary at his wilderness home."

Turnbull noted that Old Turner's ingenious beekeeping efforts were never registered with the Department of Agriculture, nor were his hives ever inspected by the Inspector of Apiaries.

"It was only proof of the ingenuity of our real pioneers," he stated.

Then W. H. Turnbull revealed a whole new explanation of Old Turner's past. It was the antithesis of him being an outlaw, and it bears some consideration.

He said his son, Corporal Bob Turnbull, was serving as the provincial policeman at Alexis Creek when Old Turner decided to apply for his old age pension. He was in his eighties by that time but local authorities needed proof of Old Turner's age.

Bob Turnbull paid him a visit at his cabin in Kleena Kleene, and going through an accumulation of personal papers, some more than half a century old, he uncovered Turner's 1903 application for a homestead in Bella Coola. That was sufficient proof of his age and residency for his pension.

But it was another discovery by the police officer that shed a whole different light on Old Turner's past. When Bob Turnbull unearthed an old Colt 45 pistol in a pack sack, with twenty-seven notches carved on its wooden handle, he asked, "What's this?"

The aging trapper gave an answer no one else had ever heard before. He told the policeman he hailed from Kansas, the same state where the infamous Dalton Gang pulled its failed last caper at Coffeyville. But instead of being an outlaw, Turner told Turnbull he was a deputy sheriff working with the legendary sheriff and gunman, Bat Masterson.

This was an era when a man had to be lightning on the draw to stay alive, and George was fast. The twenty-seven notches on the handle of his old "45" attested to that, carved in the memory of men who had challenged his skill and not lived to tell about it.

He told Bob Turnbull while he was a deputy sheriff he naturally made a number of enemies. So he decided that a quieter life in the British Columbia wilderness would give him a better chance of survival. He said he took the steamship to Bella Coola and picked about the wildest part of the country to settle down and live in peace.

Bob asked Old Turner if he could still fire the old gun, and the old man answered that he was a bit out of practice and had no ammunition for it. The officer unstrapped his own service revolver and handed it to Turner and asked if he could hit a milk can lying on the ground a dozen metres away.

He fired four shots in succession and the can jumped with every shot, Turnbull reported. Then he asked to have the can tossed in the air and he hit it three times out of four shots.

Bob Turnbull later said the old man's eyes twinkled. "He was very pleased that his skill with the six-gun was still as good as it had been fifty years earlier."

Old George Turner at Chief One-Eye's grave, indicating where he wanted to be buried. Photo Elora Alden.

Records show he applied to preempt a homestead in Bella Coola in 1903 during the time the Norwegians were colonizing the valley. George was seeking a less civilized life and he soon moved farther into the mountains, following the Atnarko River to its headwaters and over the ridge into Knot Lakes and the North Fork of the Klinaklini River.

It was there at Sleepy Hollow in the heart of the Klinaklini wilderness that George Turner made his home with his Tŝilhqot'in wife, Louisa One-Eye, and their children.

Old George didn't suffer fools lightly. He defended his turf with an iron hand. One time at a rodeo at Andy Stuart's store in Redstone, he cold-cocked a man with the butt of his pistol, who confronted him over trapping rights in Knot Lakes country. That settled the question immediately.

Old Turner and Louisa lived more than fifty years together in the rugged mountain country of the Klinaklini and Upper Atnarko. Turner Lake, source of the spectacular Hunlin Falls is named after him.

HOLDING ON TO THE OLD MYTHOLOGY

Myth and speculation being what they are, there are some people who still hold to the belief that Old George Turner was indeed a long-lost member of the Dalton Gang. Entrenching this idea is the Nature Conservancy of Canada, which recently purchased the property down the Klinaklini River once occupied by Turner and Louisa One-Eye. The name chosen by the NCC for this property is Dalton's Hideaway.

Elora Alden is another person who isn't quick to give up on the romance of Old Turner's possible outlaw past. "He would tell people when they quizzed him all sorts of stories about his past if they got too nosy," she insisted. "I knew Old Turner when I was a kid. There were two people he trusted. My dad, Leonard Butler, was one, and old Baptiste Dester was the other. He basically told Dad and Baptiste what happened at Coffeyville."

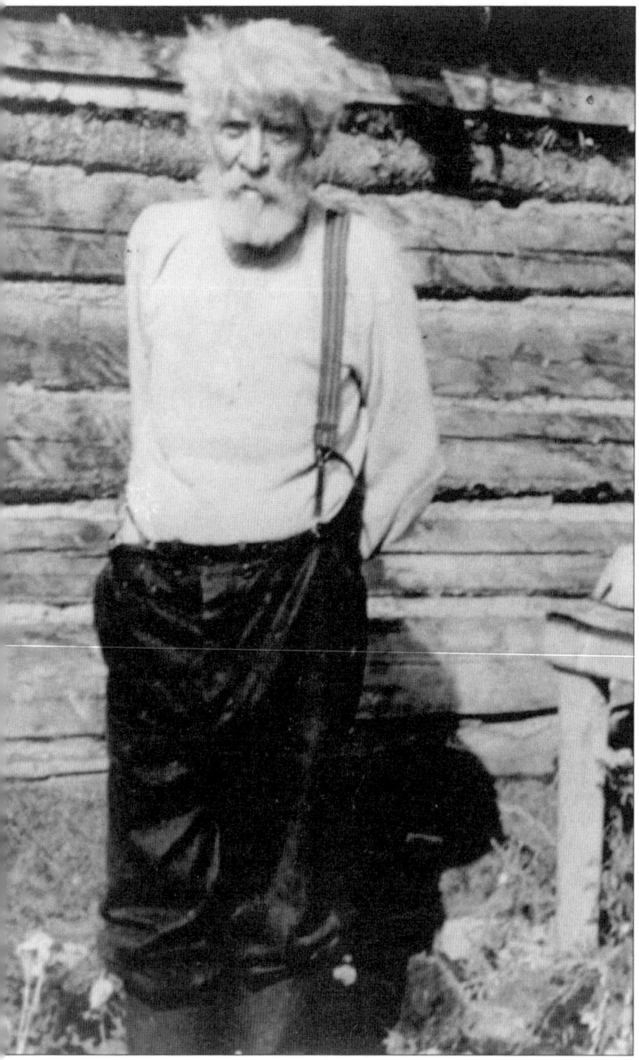

Old George Turner at Kleena Kleene, circa 1954. Photo Bill Mouat.

Elora was convinced that many of the so-called gangsters who were robbing banks and trains in the American Wild West were doing so to help the poor. "These gangs were like Robin Hood. They'd rob these banks and give money to families that were starving to death to help them along. I think the Dalton Gang was one of these. There were more gang members who got away than was known."

Elora figured that when Old Turner got up to the Canadian border, he would have changed his name. "He sure as hell wouldn't have kept the name he had when he was with the Dalton Gang."

She says the person who helped Old Turner get his pension was a judge that used to come up through the country. "He used to stay at my Uncle Clarence Mackill's lodge at Kleena Kleene. Turner was really old. He told Dad when he got up to the border down by Vancouver, he hired this Indian woman to take him around the border in her canoe. That's how he got into Canada. I think he came directly up the Klinaklini Valley."

Elora said Old Turner was 92 when he died. "I took those pictures of Old Turner at Chief One-Eye's grave when I was only 16. He wanted to show Grace Kellogg and me where he wanted to be buried."

Louisa One-Eye Turner

Louisa One-Eye was as much a legend in the lore of the Chilcotin as her white trapper husband, Old George Turner. At a young age, Louisa suffered an infirmity and her right arm was left paralyzed. It was a strange thing. Her granddaughter, Josephine Gregg, said Louisa and another young girl were sleeping in a tent beside the river when this stroke-like affliction hit both girls. But it only affected Louisa's right arm and no other part of her body. The other girl's arms and legs were okay, but one side of her face suffered a palsy-like paralysis.

Born around 1867, three years after the Chilcotin War, Louisa was raised in the Klinaklini River country of the West Chilcotin. Despite her shrivelled right arm, she grew strong and capable in every other way. Using only her left hand, she tanned hides, sewed buckskin, hunted and fished, saddled and rode horses and did domestic chores. It was said she could track through the bush on a saddle horse better than anyone in the country, including her husband.

"It was just like she had two arms," said Josephine. "She tanned hides just like she had two hands. She taught me how to make a baby basket when I was a little girl. She would use her foot to hold down the willow branch. Step on it and cut it."

Josephine remembers her grandmother making moccasins. "She made moccasins just like she had two hands. She used the treadle sewing machine left-handed, and she used it good."

One day while Josephine was watching Louisa sewing on the treadle machine, the needle went through her grandmother's hand. "I was pretty small sitting beside her, and we got no medicine to put on her hand."

Josephine's uncle, Young George Turner, was also in the cabin drinking coffee, and had a pot of coffee brewing on the stove. "He told me to get that coffee and pour it on my grandmother's hand, so I did. She healed up without a problem."

Josephine grew up with her grandmother at Kleena Kleene, as her parents, Lucy Dagg and Baptiste Dester, were often away. They worked hard to make a living, and would be gone for weeks at a time trapping down the Klinaklini River or hunting in the mountains.

Lucy and Baptiste both had Tŝilhqot'in mothers and absentee white fathers who had come from England. Though they were both raised as Tŝilhqot'in, neither Lucy nor Baptiste were granted Indian status. Baptiste officially obtained his white rights so he could own deeded land near Clearwater Lake. On the positive side, Josephine wasn't forced to go to residential school like most other Tŝilhqot'in children, so she avoided that humiliation.

She was grateful she got to spend her formative years with her grandmother. On the down side, Josephine never learned to speak English until her own children started attending school at Kleena Kleene.

"My grandmother told me everything. Sometimes she told me stories. She told me who is related to who. That's why I know everything. We don't know other Tŝilhqot'in people at Kleena Kleene. There was nobody else around us except Charlie Ekks and his family."

Louisa had several children before she met Old George Turner. Besides her son, Timothy, sired by Baptiste Stillas from Ulkatcho country, she had a couple of other sons adopted by Ulkatcho families before Josephine's mother, Lucy Dagg, was born.

Josephine Gregg holds a pair of her exquisite newly sewn buckskin gloves with daughter Joanne Gregg. Taught by her grandmother Louisa, Josephine learned to make some of the best buckskin in the Chilcotin. Her moccasins, gloves and other attire were coveted near and far. Photo Sage Birchwater.

"Timothy Stillas had a brother, Mark, and another brother, Eddie, raised at Ulkatcho Village. Lucy took care of one of her older brothers before he passed away. Old man Stillas' first name was Baptiste. So Timothy also had the last name of Baptiste. He married Maggie Charleyboy from Tsi Deldel."

Lucy's father was an Englishman by the name of George Dagg, who procreated a legacy of half-siblings across the Chilcotin landscape. Billy Dagg from Nemiah Valley, half-brother to Eagle Lake Henry, and Celestine Guichon Dagg, who married Thomas Squinas of Anahim Lake, are two, but there were others.

When Old Turner and Louisa got together in the early 1900s, Lucy was still an infant and Timothy was a toddler. Later they had two children of their own, George Turner Junior and Mary Anne (Ross).

Louisa and Old Turner traversed some of the most rugged country imaginable, from the Chilcotin Plateau to the mouth of the Klinaklini River at Knight Inlet on the coast, and up the North Fork of the Klinaklini to Knot Lakes and beyond that into the Atnarko and the Bella Coola Valley. They also trapped down the West Branch of the Homathko until a sinister incident with Harvey Theodor Valleau putting strychnine in their food cache convinced them to stay clear of there.

Although Turner Lake, the source of the world-renowned Hunlin Falls, was named after Old George Turner, it was Louisa One-Eye who showed her husband

Opposite: Louisa One-Eye Turner at Kleena Kleene around 1954. In her busy industrious life, Louisa could do more with one arm than most women could do with two. Photo Bill Mouat.

the precipitous horseback route to Turner Lake in the first place. "My grandmother could ride a horse at full speed all the time," Josephine stated. "You couldn't beat her. She knew all the old foot trails and horse trails to Bella Coola. She showed Old Turner the way."

Some people made light of Louisa's infirmity, using the nickname Sitkum Memaloost or "half-dead one side" in the Chinook dialect to refer to her. Josephine was never impressed by that name. She insisted her grandmother was anything but "half dead." "My grandmother could saddle a horse just like she's got two hands. Nothing to it. She set up a wall tent too. Just one hand. Nothing to it. When she was young she went hunting with a rifle. A shotgun too. When I knew her she would no longer shoot a gun, but she still packed a rifle on her horse. I think she could have used it if she had to."

Josephine remembered camping around the country with her grandmother and Old Turner trapping and hunting. "We'd go fishing. I remember that."

She said her grandmother's father was known as Chief One-Eye. One Eye Lake is named after him.

"He had an Indian name, but I don't know what it was. I guess some white people come along and say, what's your name. I'm Chief One-Eye, he tell them. So everybody call him Chief One-Eye."

Josephine says Louisa's mother came from the country north of Anahim Lake, and she spoke a different Athapaskan dialect than that spoken by the Tsîlhqot'in. Likely it was Dakelh.

"I understood my grandmother. I talk to her lots. I didn't know she talked differently until I went to Tl'etinqox on the other side of Alexis Creek. They say what kind of talk you talk? I felt pretty ashamed. I was kind of young. My grandmother talked in the language of her mom, but I didn't know anything about it."

Louisa and Old George Turner were both in their late 80s when the school inspector from Williams Lake, Bill Mouat, got them to pose for pictures. The portrait of Louisa taken in June 1954 is the only known image of her.

Louisa died in Chezacut a few years later and is buried next to her husband on the sidehill overlooking One Eye Lake.

And one more thing.

There were a lot of mysterious deaths in the wilds of the Chilcotin that nobody could explain. One was the death of Chief One-Eye. He had been shot by an assailant and his body was dumped in McClinchy River while Old George Turner and Louisa were trapping down the Klinaklini Valley.

Some people speculated that Old Turner might have murdered him because he didn't want the supposed Dalton Gang outlaw to marry his daughter.

Those who knew Old Turner say nothing could be further from the truth. Why would he ask to be buried next to his father-in-law if he were involved in that kind of scandal?

Afterword

The Great Photographic Record

There's an old joke, from before the invention of the digital camera, about a Japanese tour bus getting hijacked in Whistler. The authorities didn't know who did it, but they got 20,000 photos of the suspects.

The joke stems from the days when the Japanese were the champions of tourism photography. Now that we are firmly ensconced in the digital age, everyone seems manic when it comes to taking photo images, regardless of cultural or ethnic origin. Even animals get in on the act, with cameras mounted on the backs of eagles.

A big question remains: Despite the exponential increase in the number of photographs being taken, what physical visual evidence of our times will remain a century or so from now? Historical writers and researchers rely heavily on archival family photograph collections for images of people, places or events of the past. Some of these collections are well organized into albums or mounted in frames; some are prominently displayed in kitchens held fast by fridge magnets; others are kept helter-skelter in bags or boxes. But the bottom line is that these hard-copy images that you can hold in your hand are accessible.

When the digital age rocketed into our laps at the end of the twentieth century, I celebrated the technology. As a freelancer in the remote Chilcotin, sending a roll of film to a newspaper or magazine hundreds of kilometres away was iffy. First off, you were never sure whether you had captured the image you were after. Then there was the question of accurately identifying who was who, and of course, there was the time delay of sending the roll of film by bus, stage line or in the mail.

Digital imagery eliminated the guesswork. You knew instantly if you nailed your subject. Then, with e-mail, you could have the image on the editor's computer screen before your French fries had cooled.

The problem is, I've lost touch with hundreds of images I have taken since going digital. Besides the countless number stored in some imperceptible file, I no longer have the equipment to view some of the early ones. Remember the generations of floppy disks? The timeframe of obsolescence gets shorter and shorter as the information age devours us.

Since the invention of photography around 1840, photo images gradually put sketch artists and portrait painters out of business portraying likenesses of individuals and providing a reliable visual link to the times they were in.

A century ago, there were few cameras or photographers in the backwoods of British Columbia. Early camera equipment was cumbersome. Tripods, bulky camera bodies, and fragile glass plate slides were tricky enough to set up in a studio, but taking this equipment on horseback down the trail and into the wild required focused attention and dedication. An extra packhorse would be needed to lug the stuff around.

Images like the one of Culla Culla House on page 11, authenticate our collective memories and remind us of the capacity of a photograph to transport us back in time and place.

In 1793, Alexander Mackenzie described this unique structure in his journal while trekking along the Nuxalk/Dakelh Grease Trail to Bella Coola while making the first recorded crossing of North America north of Mexico. Cameras had not been invented yet so Mackenzie used words to describe what he saw.

Then eighty-three years later, in 1876, surveyor George Dawson took the only known image of the Culla Culla potlatch house, and it mirrored Mackenzie's description. A quarter of a century later, when Father François Marie Thomas trundled through the country and encouraged his converts to build the first Catholic Church at Ulkatcho Village, the Culla Culla House was gone.

Ulkatcho Village was 160 kilometres up the Grease Trail through the mountains from Bella Coola, yet the potlatch house gave visual evidence of the cultural sharing that occurred between the Coastal Nuxalk and Interior Dakelh. It sported coastal artwork and a spindly carved totem out front in "Stick Indian" country as the Nuxalk sometimes referred to their colleagues on the high plateau.

Elders told me there were several of these potlatch houses throughout Ulkatcho territory, but there is only one known image of these structures, thanks to this early photograph taken by George Dawson.

By the turn of the twentieth century, other photographers started providing high-quality photo images depicting the people and times of the Cariboo Chilcotin Coast.

Surveyor Frank Swannell is one of the pioneers. He began his career in 1899 mapping the remote hinterland of British Columbia. When he realized he was seeing areas of the province that few people would ever visit, he purchased his first camera in 1901. Thanks to Swannell's talented work, we have high-quality images of freighting on the Cariboo Road in 1901, paddlewheelers on the Fraser, and portraits of individuals who lived across the landscape. Then, in the 1920s, after a hiatus to serve in the First World War, Swannell spent a couple of survey seasons working in the Cariboo Chilcotin Coast region, and recording images of important places and individuals in the West Chilcotin and the Bella Coola Valley. His extensive photo collection spanning nearly three decades has been published by Jay Sherwood in four volumes.

The arrival of Norwegian colonists in the Bella Coola Valley in 1894 brought two photographers to the region, Simon Olsen Bangen and Iver Fougner. They took images of Norwegian settlers hacking out their homesteads in the coastal rainforest, and classic images of the old Q'umk'uts Nuxalk village at the mouth of the Bella Coola River before it slipped into obscurity.

Between 1920 and 1924, two ethnographers arrived in Bella Coola to document the traditional use of plants, animals, social organization and cultural traditions of the Nuxalk, Dakelh and Tŝilhqot'in people. Thomas McIlwraith collected

Opposite: The meeting of the Cats. This historic photograph records the handshake between bulldozer drivers Alf Bracewell (left) and George Dalshag (right) on Sept 26, 1953, signifying completion of the road over the Bella Coola Hill. Photo Leslie Kopas.

the stories and oral material, while Harlan Smith photographed a broad range of subjects. Harlan Smith's impeccable images give a lasting and vital connection to the Ulkatcho, Tŝilhqot'in and Nuxalk people of that time. A catalogue of Smith's collection was compiled by Leslie Tepper for the Canadian Museum of History in 1991.

In June 1933, Cliff Kopas and his bride, Ruth, set out from Calgary by pack horse on their honeymoon, bound for Bella Coola. Four months later, they arrived safely in the Central Coast community, after following Mackenzie's Nuxalk-Dakelh Grease Trail from the Fraser River to the Central Coast. Though Ruth died in childbirth two years later, Cliff spent a lifetime in Bella Coola as a prominent photographer, establishing his own darkroom and photography studio. While he accomplished much as a leader in the community, including spearheading the construction of the Bella Coola Road through the Coast Mountains, his photo collection remains one of his great legacies.

In Tatla Lake, Joy Graham took up photography as a hobby. Few people in the Chilcotin had cameras when Joy and her sister Eve arrived in the mid-1930s to work for K. B. Moore in Tatlayoko Valley. Most people didn't own cameras and, for those who did, getting film developed cost more time and trouble than most people could afford. But Joy was dedicated to preserving history and providing a record of the times. Her photo collection remains one of the historical treasures of the West Chilcotin, documenting the past.

So that brings us back to our original question. What physical evidence will there be for the descendants of the photographers in this digital age? Will there be a tangible record for our great-grandchildren to pick up and hold—something for them to grasp as they attempt to get their bearings of the past, before rocketing off into the future?

Something to consider for sure.

Forty years ago, I was gathering the tools and resources I would need to move out into the Chilcotin wilderness. I was on a great journey of discovery and had no intention of coming back. This was during the back-to-the-land movement where many young people were moving away from the urban environments they grew up in to get immersed in Nature.

Shortly before I left, I took a writing workshop with renowned local playwright Gwen Pharis Ringwood. Knowing my imminent plans and intent to disappear into the wild, her advice to me was simple: keep a record.

With this book of stories, anecdotes and photographs of the Cariboo Chilcotin Coast, I've aimed to do that.

Family Bonds

The Dakehl, Tŝilhqot'in and Nuxalk Peoples

On November 5, 1990, Ulkatcho Chief Jimmy Stillas disappeared in the wilderness north of Anahim Lake. The snow machine he was riding broke through the ice near a beaver dam where he was hunting moose along the ancient Nuxalk-Dakelh Grease Trail. Jimmy was hunting alone, and when he failed to come back to his cabin along the Dean River that night, his two companions, Wilfred Cassam and David Friesen, knew something was amiss. They walked through deep snow to the closest neighbours at Salmon River and got the word out that something was seriously wrong.

Ulkatcho Chief Jimmy Stillas (right) welcomes Nuxalk elder Clayton Mack (in wheelchair), who flew in from Bella Coola for the 1987 Tanya Lakes Gathering. Photo Sage Birchwater.

If it wasn't for the extraordinary effort by the Ulkatcho community to immediately launch an air search before snow covered his tracks, his body and snow machine would have never been discovered in the depths of the small lake. Jimmy's death would tragically have remained an unsolved mystery.

Jimmy was 54 years old when he died doing what he loved best, hunting in the traditional territory of his grandfather Baptiste Stillas. He only served as chief for four years, but in that brief time he brought profound changes to his community. He instilled a new sense of cultural pride, self-esteem and self-determination into the mindset of his people. Vestiges of Jimmy's inspiration can still be found, echoing throughout the Cariboo Chilcotin Coast region.

Jimmy often talked about his mother, Mary Jane McEwan, but it was only after his death that I met her. At Jimmy's funeral, she was sitting next to Nuxalk Elder Addy Saunders, and it was then that I learned about the unique family ties the two women shared. Addy was the wife of Mary Jane's biological father, Joe Saunders. It offered me some insight into the unique family connections that bind the Nuxalk and Ulkatcho communities.

Mary Jane was born before her mother, Emma Stillas, married her husband, Jamos Jack, and had their own family that included John, Henry, Benny and Minnie (Alexis).

Similarly, Mary Jane was unmarried when she conceived Jimmy with Nuxalk fisherman David Moody. Jimmy was born at his great-grandfather's ranch along the Nuxalk-Dakelh Grease Trail and was raised there in the loving care of his extended family. He always referred to his great-grandfather Baptiste Stillas as his grandfather, because it was simpler that way. Baptiste was the patriarch of the family during Jimmy's formative years.

Mary Jane eventually married Mack McEwan, and they had a number of children together.

It was an eye-opener for me to learn about the intimate family ties between the Ulkatcho, Nuxalk and Tŝilhqot'in communities. Blood is thicker than water, and these were clear lines of acceptance unclouded by moral judgement.

Jimmy once explained the importance of tracing bloodlines. Partly it was about avoiding incest and the unfortunate ramifications associated with that. But there were deeper implications.

Blood ties cut through the ramparts of political and cultural differences.

Athapaskan-speakers from the high Chilcotin Plateau, Ulkatcho and Tŝilhqot'in families were welcomed guests in Bella Coola during the Nuxalk winter potlatch season. Outside witnesses were vital to these great naming ceremonies, which lay at the root of Nuxalk government structure. These dances and feasts would go all night and continue over a three-month period, and witnesses were needed to validate the evolving social order.

In quiet moments during the mystery of dancing newly carved masks, feasting and give-aways, under the shroud of the rain coast cedar canopy and protected by the softness of the thick moss carpeting the rainforest floor, children of mixed lineage

Nuxalk elder Addie Saunders and Ulkatcho elder Mary Jane McEwan renew acquaintances and their unique family connection. Addie's husband Joe Saunders was Mary Jane's biological father. Photo Sage Birchwater.

Mary Jane Stillas McEwan on horseback with her friend Sadie Cahoose in 1934, two years before the birth of her son Jimmy Stillas. Photo Cliff Kopas.

were sometimes conceived. Later their parentage was acknowledged. And so Jimmy Stillas and his mother, Mary Jane McEwan, traced their biological dads.

This blending of bloodlines occurred on the Chilcotin Plateau as well, linking the Ulkatcho Dakelh and the Tŝilhqot'in. Baptiste Stillas's liaison with Louisa One-Eye produced a son, Timothy Stillas. And, in the custom of those times, Timothy carried the identity of his biological father in two ways. He was sometimes known as Timothy Stillas, but also as Timothy Baptiste, after his father's first name. This was a common practice among these Indigenous people until the Church got involved and insisted that offspring have their father's last name.

Then when Timothy married Maggie Charleyboy of K'l Deldel (Redbrush), the duel mystique of naming children continued. Their first-born son, Tommy Timothy, was given his father's first name for his surname, while their subsequent children, Yellicy (Hunlin), Lottie (Guichon), Emily (William), Dominic and Isadore were baptized as Baptiste. Somehow the surname Stillas disappeared off the baptismal charts.

The Nuxalk, with their entrenched naming formalities, were unparalleled in keeping track of genealogy. One day in the late 1980s, Nuxalk Elder Mabel Hall visited the Ulkatcho community in Anahim Lake and explained the lineage linking the great families of the Ulkatcho and Tŝilhqot'in people to the Nuxalk villages of

Stwic (Stuie) and Nus'qulst (Noosgulch). "Some of our family relations extend to the Lhkwanaats (Squinas) family of Anahim Lake; to the Anuxim (Alphonse family of T'letinqox through Chief ʔAnahim); to the Alexci (Charleyboy family of Tsi Deldel and Blackwater); to the St'ls (Stillas family of Ulkatcho); and to the Stwic family, whose history is unknown."

She said these five families were closely related to her grandfather Chief Tl'alamn (Clellamin), who was buried at Stwic. The Clellamin longhouse once stood in the village of Nus'qulst at the mouth of the Noosgulch River in the shadow of Mt. Nusatsum. In the late 1890s, when settlers introduced the first cameras to the valley, the magnificent Clellamin House had been reconstructed at Q'umk'uts Village at the mouth of the Bella Coola River. It stands out with its uniquely sculpted multi-peaked façade. Mabel Hall said the five peaks of Clellamin House represent the five sacred peaks of Mt. Nusatsum.

Clayton Mack described how the Ulkatcho families were linked to his home village of Nus'qulst. "Quite a few of the old Ulkatcho people came from Bella Coola. Charlie West, Antone Capoose, Old Cahoose, Domas Squinas, Baptiste Stillas, Old Alexie and Old Chantyman all spoke the Bella Coola language." He said their families all came from Nus'qulst Village.

The first trail out of the Bella Coola Valley to the high plateau follows the ridge just upstream of Noosgulch River. It is known today as the Capoose Summer Trail, and it is linked directly to the Nuxalk-Dakelh Grease Trail system, to Tanya Lakes and to Ulkatcho Village.

Clayton Mack went on to explain how the names of the Ulkatcho families connect to Bella Coola. "They came from Nus'qulst Mountain (Mt. Nusatsum). Charlie West's name was Mucklehoose, which means one side of the mountain red like when the sun shines on the mountain at the first light of day. Cahoose means frost on the mountain; Capoose means bald part of the mountain where no trees grow; Squinas means the bottom of the mountain on one side where berries grow."

In 1987, Chief Jimmy Stillas hosted a gathering at Tanya Lakes where the Ulkatcho people traditionally harvested salmon in Takia Creek, a tributary of the Dean River. Elders, including Clayton Mack, were flown in from Bella Coola. Dakelh, Tŝilhqot'in and Nuxalk youth rode in by horseback from Anahim Lake, and others came by horse-drawn wagon along the Grease Trail from Quesnel, Nazko and Lhoos'kus.

They got a chance to relive how their ancestors from the high plateau and Central Coast came together and celebrated ages ago.

The experience of the Tanya Lakes Gathering is one of the great legacies gifted to the Ulkatcho people by Chief Jimmy Stillas.

Following pages: Frank Swannell's survey party is met at Ulkatcho Village by Charlie West, Captain Harry Alexis and Baptiste Stillas (far right). Photo Frank Swannell. Image H-06534 courtesy of the Royal BC Museum and Archives.

A DOCUMENT OF CHANGE

The dynamic tension that existed between the Indigenous peoples that occupied what we now call British Columbia changed irrevocably in 1793.

When Alexander Mackenzie cracked through the ramparts of the Rocky Mountains into the Pacific coast drainage, he brought a fissure of change to the relationships the Dakelh, Secwepemc, Tsilhqot'in, St'at'imc, Nuxalk and Homalco had with each other and the land on which they lived. Within 15 years Euro-Canadians were living among the indigenous populations.

For thousands of years Indigenous societies evolved, developing their own languages, cultures and traditions tied to the land and resources that sustained them. They established territorial boundaries and defended their lands tenaciously. Sometimes monumental disputes arose that escalated into dramatic events of bloody warfare and retribution. Memory of these incidents became etched into the psyche of each nation, preserved by oral history and handed down to succeeding generations long before Euro-Canadians arrived with a written language to record history.

One example is the Chunlak massacre of 1745.

Nearly twenty years before Alexander Mackenzie was born, a Tŝilhqot'in war party destroyed the Dakelh village of Chunlac, located at the confluence of the Stuart and Nechako rivers. The destruction of the village was an act of retribution over the killing of a prominent Tŝilhqot'in leader and was a brutal affair in which the bodies of women and children were impaled on long poles—like salmon hung up to dry. Three years later, the Dakelh reciprocated, killing a large number of Tŝilhqot'in in a similar fashion.

For nearly three centuries, memory of this conflict festered like an open wound.

After fur traders and settlers arrived and stamped their Euro-Canadian brand on the region, conflicts among Indigenous peoples continued to occur. Hudson's Bay Company records, for example, document an incident in 1826 when three Dakelh hunters making a hunting foray into Tŝilhqot'in territory were killed. War ensued.

The Dakelh dispatched a raiding party from Fort Alexandria on April 19 and returned with twelve Tŝilhqot'in scalps. In June and September, the Tŝilhqot'in sent two armies of warriors to kill the Dakelh. Only intervention by the HBC, who supplied the Dakelh with guns and ammunition, prevented a massacre.

Similar conflicts occurred between the Tŝilhqot'in and the St'at'imc of Lillooet. In 1839, a raiding party of St'at'imc attacked a Tŝilhqot'in village on Chilko Lake, and Tŝilhqot'in warriors from Bendziny to ʔEsdilagh reciprocated, giving chase to the enemy.

Relations between the Tŝilhqot'in and the Homalco were never particularly friendly. Oral history tells of a war around 1844 where the Tŝilhqot'in attacked and massacred many Homalco and the two peoples remained in a state of conflict for several years afterwards.

Around 1900, the Tŝilhqot'in and St'at'imc officially put an end to war between their two nations. They camped together at Graveyard Valley, where many wars had been fought over the centuries. There, in the high mountain country that both peoples shared, the graves of many Elders, women, children and warriors from both nations lay side by side. As Terry Glavin put it in his 1992 book, *Nemiah: The Unconquered Country*, instead of warring they gambled away generations of hostility with horse races, wrestling matches and lahal.

The ancient hurt of the Chunlak massacre still lingered in tribal memory when Dakelh Chief Martin Louie of Nadleh Whut'en drove five hours from his home at Fort Fraser to Williams Lake in early November 2013 to help send off Tŝilhqot'in Elders to attend a case being heard by the Supreme Court of Canada in Ottawa.

In the darkness of the predawn morning, Chief Martin drummed and sang a powerful song of support for the Elders as they boarded a bus for the five-day trek across the country. They were heading to Ottawa where Chief Roger William's case over indigenous title to the Tŝilhqot'in traditional territory was to be heard in

Xeni Gwet'in Chief Roger William began and ended every meeting with federal government law makers in Ottawa by drumming and singing traditional songs essential to his culture. Joining him at this meeting are Tŝilhqo'tin Tribal Chair Chief Joe Alphonse of Tl'etinqox, and National Chief Shawn Atleo. Photo Sage Birchwater.

a week's time. The Supreme Court was asked to grant the Tŝilhqot'in Nation title to 1,900 square kilometres of land in Xeni Gwet'in territory.

At no time in Canadian history had a court declared Indigenous title to lands outside a reserve.

Clearly, the fight of the Xeni Gwet'in and the Tŝilhqot'in Nation was a fight for all Indigenous people in Canada, and this wasn't lost on Chief Martin Louie.

Then when the eight Supreme Court justices unanimously ruled in favour of the Tŝilhqot'in claim on June 26, 2014, Chief Martin Louie attended the jubilant celebration held in Nemiah Valley on July 4. That's when he invited the Tŝilhqot'in leadership to Nadleh to take part in a ceremony that aimed for mutual peace and forgiveness over the atrocities that occurred at Chunlak (duchun nidulak) and the subsequent retaliations that had occurred more than two centuries earlier.

Also attending the July 4 celebration in Nemiah Valley was a delegation of Wet'su'wet'en chiefs from Smithers and Moricetown. The Tŝilhqot'in leadership publicly thanked them for taking the Delgamuukw case over Indigenous title to the Supreme Court of Canada in 1997. The Tŝilhqot'in acknowledged that this previous case had paved the way for the Xeni Gwet'in victory.

Although the Gitksan and Wet'su'wet'en nations were denied title by the Supreme Court, the case accomplished one important landmark success. The court gave greater weight to oral history than written evidence. Key to the Xeni Gwet'in Supreme Court victory was its strong reliance on oral history.

So on the Labour Day weekend 2014, thirty Tŝilhqot'in leaders, Elders, youth and community members drove up to Nadleh to sign a Commitment to an Accord of Peace, Respect and Responsibility between the Dakelh and Tŝilhqot'in peoples. The agreement outlined how the two nations would work together to develop a lasting accord. The chiefs spoke of their interest in having a ceremony at Chunlak, the battleground where the Tŝilhqot'in and Dakelh had fought many generations ago, in order to finalize the accord.

On August 30, 2014, Tribal Chair Chief Joe Alphonse and Vice-Tribal Chair Chief Roger William signed on behalf of the Tŝilhqot'in National Government. Chief Martin Louie signed on behalf of Nadleh Whut'en, and Councillor Tannis Reynolds (Dzih Bhen) for the Stellat'en First Nation. Tl'esqox Chief Francis Laceese, Chief Madeek of the Wet'su'wet'en (Moricetown) and Dziiggot (Ron Austin) of the Wet'su'wet'en signed as witnesses.

Chief Roger William says the Supreme Court win of 2014 was all about these changing times. "Proving our rights and title was our goal. The Supreme Court decision changed how government has to deal with First Nations in Canada. Government has to consult with First Nations and prove to us it's not infringing on our rights. Lots of stories and legends give us knowledge of the land."

A jubilant Xeni Gwet'in Chief Roger William celebrates the dawn of a new age of Indigenous relations in Canada. Photo Sage Birchwater.

Timeline

1579: Sir Francis Drake heads north from California seeking the Sea of Anian or the Northwest Passage. He gets as far as Coos Bay and the Oregon Dunes, then returns south again, seeking safe harbour.

1592: Juan de Fuca possibly sails into the Juan de Fuca Strait, claiming it to be the Sea of Anian.

1596: Juan de Fuca meets British citizen Michael Lok (Locke) in the Italian city of Venice and tells his story of exploration up the west coast of North America.

1756: Start of the Seven Years War/French and Indian War.

1763: On February 10, the Seven Years War/French and Indian War ends with the signing of the Treaty of Paris 1763. On October 7, King George III signs the Royal Proclamation of 1763, which states that Indigenous peoples in North America have title to and ownership of the land they occupy west of the Appalachian Mountains. The proclamation forbids settlement of this land unless a treaty is first negotiated and that only the Crown and not settlers may purchase land from Indigenous peoples.

1768: Captain James Cook, aged 39, sails into the Pacific Ocean for the first time, on the first of his three voyages of exploration (1768–1771), visiting New Zealand and Australia. On his second voyage (1772–1775), he circumnavigates the globe from east to west, becoming one of the first Europeans to cross the Antarctic Circle. On his third journey (1776–1779), he explores the west coast of North America, searching for the Northwest Passage. In 1778, Cook charts the west coast waters of what would become British Columbia. On February 14, 1779, Cook is killed in Hawaii, known then as the Sandwich Islands.

1776: May 20: Simon Fraser is born in Mapleton, New York, part of the Thirteen Colonies. (His family had arrived in North America in 1773, and his father, Captain Simon Fraser, a member of the 84th Highland Regiment, fought on the side of Great Britain in the American Revolutionary War. He was captured in August 1777 and died in prison in 1779, when Simon Jr. was less than three years old.)

1776: The American Revolution begins in July with the Thirteen Colonies declaring independence from Great Britain. Fighting ends in 1781. The Treaty of Paris of 1783 recognizes United States sovereignty.

1783: Simon Fraser moves to Canada with his mother Isabella and settles in Cadillac, Quebec. In 1790, aged 14, Simon Fraser attends school in Montreal, where two of his uncles are active in the fur trade. In 1792, aged 16, Fraser begins an apprenticeship with the North West Company. From 1792 to 1805, he works in the fur trade in the Athabasca District.

1788: American merchant sea captain Robert Gray finds the mouth of the Columbia River at latitude 46°N on the west coast of North America, but is prevented from entering the river by sandbars and tides.

1789: Alexander Mackenzie is commissioned to find a navigable river to the Pacific Ocean.

1792: Captain George Vancouver explores and charts northwest North America for Great Britain. In May, American Captain Robert Gray is the first explorer to enter the Columbia River at latitude 46°N. He claims it for the United States, and names the river after his ship, the *Columbia Rediviva*. In October, Captain Vancouver sends William Robert Broughton to explore the Columbia River, already claimed by Gray for the United States.

1793: Alexander Mackenzie makes the first recorded crossing of North America north of Mexico, arriving in Bella Coola in July. Captain Robert Gray returns to Boston in July with news of finding and charting the mouth of the Columbia River.

1803: James Douglas is born in British Guiana.

1804: Meriwether Lewis and William Clark set off in May to explore the Louisiana Purchase and find a land route to Captain Gray's Columbia River for the United States.

1805: Simon Fraser leaves Fort William to establish trading posts for the North West Company west of the Rocky Mountains. His mandate is to follow the great river Mackenzie paddled on his journey to Bella Coola, believed by then to be a northern tributary of Gray's Columbia River. He establishes forts at Hudson's Hope and Fort McLeod.

1806: Fraser establishes forts at Nak'azdli (Fort St. James) and Nadleh (Fort Fraser). Chief K'wah keeps the fur traders from starving at Nak'azdli by providing them with 30,000 dried salmon.

1807: Fraser establishes Fort George on the Fraser River at the mouth of the Nechako River as a launching point for his great expedition to the Salish Sea the following year.

1808: Fraser descends the Fraser River to its mouth and successfully returns without the loss of any crew members. He is disappointed to realize that the great river he has followed isn't the Columbia when he records the latitude of its mouth at 49°N. He is also disappointed that the river is not navigable for the fur trade.

1812: John Stuart is commissioned by the North West Company to find a route from New Caledonia to the Columbia River. The following summer, he takes nine men in two canoes from Fort St. James to the first bad rapids on the Fraser River (where Mackenzie had stopped) and continues overland by horseback to Fort Kamloops and on to Fort Okanagan, where they continue by canoe to the ocean.

1814: The Northwest Company establishes Fort Alexandria on the east side of the Fraser River.

1816: Charles Touin (Twan) is born.

1821: The Hudson's Bay Company and the North West Company merge under the HBC banner.

1824: Fort Vancouver is established on the Columbia River by the Hudson's Bay Company, with Dr. John McLoughlin appointed its first chief factor. The region is known by the HBC as the Columbia District and as the Oregon Country by the Americans. Great Britain and the United States share an interest in this territory until 1846, when the Oregon Treaty sets the Canada–United States boundary at the 49th parallel.

1828: Chief K'wah saves the life of James Douglas at Fort St. James after members of the Nak'azdli Village enter Fort St. James and hold Douglas at knifepoint for killing a Dakelh man.

1829: The Hudson's Bay Company opens Fort Chilcotin on the Chilcotin River.

1830: James Douglas is posted to Fort Vancouver from Fort St. James by the HBC. Tsholiranlna (Nancy Alexis Swanson) is born near Puntzi Lake. She is a sister of Chief Alexis.

1833: Charles Touin (Twan), aged 17, joins the HBC fur brigade and arrives in New Caledonia and the Columbia District.

1835: Peter Curan Dunlevy is born in Pittsburgh.

1837: Fort Alexandria is moved to the west side of the Fraser River in the hopes of attracting the Tŝilhqot'in to trade. Reverend Christian Saugstad, founder of the Norwegian colony in Bella Coola, is born in Norway.

1838: The first priests, Father Modeste Demers and Father Francois Norbert Blanchet, arrive in the Columbia District, travelling from Fort William on Lake Superior to Fort Vancouver.

1840: Photography is invented.

1842: Father Modeste Demers becomes the first priest to visit the Cariboo when he arrives at Fort Alexandria with Peter Skene Ogden and the HBC fur brigade from Fort Vancouver. Benny Franklin is born in Maine.

1843: James Douglas builds Fort Victoria on Vancouver Island. The Hudson's Bay Company closes Fort Chilcotin.

1845: Father John Nobili, a Jesuit from France, is the second Catholic missionary to visit the Cariboo and New Caledonia. After performing 629 baptisms of Dakelh, Secwepemc and Tŝilhqot'in people, he returns to Fort Vancouver in 1847.

1846: The Oregon Treaty is signed, which establishes the 49th parallel as the border between the United States and British Columbia.

1847: Father Modeste Demers becomes the first Catholic bishop of the colonies of Vancouver Island and British Columbia.

1848: Jacob Lunas is born in Norway.

1849: The Colony of Vancouver Island is created by the British government, with Victoria as its capital. The California gold rush begins and Father Nobili heads to San Francisco.

1853: Marie Cletses gives birth to John Sanford Twan at Fort Alexandria (ʔEsdilagh).

1854: Domas Squinas is born in Ulkatcho territory.

1857: Gold is discovered in the Fraser River.

1858: In April, the Fraser Canyon gold rush brings an estimated 30,000 miners from California to British Columbia. Violent confrontations erupt between American miners and the Indigenous inhabitants of the Fraser Canyon, reminiscent of the Indian Wars. On November 19, the colony of British Columbia is founded, with New Westminster its capital. James Douglas is named governor of both the British Columbia and Vancouver Island colonies. The Catholic Missionary Order Oblates of Mary Immaculate establishes its colonial headquarters in Esquimalt, near Victoria.

1859: The first gold discoveries are made in the Cariboo at Horsefly and Barkerville. Gentleman gold miner Peter Dunlevy and four companions attend a gathering of Indigenous people at Lac La Hache, where Tŝilhqot'in Chief ʔAnahim tries to convince the Dakelh and Secwepemc chiefs to join the Tŝilhqot'in in a war against the white gold miners invading the country. Dakelh Chief Lolo and Secwepemc Chief William refuse to engage in a battle they feel they cannot win. Father Adrian Gabriel Morice is born in Nancy, France.

1860: Settlers follow the gold rush to the Cariboo. Despite colonial policy forbidding settlers to stake lands occupied by Indigenous people, settler Thomas W. Davidson pre-empts the home of T'exelc Chief William, which lies where the city of Williams Lake is today. Land speculators led by George Cary stake land at Bella Coola harbour in the North Bentinck Arm. Fort Alexandria's post manager scouts out a road from the Fraser River to Bella Coola.

1861: In the spring, Chief ʔAnahim provides a party of nine men to guide road surveyors to Bella Coola, where Chief Pootlass gives a welcoming feast at Q'umk'uts for land speculators and road-builders. In August, Governor James Douglas gives Ranald McDonald a licence to create a toll road from the Bentinck Arm to the Fraser River. In November, George Cary purchases McDonald's licence for the Bentinck Arm Road.

1862: Lt. Henry Spencer Palmer surveys a route from North Bentinck Arm (Bella Coola) to the Cariboo goldfields. In the spring, Alfred Waddington hires an exploratory expedition to map a route from Bute Inlet to Fort Alexandria. A smallpox epidemic kills an estimated two-thirds of the Indigenous population of British Columbia in a twelve-month period. In September, Waddington starts constructing his toll road at Bute Inlet.

1863: From April to November, Alfred Waddington continues construction of his road from Bute Inlet to the Cariboo goldfields.

1864: The Chilcotin War begins April 29 as Lha Tŝ'aŝʔin leads an attack on Alfred Waddington's road-building crew in the Homathko Canyon, killing fourteen workers. A few days later, William Manning is killed at Bendziny (Puntzi Lake). On May 30, Alex McDonald, Peter McDougall, Clifford Higgins and Klymtedza are killed near Nagwuntl'oo. In September, Nancy Swanson (Tsholiralna) is forced to testify at the Chilcotin War trial in Quesnel. On October 26, five chiefs are hanged at Quesnel. Chief Louis Billy Prince, grandson of K'wah and father of Lizette Hall, is born at Nak'azdli.

1865: The Oblates of Mary Immaculate move their colonial headquarters from Victoria to New Westminster. Chief Ahan is hanged in New Westminster.

1866: Augustine Franklin is born in Brantford, Ontario. George Turner is born in the American West. Father James Maria McGuckin is sent to the Cariboo to establish St. Joseph's Mission near Williams Lake.

1867: Louisa One-Eye Turner is born. The St. Joseph's Mission opens on July 5. The Fort Alexandria trading post closes.

1868: Father François Marie Thomas is born in Brittany, France. Alex P. McInnis is born in Barkerville on April 11.

1871: Jesse Swanson is born at Swanson Flat. Robert "Bob" Graham is born in County Antrim, Ireland. David Hamm is born in Odessa, Russia.

1872: Father McGuckin opens a school for white and half-Indigenous boys at St. Joseph's Mission.

1873: John Clayton arrives in Bella Coola from the Cariboo goldfields and starts working in the Hudson's Bay Company store.

1876: The Sisters of St. Anne open a school for girls at St. Joseph's Mission. George Dawson photographs the Culla Culla House at Ulkatcho Village.

1877: Willie Mack, son of John Clayton and Q'uit, a Nuxalk woman, is born in Bella Coola. Annie Swanson Mackill is born at Swanson Flat.

1878: Robert Cecil (R. C.) Cotton is born in Hampton Court, England.

1879: T'exelcemc Chief William writes an appeal for land and justice in the Victoria *Colonist* newspaper. Sara Dyck Hamm is born in Stanley, Manitoba.

1880: T'exelcemc people are granted land at the head of Williams Lake.

1882: Father Morice is sent to St. Joseph's Mission in Williams Lake. Annie Lunas Engebretson is born in Minnesota.

1883: Gerald Dester arrives in Canada from Bath, England, to work on the construction of the Canadian Pacific Railway (CPR). He takes a Tsîlhqot'in woman, Jessie Peltashaata, as his country bride and they have two daughters, Isabel (b. 1889) and Lottie (b. 1894).

1884: Canada's Indian Act bans potlatches. The T'exelcemc (Williams Lake Indian Band) are granted 4,100 acres of land at Sugar Cane. The grant is formalized by the federal government.

1885: Nine Nuxalk men spend a year in Germany demonstrating their culture for Europeans. Father Morice is sent to Fort St. James, where he spends the next nineteen years. Tommy Hodgson is born in Yorkshire, England. John Clayton buys the Hudson's Bay Company trading post in Bella Coola. The last spike of the CPR is pounded at Craigellachie.

1886: Benny and Augustine Franklin pre-empt land at Tatla Lake. Benny offers the Tŝilhqot'in people he met there a big caddy of tobacco as a peace offering. The St. Joseph's Mission residential school opens. Eagle Lake Henry is born at Neghatalhchuẑ.

1889: Isabel Dester is born at Riske Creek.

1890: John Clayton returns to England and marries Elizabeth Orden.

1891: K. B. Moore is born in Boston. Bob Graham comes to Alexis Creek and stakes land where the present village site is located today.

1892: Gerald Dester opens a store at Riske Creek in partnership with Fred Becher and becomes the first "Chilcoten" postmaster. On October 5, the Dalton Gang is foiled in a dual bank heist in Coffeyville, Kansas. Four gang members are killed; Emmit Dalton survives and goes to jail; and one man, the pony boy, escapes. Some believe this was Old George Turner.

1894: Lottie Dester Johnny Chell is born at Riske Creek. On October 30, the first Norwegian colonists arrive in Bella Coola from Minnesota.

1895: The second and third boatloads of Norwegian settlers come to Bella Coola.

1896: William "Billy" Swanson dies at Swanson Flat, aged 65.

1897: R. C. Cotton comes to the Chilcotin to work as a mud pup for Mortimer Drummond at Riske Creek. Father François Marie Thomas arrives at St. Joseph's Mission. Reverend Christian Saugstad dies in Bella Coola aged 60. Gerald Dester marries Caroline Magee and she moves to Riske Creek. Tommy Hodgson moves to Canada from Yorkshire with his parents when he is 12 years old.

1898: Caroline Magee Dester heads to Vancouver for the birth of her daughter, Evelyn, in January and never returns to Riske Creek.

1899: Frank Swannell starts his illustrious surveying career. Father Thomas baptizes Annie Swanson and records her age to be about 70. Jim Robertson comes to Canada and gets a job in a Bella Coola cannery.

1900: R. C. Cotton buys Riske Creek Ranch from Mortimer Drummond and renames it the Cotton Ranche. Gerald Dester takes his daughter Isabel to England to get a proper English education.

1901: Jacob Lunas and Tom and Annie Engebretson stake land at Towdystan. Baptiste Dester is born in August. Frank Swannell buys a camera and starts photographing people and places in remote parts of British Columbia.

1902: Scotty Shields is born in Scotland. Tom Chignell is born in England. Billy Dagg is born at Naghatalhchuẑ. Benny Franklin sells Tatla Lake Ranch to Bob Graham and George Dagg for $1,700. Gerald Dester dies at Alkali Lake.

1903: George Turner stakes land in Bella Coola.

1904: Annie Nicholson is born at Rosthern, Saskatchewan.

1906: Father A. G. Morice publishes his major work, *The History of Northern British Columbia (1660–1880).* Alexina Reay is born in England.

1907: Margaret Robertson Reay comes to the Nemiah Valley to visit her brother Jim Robertson. Bern Mullin is born in Bathurst, New Brunswick.

1908: K. B. Moore arrives in the Chilcotin.

1909: Hilda Mackill Butler is born at Soda Creek. Bob Graham woos Margaret Reay and they marry in Ashcroft.

1910: John Clayton dies in Bella Coola. Clayton Mack is born in Bella Coola. Fred Engebretson is born in Bella Coola.

1911: Betty Graham is born in Scotland.

1912: Margaret Graham brings her daughters, Alexina and Betty, to Canada, accompanied by two of her brothers and two sisters. Tommy Hodgson starts driving weekly mail runs to Alexis Creek.

1914: K. B. Moore rides his horse to Tatlayoko, gets engaged to Dolly Church, then joins the army to fight in Europe.

1915: Bill Graham is the first baby born in the new Alexis Creek outpost hospital.

1916: Jim Robertson dies of unusual circumstances in the Nemiah Valley. Pete McCormick moves to the Chilcotin.

1919: K. B. Moore stakes land in Tatlayoko. Alex Graham is born at Alexis Creek. Andy Stuart takes over the Redstone Store.

1920: Thomas McIlwraith and Harlan Smith begin their ethnology work in Bella Coola.

1923: Mary Jane Dagg (Baptist) is born at Mountain House. Annie Hamm and Bob Nicholson marry in Rosthern, Saskatchewan.

1924: Andy Christensen and Dorothy Clayton marry in January.

1925: Eagle Lake Henry guides the Victor Dolmage survey party. Valleau beats up Neganie at Bluff Lake. After his wife and infant son die, Billy Dagg gives his two-year-old daughter Mary Jane to Eagle Lake Henry and Alyetta to raise as their own child.

1926: Neganie dies in suspicious circumstances.

1928: Leonard Butler and Hilda Mackill marry. Nancy Swanson (Tsholiralna) dies at Riske Creek. Betty Graham starts a store at Tatla Lake.

1929: D'Arcy Christensen is born at Ocean Falls. Bern Mullin arrives in the West Branch.

1930: Scotty Shields retrieves his runaway horse from Valleau. Bob Graham starts work on the "Big House" at Tatla Lake.

1931: Valleau meets destitute prairie farmers Johnny Hamm, Bob Nicholson and Charlie Godfrey in Williams Lake and invites them to the West Branch. Lee Butler is born at Alexis Creek.

1932: Bob and Annie Nicholson put their children into school in Tatla Lake. Bob Nicholson, Johnny Hamm and Charlie Godfrey stake pre-emptions in West Branch. The Graham Ranch "Big House" is finished.

1933: Don and Phyllis Munday hire Pete McCormick to take them to Mount Waddington via the West Branch. Pete hires Valleau with nine horses to help with the expedition. In September, Valleau is arrested for firing his rifle at Johnny Hamm.

1934: In March, Sir Norman Watson hires Pete McCormick to take ski mountaineers to Mt. Waddington. Pete McCormick comes home from Vancouver with a lady. Valleau gets out of jail and raises hell.

1935: Bob Nicholson is arrested for stealing and branding Jim Mackill's horse. Valleau pulls out of the country. August Schnarr sells his trapline to Johnny Hamm.

1936: Chief Jimmy Stillas is born at Ulkatcho. Bob Nicholson pulls out of the country. Bert Hamm arrives in the West Branch with his parents, David and Sara, three younger siblings and a nephew, Joe Schuk, from Rosthern.

1937: Provincial policeman Johnny Blatchford arrests Eagle Lake Henry in Williams Lake for raising hell with his family. Bob Pyper dies at Chilanko Forks.

1939: Betty Graham opens a new store in Tatla Lake.

1940: Pete McCormick dies in the Klinaklini Valley. June Draney is born at Mountain House.

1945: Tommy Hodgson dies.

1946: John Sanford Twan dies in Quesnel at 93 years old.

1952: Bob Graham dies at Tatla Lake.

1953: The Bella Coola Road is built through the Coast Mountains to Anahim Lake. The Kenny Dam floods the Nechako River to create Ootsa Lake reservoir, putting much traditional Ulkatcho trapping and hunting territory and homes under water. Alyetta Henry dies at Mountain House.

1954: K. B. Moore dies in Vancouver. Eagle Lake Henry marries Millie Setah.

1955: Old George Turner dies at Kleena Kleene and is buried next to Chief One-Eye at One Eye Lake.

1956: Louisa One-Eye dies at Chezacut and is buried next to her husband at One Eye Lake.

1957: Father Thomas dies in Edmonton at age 89.

1958: Margaret Graham dies at Tatla Lake.

1965: Roger William born in Nemiah Valley.

1967: Eagle Lake Henry dies in Williams Lake.

1969: Fred Linder dies at Tatla Lake.

1973: Alex Graham dies at Tatla Lake. Leonard Butler dies in West Branch.

1976: Rosalie Twan dies in Quesnel, aged 97. Graham family sells Tatla Lake Ranch.

1980: Betty Graham dies.

1983: Bill Graham dies.

1989: Aug 23, the Xeni Gwet'in declare traditional lands as the Nemiah Aboriginal Wilderness Reserve.

1990: Xeni Gwet'in launch court case in BC Supreme Court to prevent logging in their territory.

1992: Xeni Gwet'in community blocks loggers attempting to cross Henry's Crossing bridge.

2007: April 11, the 339-day trial before Mr Justice Vickers concludes.

2014: June 26, Eight justices of the Supreme Court rule in favour of the Xeni Gwet'in court case, awarding title to 1,900 square kilometres of land to the Tŝilhqot'in Nation.

Reference List and Sources

Books

Adams, John. *Old Square-Toes and His Lady: The Life of James and Amelia Douglas*. Victoria: Horsdal & Schubart, 2001.

Barker, John, and Douglas Cole, editors. *At Home with the Bella Coola Indians: T. F. McIlwraith's Field Letters, 1922–4*. Vancouver: UBC Press, 2003.

Bawlf, Sam. *The Secret Voyage of Sir Francis Drake, 1577–1580*. Vancouver: Douglas & McIntyre, 2003.

Beeson, Edith. *Dunlevey: From the Diaries of Alex P. McInnes*. Lillooet, BC: Lillooet Publishers, 1971.

Berger, Thomas R. *A Long and Terrible Shadow: White Values, Native Rights in the Americas, 1492–1992*. Vancouver: Douglas & McIntyre, 1991.

Birchwater, Sage. *Ulkatchot'en: The People of Ulkatcho*. Anahim Lake, BC: Ulkatcho First Nation, 1991.

———. *Chiwid*. Vancouver: New Star Books, 1995.

Birchwater, Sage, et al. *Ulkatcho Stories of the Grease Trail*. Anahim Lake, BC: Ulkatcho First Nation, 1993.

Birchwater, Sage, et al. *Ulkatcho Food & Medicine Plants*. Anahim Lake, BC: Ulkatcho First Nation, 1996.

Bliss, Irene E., Veera Bonner, Hazel H. Litterick (Witte sisters). *Chilcotin: Preserving Pioneer Memories*. Surrey, BC: Heritage House Publishing, 1995.

Bostock, Hugh Samuel. *Pack Horse Tracks: Recollections of a Geologist's Life in British Columbia and the Yukon, 1924–1954*. Ottawa: Geological Survey of Canada, 1979.

Bracewell, Gerry. *Gerry Get Your Gun*. Halfmoon Bay, BC: Caitlin Press, 2015.

Bridge between Nations: A History of First Nations in the Fraser River Basin. Vancouver: Fraser Basin Council, 2013.

Brown, R. C. Lundin. *Klatsassan and Other Reminiscences of Missionary Life in British Columbia*. London: Society for Promoting Christian Knowledge, 1873.

Collier, Eric. *Three Against the Wilderness*. London: Hutchinson & Co., 1960.

Duff, Wilson. *The Indian History of British Columbia*, Vol. 1. Victoria, BC: BC Provincial Museum, 1965.

Elliot, Marie. *Fort St. James and New Caledonia: Where British Columbia Began*. Madeira Park, BC: Harbour Publishing, 2009.

Furniss, Elizabeth. *The Victims of Benevolence: Discipline and Death at the Williams Lake Indian Residential School, 1891–1920*. Williams Lake, BC: Cariboo Tribal Council, 1992.

———. *Changing Ways: Southern Carrier History, 1793–1940*. Quesnel, BC: Quesnel School District 28, 1993.

———. *Dakelh Keyoh: The Southern Carrier in Early Times*. Quesnel, BC: Quesnel School District 28, 1993.

Glavin, Terry. *A Death Feast in Dimlahamid*. Vancouver: New Star Books, 1990.
———. *Nemiah: The Unconquered Country*. Vancouver: New Star Books, 1992.
Goodenough, Maurine. *Only in Nazko*. Quesnel, BC: Self-published, 2008.
Gough, Barry. *Juan de Fuca's Strait: Voyages in the Waterways of Forgotten Dreams*. Madeira Park: Harbour Publishing, 2012.
Hall, Lizette. *The Carrier, My People*. Quesnel, BC: Self-published, 1992.
Hume, Stephen. *Simon Fraser: In Search of Modern British Columbia*. Madeira Park, BC: Harbour Publishing, 2008.
Keddell, Georgina. *The Newspapering Murrays*. Toronto: McClelland & Stewart, 1967.
Kopas, Cliff, with Leslie Kopas. *No Path but my Own: Horseback Adventures in the Chilcotin & the Rockies*. Madeira Park, BC: Harbour Publishing, 1996.
Kopas, Leslie; photographs by Cliff Kopas. *Bella Coola Country*. Vancouver: Self-published, 2003.
Lamb, W. Kaye, ed. *Simon Fraser Letters & Journals, 1806–1808*. Toronto: Macmillan Company of Canada, 1960.
Mack, Clayton, with Harvey Thomassen, ed. *Grizzlies & White Guys*. Madeira Park, BC: Harbour Publishing, 1993.
Mack, Clayton, with Harvey Thomassen, ed. *Bella Coola Man*. Madeira Park, BC: Harbour Publishing, 1994.
Marriott, Harry. *Cariboo Cowboy*. Sidney, BC: Gray's Publishing, 1966.
McIlwraith, Thomas Forsyth. *The Bella Coola Indians*, Vol. 1 and 2. Toronto: University of Toronto Press, 1948.
Morice, Adrien Gabriel. *The History of the Northern Interior of British Columbia*. London: John Lane, The Bodley Head, 1906.
Munday, Don. *The Unknown Mountain*. London: Hodder and Stoughton, 1948.
Patenaude, Branwen. *Trails to Gold: Volume Two, Roadhouses of the Cariboo*. Surrey, BC: Heritage House, 1996.
Roberts, John A. *Cariboo: An Historical Narrative*. Williams Lake, BC: Self-published, 2002.
Schreiber, John. *Old Lives in the Chilcotin Backcountry*. Halfmoon Bay, BC: Caitlin Press, 2011.
Sheppe, Walter. *First Man West*. Montreal: McGill University Press, 1962.
Sherwood, Jay. *Surveying Central British Columbia: A Photojournal of Frank Swannell, 1920–28*. Victoria: Royal BC Museum, 2007.
———. *Surveying Southern British Columbia: A Photojournal of Frank Swannell, 1901–07*. Halfmoon Bay, BC: Caitlin Press, 2014.
Solhjell, Peter. *Spuds among the Stumps: Norwegian Immigrant Settlement Photos, Bella Coola, 1896–97*. Hagensborg, BC: Solly's Publishing, 2008.
Stangoe, Irene. *Cariboo-Chilcotin: Pioneer People and Places*. Surrey, BC: Heritage House Publishing, 1994.
———. *Looking Back: At the Cariboo-Chilcotin*. Surrey, BC: Heritage House Publishing, 1997.

———. *History and Happenings in the Cariboo-Chilcotin*. Surrey, BC: Heritage House Publishing, 2000.

Swanky, Shawn. *The Great Darkening*. Vancouver: Dragon Heart, 2013.

Swanky, Tom. *The True Story of Canada's "War" of Extermination on the Pacific plus The Tsilhqot'in and other First Nations Resistance*. Vancouver: Dragon Heart, 2012.

———. *A Missing Genocide and the Demonization of its Heroes, a Review of the CanadianMysteries.ca Website: We Do not Know His Name: Klatsassin and the Chilcotin War*. Vancouver: Dragon Heart, 2014.

Tatla Lake School Heritage Project. *Hoofprints in History*, Vols. 1–8. Tatla Lake, BC: Tatla Lake Elementary Junior Secondary School, 1986–1998.

Tepper, Leslie H., ed. *The Bella Coola Valley: Harlan I. Smith's Fieldwork Photographs, 1920–1924*. Hull (Gatineau), QC: Canadian Museum of Civilization (History), 1991.

Turnbull, W. H. *One hundred years of beekeeping in British Columbia, 1858-1958*. B.C. Honey Producers' Association,1958.

Waddington, Alfred. *Fraser Mines Vindicated*. Fairfield, Washington: Ye Galleon Press, 1980.

Watson, Sir Norman, and E. J. King. *Round Mystery Mountain: A Ski Adventure*. London: Edward Arnold & Co, 1935.

William, Chief Roger, and Jack Woodward. *Sechanalyagh: A Book of Gratitude*. Woodward and Company, 2007.

Documentary Films

Grossman, Barb. *The Hill: Meeting of the Cats*. Williams Lake, BC: Self-produced, 2003.

Hager, Barbara. *From Bella Coola to Berlin*. Victoria, BC: Self-produced, 2006.

Haig-Brown, Helen. *My Legacy*. Yunesit'in. Independent, 2014.

Special Thanks

Thank you to Craig and Christa Smith for giving many of these stories first light of day in the *Stew Magazine* (thestew.ca).

Interviews, consultation and assistance:

Elora Alden
Bella Alphonse
Chief Joe Alphonse
Chief Marilyn Baptistc
Johnny & Phyllis Blatchford
Irene & Bill Bliss
Veera Bonner
Gerry & Alf Bracewell
Caroline Brunet
Lee & Bev Butler
Susan Cahoose
Alfred Casimer
Chief Ervin Charleyboy
Tom Chignell
D'Arcy Christensen
Antoinette Danaher
June Draney
Lorena Draney
Donald & Emily Ekks
Al Elsey
David Friesen
Caterina Geuer
Sunniva Geuer
Rick Gilbert
Josephine Gregg
Chief Percy Guichon
Lizette Hall
Mabel Hall
Bert Hamm
Susan Hance
Grace Hans
Harry Haynes
Laurie Haynes
Lou Haynes
Wilfred Hodgson
Theresa Holte
Penny Hutchinson
Henry Jack
Janie Jack
Patrick Jack
Dieter Kellinghusen
Ollie Knoll
Chief Francis Laceese
Hank Law
Chief Martin Louie
Casimer Lulua
Dinah & Jim Lulua
Doris Lulua
Chief Bernie Mack
Clayton Mack
Fred McEwan
Mary Jane McEwan
Olive McInroy
Thelma McInroy
Rene Morton
Bern Mullin
Randolph Mulvahill
Chris Nelson
Lance Nelson
Annie Nicholson
Ann Porter
Bill Poser
Alexina Renshaw
Phil & Joyce Robertson
Mary Ann Ross
Chief Russell Myers Ross
Joe Schuk
Johnny Schuk
Scotty Shields
Elaine Sirois
Andy & Lillian Siwallace
Peter Solhjell
Mabel Solomon
Mac Squinas
Thomas Squinas
Irene Stangoe
Chief Jimmy Stillas
Tom Swanky
Leona Toney
Danny Twan
Laurie Vaughan
Theresa Vogel
Lorraine Weir
Chief Roger William
Boise Williams
Lorie Wilson
Chris Wycotte Sr.

INDEX

J

K

L

M

N

U

V

W

X

Y